Geasford, Photo.

THE POEMS

OF

RICHARD WATSON GILDER

BOSTON AND NEW YORK

HOUGHTON MIFFLIN COMPANY

The Riverside Press Cambridge

CONTENTS

THE NEW DAY

THE CELESTIAL PASSION

PART I

PART II

PART III

PART II

PART III

TWO WORLDS AND OTHER POEMS

PART I

PART II

PART III

PART IV

PART V

PART VI

THE GREAT REMEMBRANCE

PART I

PART II

PART III

PART IV

IN PALESTINE AND OTHER POEMS

PART I

PART II

PART III

"IN THE HIGHTS"

THE FIRE DIVINE

IN HELENA'S GARDEN

PART I

PART II

Frontispiece: Photograph by Gessford.
Decorations by H. de K. G.

THE NEW DAY

A POEM IN SONGS AND SONNETS

THE NEW DAY

PRELUDE

THE night was dark, tho' sometimes a faint star
A little while a little space made bright.
The night was dark and still the dawn seemed far
When, o'er the muttering and invisible sea,
Slowly, within the East, there grew a light
Which half was starlight, and half seemed to be
The herald of a greater. The pale white
Turned slowly to pale rose, and up the hight
Of heaven slowly climbed. The gray sea grew
Rose-colored like the sky. A white gull flew
Straight toward the utmost boundary of the East
Where slowly the rose gathered and increased.
There was light now, where all was black before:
It was as on the opening of a door
By one who in his hand a lamp doth hold
(Its flame being hidden by the garment's fold), —
The still air moves, the wide room is less dim.

More bright the East became, the ocean turned
Dark and more dark against the brightening sky —
Sharper against the sky the long sea line.
The hollows of the breakers on the shore
Were green like leaves whereon no sun doth shine,
Tho' sunlight make the outer branches hoar.
From rose to red the level heaven burned;
Then sudden, as if a sword fell from on high,
A blade of gold flashed on the ocean's rim.

PART I

I—SONNET

(AFTER THE ITALIAN)

I KNOW not if I love her overmuch;
  But this I know, that when unto her face
  She lifts her hand, which rests there, still, a space,
  Then slowly falls — 't is I who feel that touch.
And when she sudden shakes her head, with such
  A look, I soon her secret meaning trace.
  So when she runs I think 't is I who race.
  Like a poor cripple who has lost his crutch
I am if she is gone; and when she goes,
  I know not why, for that is a strange art —
  As if myself should from myself depart.
I know not if I love her more than those
  Who long her light have known; but for the rose
  She covers in her hair, I'd give my heart.

II—SONNET

(AFTER THE ITALIAN)

I LIKE her gentle hand that sometimes strays,
  To find the place, through the same book with
     mine;
  I like her feet; and O, those eyes divine!
  And when we say farewell, perhaps she stays
Love-lingering — then hurries on her ways,
  As if she thought, "To end my pain and thine."
  I like her voice better than new-made wine;
  I like the mandolin whereon she plays.

And I like, too, the cloak I saw her wear,
  And the red scarf that her white neck doth cover,
  And well I like the door that she comes through;
I like the riband that doth bind her hair —
  But then, in truth, I am that lady's lover,
  And every new day there is something new.

III — "A BARREN STRETCH THAT SLANTS TO THE SALT SEA'S GRAY"

A BARREN stretch that slants to the salt sea's gray, —
  Rock-strewn, and scarred by fire, and rough with
    stubble, —
With here and there a bold, bright touch of color —
Berries and yellow leaves, that make the dolor
  More dolorous still. Above, a sky of trouble.

But now a light is lifted in the air;
  And tho' the sky is shadowed, fold on fold,
  By clouds that have the lightnings in their hold,
That western gleam makes all the dim earth fair —
  And the gray sea gold.

IV — HESITATION

(A PORTRAIT)

To-DAY I saw the picture of a man
  Who, issuing from a wood, doth thrust apart
  Strong-matted, thorny branches, whose keen smart
  He heeds in nowise, if he only can
Win the red rose a maiden, like a fan,
  Holds daintily. She, listening to her heart,
  Hath looked another way. Ah, would she start,
  And weep, and suffer sorrow, if he ran —

For utter love of her, forever back
　　Into the shadows, which thrice darker were
　　Because her whiteness made their black more black!
A little while he waits, lest he should err.
　　Awhile he wonders, secretly.—Alack!
　　He could so gladly die or live for her.

V—LOVE GROWN BOLD

THIS is her picture painted ere mine eyes
　　Her ever holy face had looked upon.
　　She sitteth in a silence of her own;
　　Behind her, on the ground, a red rose lies;
Her thinking brow is bent, nor doth arise
　　Her gaze from that shut book whose word unknown
　　Her firm hands hide from her; there all alone
　　She sitteth in thought-trouble, maidenwise.
And now her lover waiting wondereth
　　Whether the joy of joys is drawing near;
　　Shall his brave fingers like a tender breath
That shut book open for her, wide and clear?
　　From him who her sweet shadow worshipeth
　　Now will she take the rose, and hold it dear?

INTERLUDE

THE sun rose swift and sent a golden gleam
Across the moving waters to the land;
Then for a little while it seemed to stand
In a clear place, midway 'twixt sea and cloud;
Whence rising swift again it past behind
Full many a long and narrow cloud-wrought beam
Encased in gold unearthly, that was mined
From out the hollow caverns of the wind.

These first revealed its face and next did shroud,
While still the daylight grew, and joy thereby
Lit all the windy stretches of the sky —

Until a shadow darkened from the east
And sprang upon the ocean like a beast.

PART II

I

THERE was a field green and fragrant with grass and flowers, and flooded with sunlight, and the air above it throbbed with the songs of birds. It was yet morning when a great darkness spread over the earth, and out of the darkness lightning, and after the lightning fire that consumed every green thing; and the singing birds fell dying upon the blackened grass. The thunder and the flame past, but it was still dark — till a ray of light touched the field's edge and grew, little by little. Then one who listened heard — not the songs of birds again, but the flutter of broken wings.

II — THE TRAVELER

I MET a traveler on the road
Whose back was bent beneath a load;
His face was worn with mortal care,
His frame beneath its burden shook,
Yet onward, restless, he did fare
With mien unyielding, fixt, a look
Set forward in the empty air
As he were reading an unseen book.

What was it in his smile that stirred
My soul to pity! When I drew
More near it seemed as if I heard
The broken echo of a tune
Learned in some far and happy June.
His lips were parted, but unmoved
By words. He sang as dreamers do,
And not as if he heard and loved
The song he sang: I hear it now!
   He stood beside the level brook,
Nor quenched his thirst, nor bathed his brow,
Nor from his back the burden shook.
He stood, and yet he did not rest;
His eyes climbed up in aimless quest,
Then close did to that mirror bow —
And, looking down, I saw in place
Of his, my own familiar face.

III — "COME TO ME YE WHO SUFFER"

Come to me ye who suffer, for to all
  I am a brother now! 'T was not in vain
  I saw the face of Sorrow; she who slain
  Yet lives; whose voice when she doth weep and call
Is silent. When she weeps? Nay, nay! the pall
  Is on her tears too — they are dead. The rain
  Is molten-hot, dust-dry from her dull pain,
  Like ashes from the burning heavens that fall.
I know the world-wide, lovely, living lie;
  I know the truth that better were unknown;
  I know the joyful laugh that is a cry
Torn from a heart whence hope and faith have flown,
  And yet beats on, and will not, dare not die.
  I know the anguish without word or moan.

IV — WRITTEN ON A FLY-LEAF OF "SHAKESPEARE'S SONNETS"

WHEN shall true love be love without alloy —
   Shine free at last from sinful circumstance!
   When shall the canker of unheavenly chance
   Eat not the bud of that most heavenly joy!
When shall true love meet love not as a coy
   Retreating light that leads a deathful dance,
   But as a firm fixt fire that doth enhance
   The beauty of all beauty! Will the employ
Of poets ever be too well to show
   That mightiest love with sharpest pain doth writhe;
   That underneath the fair, caressing glove
Hides evermore the iron hand; and tho'
   Love's flower alone is good, if we would prove
   Its perfect bloom, our breath slays like a scythe!

V — "AND WERE THAT BEST!"

AND were that best, Love, dreamless, endless sleep!
   Gone all the fury of the mortal day —
   The daylight gone, and gone the starry ray!
   And were that best, Love, rest serene and deep!
Gone labor and desire; no arduous steep
   To climb, no songs to sing, no prayers to pray,
   No help for those who perish by the way,
   No laughter 'mid our tears, no tears to weep!
And were that best, Love, sleep with no dear dream,
   Nor memory of anything in life —
   Stark death that neither help nor hurt can know!
O, rather, far, the sorrow-bringing gleam,
   The living day's long agony and strife!
   Rather strong love in pain; the waking woe!

VI — "THERE IS NOTHING NEW UNDER
THE SUN"

THERE is nothing new under the sun;
　　There is no new hope or despair;
The agony just begun
　　Is as old as the earth and the air.
My secret soul of bliss
　　Is one with the singing stars,
And the ancient mountains miss
　　No hurt that my being mars.

I know as I know my life,
　　I know as I know my pain,
That there is no lonely strife,
　　That he is mad who would gain
A separate balm for his woe,
　　A single pity and cover;
The one great God I know
　　Hears the same prayer over and over.

I know it because at the portal
　　Of Heaven I bowed and cried,
And I said: "Was ever a mortal
　　Thus crowned and crucified!
My praise Thou hast made my blame;
　　My best Thou hast made my worst;
My good Thou hast turned to shame;
　　My drink is a flaming thirst."

But scarce my prayer was said
　　Ere from that place I turned;
I trembled, I hung my head,
　　My cheek, shame-smitten, burned;

For there where I bowed down
  In my boastful agony,
I thought of thy cross and crown —
  O Christ! I remembered thee.

VII — LOVE'S CRUELTY

"AND this, then, is thy love," I hear thee say,
  "And dost thou love, and canst thou torture so?
  Ah, spare me, if thou lov'st me, this last woe!"
  But I am not my own; I must obey
My master; I am slave to LOVE; his sway
  Is cruel as the grave. When he says Go!
  I go; when he says Come! I come. I know
  No law but his. When he says Slay! I slay.
As cruel as the grave? Yes — crueler:
  Cruel as light that pours its stinging flood
  Across the dark, and makes an anguished stir
Of life; cruel as life that sends through blood
  Of mortal the immortal pang and spur;
  Cruel as thy remorseless maidenhood.

INTERLUDE

THE cloud was thick that hid the sun from sight
And over all a shadowy roof outspread,
Making the day dim with another night —
Not dark like that which past, but O, more dread
For the clear sunlight that had gone before
And prophecy of that which yet should be.
Like snow at night the wind-blown hills of sand
Shone with an inward gleam far down the land:
Beneath the lowering sky black was the sea
Across whose waves a bird came flying low, —
Borne swift on the wind with wing-beat halt and slow, —

From out the dull east toward the foamy shore.
There was an awful waiting in the earth
As if a mystery greatened to its birth.
Tho' late it seemed, the day was just begun
When lo! at last, the many-colored bow
Stood in the heavens over against the sun.

PART III

I — "THE PALLID WATCHER OF THE EASTERN SKIES"

THE pallid watcher of the eastern skies
  Who, through the suffering night, did wait forlorn,
  When comes the first faint purple of the morn
  Waiteth no longer. To his happy eyes
The promised near the promise following flies,
  Nor is his soul with sullen anguish torn,
  Nor curseth he the day when he was born.
  From the damp ground he doth in wonder rise,
Firm set his face against the gathering glory —
  So to be sure that this, at last, is this,
  And not the ancient, bitter-lying story.
And now he prays for strength to bear the bliss,
  While, bending o'er the mountain, red and hoary,
  The morning crowns him with a golden kiss.

II — "MY LOVE FOR THEE DOTH MARCH LIKE ARMÈD MEN"

MY love for thee doth march like armèd men,
  Against a queenly city they would take.
  Along the army's front its banners shake;
  Across the mountain and the sun-smit plain

It stedfast sweeps as sweeps the stedfast rain;
And now the trumpet makes the still air quake,
And now the thundering cannon doth awake
Echo on echo, echoing loud again.
But, lo! the conquest higher than bard e'er sung:
Instead of answering cannon, proud surrender!
Joyful the iron gates are open flung
And, for the conqueror, welcome gay and tender!
O, bright the invader's path with tribute flowers,
While comrade flags flame forth on wall and towers!

III — "WHAT WOULD I SAVE THEE FROM?"

WHAT would I save thee from, dear heart, dear heart?
Not from what Heaven may send thee of its pain;
Not from fierce sunshine or the scathing rain:
The pang of pleasure; passion's wound and smart;
Not from the long, glad anguish of thine art;
Nor loss of faithful friends, nor any gain
Of growth by grief; I would not thee restrain
From needful death. But O, thou other part
Of me! — through whom the whole world I behold,
As through the blue I see the stars above!
In whom the world I find, hid fold on fold!
Thee would I save from this — nay, do not move;
Fear not, it may not flash, the air is cold;
Save thee from this — the lightning of my love.

IV — "WHAT WOULD I WIN THEE TO?"

WHAT would I win thee to? dear heart and true!
A thought of bliss, a thornless life? Ah no!
Through weeping pain, Love, I would let thee go;
Through weary days and widowed nights; yea, through

The Valley of the Shadow, without rue,
    If thou couldst gain the goal, Love, even so.
    I would not win thee to a fruitful woe;
    To best of earth or best beyond the blue.
And most of all would thy true lover scorn
    To win thee to himself; thou shalt be free
    To have or hate! But O, my golden morn!
Behold thy lover's passionate bravery —
    Mighty, unresting, stedfast, heaven-born —
    To win thee to the light, which is — to thee!

V — "I WILL BE BRAVE FOR THEE"

I WILL be brave for thee, dear heart; for thee
    My boasted bravery forego. I will
    For thee be wise, or lose my little skill;
    Coward or brave; wise, foolish; bond or free.
No grievous cost in anything I see
    That brings thee bliss, or only keeps thee, still,
    In painless peace. So Heaven thy cup but fill,
    Be empty mine unto eternity!
Come to me, Love, and let me touch thy face!
    Lean to me, Love; breathe on me thy dear breath!
    Fly from me, Love, to some far hiding-place,
If thy one thought of me or hindereth
    Or hurteth thy sweet soul — then grant me grace
    To be forgotten, tho' that grace be death!

VI — "LOVE ME NOT, LOVE, FOR THAT I FIRST LOVED THEE"

LOVE me not, Love, for that I first loved thee;
    Nor love me, Love, for thy sweet pity's sake,
    In knowledge of the mortal pain and ache
    Which is the fruit of love's blood-veinèd tree.

Let others for my love give love to me;
From other souls, O, gladly will I take,
This burning, heart-dry thirst of love to slake,
What seas of human pity there may be!
Nay, nay, I care no more how love may grow,
So that I hear thee answer to my call;
Love me because my piteous tears do flow,
Or that my love for thee did first befall.
Love me or late or early, fast or slow —
But love me, Love, for love is all in all!

VII — BODY AND SOUL

I

O THOU my Love, love first my lonely soul!
Then shall this too unworthy body of mine
Be loved by right and accident divine.
Forget the flesh, that the pure spirit's goal
May be the spirit; let that stand the whole
Of what thou lov'st in me. So will the shine
Of soul that strikes on soul make fair and fine
This earthy tenement; thou shalt extol
The inner, that the outer lovelier seem.
Thy lover, who thy love implores, doth fear
No deadlier foe than the impassioned dream
Should drive thee to him, and should hold thee near —
Near to the body, not the soul of him:
Love first my soul and then both will be dear.

II

But, Love, for me thy body was the first.
One day I wandered idly through the town,
Then entered a cathedral's silence brown
Which sudden thrilled with a strange heavenly burst

Of light and music. Lo! that traveler durst
  Do nothing now but worship and fall down.
  He thought to rest, as doth some tired clown
  Who sinks in longed-for sleep, but there immersed
Finds restless vision on vision of beauty rare.
  Moved by thy body's outer majesty
  I entered in thy silent, sacred shrine;
'T was then, all suddenly and unaware,
  Thou didst reveal, O, maiden Love! to me,
  This beautiful, singing, holy soul of thine.

VIII — "THY LOVER, LOVE, WOULD HAVE SOME NOBLER WAY"

THY lover, Love, would have some nobler way
  To tell his love, his noble love to tell,
  Than rhymes set ringing like a silver bell.
  O, he would lead an army, great and gay,
From conquering to conquer, day by day!
  And when the walls of a proud citadel
  At summons of his guns far-echoing fell —
  That thunder to his Love should murmuring say:
Thee only do I love, dear Love of mine!
  And while men cried: Behold how brave a fight!
  She should read well, O, well! each new emprize:
This to her lips, this to my lady's eyes!
  And tho' the world were conquered, line on line,
  Still would his love be speechless, day and night.

IX — LOVE'S JEALOUSY

OF other men I know no jealousy,
  Nor of the maid who holds thee close, O, close!
  But of the June-red, summer-scented rose,
  And of the barred and golden sunset sky

That wins the soul of thee through thy deep eye;
  And of the breeze by thee beloved, that goes
  O'er thy dear hair and brow; the song that flows
  Into thy heart of hearts, where it may die.
I would I were one moment that sweet show
  Of flower; or breeze beloved that toucheth all;
  Or sky that through the summer eve doth burn.
I would I were the song thou lovest so,
  At sound of me to have thine eyelids fall; —
  But I would then to something human turn.

X — LOVE'S MONOTONE

THOU art so used, Love, to thine own bird's song, —
  Sung to thine ear in love's low monotone,
  Sung to thee only, Love, to thee alone
  Of all the listening world, — that I among
My doubts find this the leader of the throng:
  Haply the music hath accustomed grown
  And no more music is to thee; my own
  Too faithful argument works its own wrong.
Love, Love, and must I learn for thy sweet sake
  The art of silence? — Ah, then hide the light
  Of thy dear countenance, lest the music wake!
Yet should thy bird at last fall silent quite,
  Would not thy heart an unused sorrow take?
  Think not of me but of thyself to-night.

XI — "ONCE ONLY"

ONCE only, Love, may love's sweet song be sung;
But once, Love, at our feet love's flower is flung;
Once, Love, once only, Love, can we be young;
    Say shall we love, dear Love, or shall we hate!

Once only, Love, will burn the blood-red fire;
But once awakeneth the wild desire;
Love pleadeth long, but what if love should tire!
    Now shall we love, dear Love, or shall we wait!

The day is short, the evening cometh fast;
The time of choosing, Love, will soon be past;
The outer darkness falleth, Love, at last;
    Love, let us love ere it be late — too late!

XII — DENIAL

WHEN some new thought of love in me is born,
    Then swift I seek a token fair and meet
    That may unblamed thy blessèd vision greet;
    Whether it be a rose, not bloodless torn
From that June tree which hideth many a thorn,
    Or but a simple, loving message, sweet
    With summer's heart and mine, — these at thy feet
I straightway fling; but all with maiden scorn
Thou spurnest. What to thee is token or sign,
    Who dost deny the thing wherefor it stands!
    Then I seem foolish in my sight and thine,
Like one who eager proffers empty hands.
    Thou only callest these my gifts unfine,
    While men are praising them in distant lands.

XIII — "ONCE WHEN WE WALKED WITHIN A SUMMER FIELD"

ONCE when we walked within a summer field
    I pluckt the flower of immortality,
    And said, "Dear Love of mine, I give to thee
    This flower of flowers of all the round year's yield!"

'T was then thou stood'st, and with one hand didst
    shield
  Thy sun-dazed eyes, and, flinging the other free,
  Spurned from thee that white blossom utterly.
  But, Love, the immortal cannot so be killed.
The generations shall behold thee stand
  Against that western glow in grass dew-wet —
  Lord of my life, and lady of the land.
Nor maid nor lover shall the world forget,
  Nor that disdainful wafture of thy hand.
  Thou scornful! sun and flower shall find thee yet.

XIV — SONG

  I LOVE her gentle forehead,
    And I love her tender hair;
  I love her cool, white arms,
    And her neck where it is bare.

  I love the smell of her garments;
    I love the touch of her hands;
  I love the sky above her,
    And the very ground where she stands.

  I love her doubting and anguish;
    I love the love she withholds;
  I love my love that loveth her
    And anew her being molds.

XV — LISTENING TO MUSIC

WHEN on that joyful sea
Where billow on billow breaks; where swift waves follow
Waves, and hollow calls to hollow;
Where sea-birds swirl and swing,

And winds through the rigging shrill and sing;
Where night is one vast starless shade;
Where thy soul not afraid,
Tho' all alone unlonely,
Wanders and wavers, wavers wandering;
On that accursèd sea
One moment only,
Forget one moment, Love, thy fierce content;
Back let thy soul be bent —
Think back, dear Love, O Love, think back to me!

XVI — "A SONG OF THE MAIDEN MORN"

A SONG of the maiden morn,
A song for my little maid,
Of the silver sunlight born!

But I am afraid, afraid,
When I come my maid may be
Nothing, there, but a shade.

But O, her shadow is more to me
Than the shadowless light of eternity!

XVII — WORDS IN ABSENCE

I WOULD that my words were as my fingers,
So that my Love might feel them move
Slowly over her brow, as lingers
The sunset wind o'er the world of its love.
I would that my words were as the beating
Of her own heart, that keeps repeating
My name through the livelong day and the night;
And when my Love her lover misses, —
Longs for and loves in the dark and the light, —

I would that my words were as my kisses.
I would that my words her life might fill —
  Be to her earth, and air, and skies.
I would that my words were husht and still —
  Lost in the light of her eyes.

XVIII — SONG

THE birds were singing, the skies were gay;
  I looked from the window on meadow and wood,
    On green, green grass that the sun made white;
  Beyond the river the mountain stood —
    Blue was the mountain, the river was bright;
  I looked on the land and it was not good,
For my own dear Love she had flown away.

XIX — THISTLE–DOWN

FLY, thistle-down, fly
From my lips to the lips that I love!
Fly through the morning light,
Flee through the shadowy night,
Over the sea and the land,
Quick as the lark
Through twilight and dark,
Through lightning and thunder;
Till no longer asunder
We stand;
For thy touch like the lips of her lover
Moves her being to mine —
We are one in a swoon divine!

Fly, thistle-down, fly
From my lips to the lips that I love!

XX — "O SWEET WILD ROSES THAT BUD AND BLOW"

O SWEET wild roses that bud and blow
Along the way that my Love may go;
O moss-green rocks that touch her dress,
And grass that her dear feet may press;

O maple-tree whose brooding shade
For her a summer tent has made;
O goldenrod and brave sunflower
That flame before my maiden's bower;

O butterfly on whose light wings
The golden summer sunshine clings;
O birds that flit o'er wheat and wall,
And from cool hollows pipe and call;

O falling water whose distant roar
Sounds like the waves upon the shore;
O winds that down the valley sweep,
And lightnings from the clouds that leap;

O skies that bend above the hills;
O gentle rains and babbling rills;
O moon and sun that beam and burn —
Keep safe my Love till I return!

XXI — THE RIVER

I KNOW thou art not that brown mountain-side,
Nor the pale mist that lies along the hills
And with white joy the deepening valley fills;
Nor yet the solemn river moving wide

Into that valley, where the hills abide
    But whence those morning clouds on noiseless
        wheels
    Shall lingering lift and, as the moonlight steals
    From out the heavens, so into the heavens shall
        glide.
I know thou art not this gray rock that looms
    Above the water, fringed with scarlet vine;
    Nor flame of burning meadow; nor the sedge
That sways and trembles at the river's edge.
    But through all these, dear heart! to me there comes
    Some melancholy, absent look of thine.

XXII — THE LOVER'S LORD AND MASTER

I PRAY thee, dear, think not alone of me,
    But sometimes think of my great master, LOVE;
    His faithful slave he is so far above
    That for his sake I would forgotten be —
Tho' well I know that hidden thus from thee
    Not far away my image then might rove,
    And his sweet, heavenly countenance would move
    Ever thy soul to gentler charity.
So when thy lover's self leaps from his song
    Thou him may love not less for his fair Lord.
    But that thy love for me grow never small
(As bow long bent twangs not the arrowed cord,
    And he doth lose his star who looks too long),
    Sometimes, dear heart, think not of me at all.

XXIII — SONG

MY love grew with the growing night,
    And dawned with the new daylight.

XXIV — "A NIGHT OF STARS AND DREAMS"

A NIGHT of stars and dreams, of dreams and sleep;
  A waking into another empty day —
  But not unlovely all, for then I say:
  "To-morrow!" Through the hours this light doth creep
Higher in the heavens, as down the heavenly steep
  Sinks the slow sun. Another evening gray,
  Made glorious by the morn that comes that way;
  Another night, and then To-day doth leap
Upon the world! O, quick the hours do fly,
  Of that new day which brings the moment when
  We meet at last! Swift up the shaking sky
Rushes the sun from out its dismal den;
  And then the wisht for time doth yearn more nigh;
  A white robe glimmering in the dark — and then!

XXV — A BIRTHDAY SONG

I THOUGHT this day to bring to thee
A flower that grows on the red rose tree.
I searched the branches — O, despair!
Of roses every branch was bare.

I thought to sing thee a birthday song
As wild as my love, as deep and strong.
The song took wing like a frightened bird,
And its music my maiden never heard.

But, Love, the flower and the song divine
One day of the year will yet be thine;
And thou shalt be glad when the rose I bring,
And weep for joy at the song I sing.

XXVI — "WHAT CAN LOVE DO FOR THEE, LOVE?"

WHAT can love do for thee, Love?
Can it make the green fields greener;
Bluer the skies, and bluer
The eyes of the blue-eyed flowers?
Can it make the May-day showers
More warm and sweet; serener
The heavens after the rain?
The sunset's radiant splendor
More exquisite and tender?
The Northern Star more sure?
Can it take the pang from pain?
(O Love, remember the curtain
Of cloud that lifted last night
And showed the silver light
Of a star!) Can it make more certain
The heart of the heart of all,
The good that works at the root —
The singing soul of love
That throbs in flower and fruit,
In man and earth and brute,
In hell, and heaven above?
Can its low voice musical
Make dear the day and the night?

XXVII — "THE SMILE OF HER I LOVE"

THE smile of her I love is like the dawn
Whose touch makes Memnon sing.
O, see where wide the golden sunlight flows —
The barren desert blossoms as the rose!

The smile of her I love — when that is gone,
O'er all the world Night spreads her shadowy wing.

XXVIII — FRANCESCA AND PAOLO

WITHIN the second dolorous circle where
   The lost are whirled, lamenting — thou and I
   Stood, Love, to-day with Dante. Silently
   We looked upon the black and trembling air;
When lo! from out that darkness of despair
   Two shadows, light upon the wind, drew nigh,
   Whose very motion seemed to breathe a sigh —
   And there Francesca, and her lover there.
These when we saw, the wounds whereat they bled,
   Their love which was not with their bodies slain —
   These when we saw, great were the tears we shed:
As, Love, for thee and me love's tears shall rain —
   The mortal agony; the nameless dread;
   The longing, and the passion, and the pain.

XXIX — THE UNKNOWN WAY

Two travelers met upon a plain
Where two straight, narrow pathways crossed;
They met and, with a still surprise,
They looked into each other's eyes
And knew that never, O, never again!
Could one from the other soul be lost.

But lo! these narrow pathways lead
Now each from each apart, and lo!
In neither pathway can they go
Together, in their new, strange need.

Far-off the purple mountains loom, —
Vague and far-off, and fixt as fate, —
Which hide from sight that land unknown
Where, ever, like a carven stone
The setting sun doth stand and wait,
And men cry not: "Too late! too late!"
And sorrow turns to a golden gloom.
But O, the long journey all unled
By track of traveler o'er the plain —
The stony desert, bleak and rude,
The bruisèd feet and the tired brain;
And O, the twofold solitude,
The doubt, the danger, and the dread!

XXX — THE SOWER

I

A SOWER went forth to sow;
His eyes were dark with woe;
He crusht the flowers beneath his feet,
Nor smelt the perfume, warm and sweet,
That prayed for pity everywhere.
He came to a field that was harried
By iron, and to heaven laid bare;
He shook the seed that he carried
O'er that brown and bladeless place.
He shook it, as God shakes hail
Over a doomèd land,
When lightnings interlace
The sky and the earth, and His wand
Of love is a thunder-flail.
Thus did that Sower sow;
His seed was human blood,
And tears of women and men.

And I, who near him stood,
Said: When the crop comes, then
There will be sobbing and sighing,
Weeping and wailing and crying,
Flame, and ashes, and woe.

II

It was an autumn day
When next I went that way.
And what, think you, did I see,
What was it that I heard,
What music was in the air?
The song of a sweet-voiced bird?
Nay — but the songs of many,
Thrilled through with praise and prayer.
Of all those voices not any
Were sad of memory;
But a sea of sunlight flowed,
A golden harvest glowed,
And I said: Thou only art wise,
God of the earth and skies!
And I praise Thee, again and again,
For the Sower whose name is Pain.

XXXI — "WHEN THE LAST DOUBT IS DOUBTED"

WHEN the last doubt is doubted,
　　The last black shadow flown;
When the last foe is routed;
　　When the night is over and gone —
Then, Love, O then! there will be rest and peace:
Sweet peace and rest that never thou hast known.

When the hope that in thee moveth
    Is born and brought to sight;
When past is the pain that proveth
    The worth of thy new delight —
O then, Love! then there will be joy and peace:
Deep peace and joy, bright morning after night.

INTERLUDE

As melting snow leaves bare the mountain-side
In spaces that grow wider and more wide,
So melted from the sky the cloudy veil
That hid the face of sunrise. Land and ledge
And waste of glittering waters sent a glare
Back to the smiting sun. The trembling air
Lay, sea on sea, along the horizon's edge;
And on that upper ocean, clear as glass,
The tall ships followed with deep-mirrored sail
Like clouds wind-moved that follow and that pass;
And on that upper ocean, far and fair,
Floated low islands all unseen before.
Green grew the ocean shaken through with light,
And blue the heavens faint-fleckt with plumy white.
Like pennants on the wind, from o'er the rocks
The birds whirled seaward in shrill-piping flocks —
And through the dawn, as through the shadowy night,
The sound of waves that break upon the shore!

PART IV

I — SONG

LOVE, Love, my love,
   The best things are the truest!
When the earth lies shadowy dark below,
   O then the heavens are bluest!
Deep the blue of the sky,
   And sharp the gleam of the stars,
And O, more bright against the night
   The Aurora's crimson bars!

II — THE MIRROR

THAT I should love thee seemeth meet and wise,
   So beautiful thou art that he were mad
   Who in thy countenance no pleasure had;
   Who felt not the still music of thine eyes
Fall on his forehead, as the evening skies
   The music of the stars feel and are glad.
   But o'er my mind one doubt still cast a shade
   Till in my thought this answer did arise:
That thou shouldst love me is not wise or meet,
   For like thee, Love, I am not beautiful;
   And yet I think that haply in my face
Thou findest a true beauty; — this poor, dull,
   Disfigured mirror dimly may repeat
   A little part of thy most heavenly grace.

III — LIKENESS IN UNLIKENESS

WE are alike, and yet, — O strange and sweet! —
   Each in the other difference discerns;

So the torn strands the maiden's finger turns
  Opposing ways, when they again do meet
Clasp each in each, as flame clasps into heat;
  So when this hand on this cool bosom burns,
  Each sense is lost in the other. So two urns
  Do, side by side, the selfsame lines repeat,
But various color gives a lovelier grace,
  And each by contrast still more fine has grown.
  Thus, Love, it was, I did forget thy face
As more and more to me thy soul was known;
  Vague in my mind it grew till, in its place,
  Another came I knew not from my own.

IV — SONG

Not from the whole wide world I chose thee —
  Sweetheart, light of the land and the sea!
The wide, wide world could not inclose thee,
  For thou art the whole wide world to me.

V — ALL IN ONE

Once when a maiden maidenly went by,
  Or when I found some wonder in the grass,
  Or when a purple sunset slow did pass,
  Or a great star rushed silent through the sky;
Once when I heard a singing ecstasy,
  Or saw the moon's face in the river's glass —
  Then I remembered that for me, alas!
  This beauty must for ever and ever die.
But now I may thus sorrow never more;
  From fleeting beauty thou hast torn the pall;
  Of beauty, Love, thou art the soul and core;

And tho' the empty shadow fading fall, —
  Tho' lesser birds lift up their wings and soar, —
  In having thee alone, Love, I have all.

VI — "I COUNT MY TIME BY TIMES THAT I MEET THEE"

I count my time by times that I meet thee;
  These are my yesterdays, my morrows, noons,
  And nights; these my old moons and my new moons.
  Slow fly the hours, or fast the hours do flee,
If thou art far from or art near to me;
  If thou art far, the bird tunes are no tunes;
  If thou art near, the wintry days are Junes —
  Darkness is light, and sorrow cannot be.
Thou art my dream come true, and thou my dream;
  The air I breathe, the world wherein I dwell;
  My journey's end thou art, and thou the way;
Thou art what I would be, yet only seem;
  Thou art my heaven and thou art my hell;
  Thou art my ever-living judgment-day.

VII — SONG

Years have flown since I knew thee first,
And I know thee as water is known of thirst;
Yet I knew thee of old at the first sweet sight,
And thou art strange to me, Love, to-night.

VIII — THE SEASONS

O strange Spring days, when from the shivering
    ground
Love riseth, wakening from his dreamful swound
And, frightened, in the stream his face hath found!

O Summer days, when Love hath grown apace,
And feareth not to look upon Love's face,
And lightnings burn where earth and sky embrace!

O Autumn, when the winds are dank and dread,
How brave above the dying and the dead
The conqueror, Love, uplifts his banner red!

O Winter, when the earth lies white and chill!
Now only hath strong Love his perfect will,
Whom heat, nor cold, nor death can bind nor kill.

IX — "SUMMER'S RAIN AND WINTER'S SNOW"

SUMMER'S rain and winter's snow
With the seasons come and go;
Shine and shower;
Tender bud and perfect flower;
Silver blossom, golden fruit;
Song and lute,
With their inward sound of pain;
Winter's snow and summer's rain;
Frost and fire;
Joy beyond the heart's desire —
And our June comes round again.

X — THE VIOLIN

BEFORE the listening world behold him stand;
The warm air trembles with his passionate play;
Their cheers shower round him like the ocean spray
Round one who waits upon the stormy strand.
Their smiles, sighs, tears all are at his command;

And now they hear the trump of judgment-day,
And now one silver note to heaven doth stray
And fluttering fall upon the golden sand.
But like the murmur of the distant sea
    Their loud applause, and far off, faint, and weak
    Sounds his own music to him, wild and free —
Far from the soul of music that doth speak
    In wordless wail and lyric ecstasy
    From that good viol prest against his cheek.

XI — "O MIGHTY RIVER, TRIUMPHING TO THE SEA"

O MIGHTY river, triumphing to the sea,
Strong, calm, and solemn as thy mountains be!
Poets have sung thy ever-living power,
Thy wintry day, and summer sunset hour;
Have told how rich thou art, how broad, how deep;
What commerce thine, how many myriads reap
The harvest of thy waters. They have sung
Thy moony nights, when every shadow flung
From cliff or pine is peopled with dim ghosts
Of settlers, old-world fairies, or the hosts
Of savage warriors that once plowed thy waves —
Now hurrying to the dance from hidden graves;
The waving outline of thy wooded mountains,
Thy populous towns that stretch from forest fountains
On either side, far to the salty main,
Like golden coins alternate on a chain.

    Thou pathway of the empire of the North,
Thy praises through the earth have traveled forth!
I hear thee praised as one who hears the shout
That follows when a hero from the rout
Of battle issues: "Lo, how brave is he,

How noble, proud, and beautiful!" But she
Who knows him best: "How tender!" So thou art
The river of love to me!
      — Heart of my heart,
Dear love and bride — is it not so indeed? —
Among your treasures keep this new-pluckt reed.

XII — "MY SONGS ARE ALL OF THEE"

My songs are all of thee, what tho' I sing
 Of morning when the stars are yet in sight,
 Of evening, or the melancholy night,
 Of birds that o'er the reddening waters wing;
Of song, of fire, of winds, or mists that cling
 To mountain-tops, of winter all in white,
 Of rivers that toward ocean take their flight,
 Of summer when the rose is blossoming.
I think no thought that is not thine, no breath
 Of life I breathe beyond thy sanctity;
 Thou art the voice that silence uttereth,
And of all sound thou art the sense. From thee
 The music of my song, and what it saith
 Is but the beat of thy heart, throbbed through me.

XIII — AFTER MANY DAYS

Dear heart, I would that after many days,
 When we are gone, true lovers in a book
 Might find these faithful songs of ours. "O look!"
 I hear him murmur while he straightway lays
His finger on the page, and she doth raise
 Her eyes to his. Then, like the winter brook
 From whose young limbs a sudden summer shook
 The fetters, love flows on in sunny ways.

I would that when we are no more, dear heart,
　The world might hold thy unforgotten name
　Inviolate in these eternal rhymes.
I would have poets say: "Let not the art
　Wherewith they loved be lost! To us the blame
　Should love grow less in these our modern times."

XIV — WEAL AND WOE

O HIGHEST, strongest, sweetest woman-soul!
　Thou holdest in the compass of thy grace
　All the strange fate and passion of thy race;
　Of the old, primal curse thou knowest the whole.
Thine eyes, too wise, are heavy with the dole,
　The doubt, the dread of all this human maze;
　Thou in the virgin morning of thy days
　Hast felt the bitter waters o'er thee roll.
Yet thou knowest, too, the terrible delight,
　The still content, and solemn ecstasy;
　Whatever sharp, sweet bliss thy kind may know.
Thy spirit is deep for pleasure as for woe —
　Deep as the rich, dark-caverned, awful sea
　That the keen-winded, glimmering dawn makes
　　white.

XV — "O, LOVE IS NOT A SUMMER MOOD"

O, LOVE is not a summer mood,
　Nor flying phantom of the brain,
Nor youthful fever of the blood,
　　Nor dream, nor fate, nor circumstance.
　　Love is not born of blinded chance,
　　Nor bred in simple ignorance.

Love is the flower of maidenhood;
　Love is the fruit of mortal pain;
And she hath winter in her blood.
　　　True love is stedfast as the skies,
　　　And once alight she never flies;
　　　And love is strong, and love is wise.

XVI — "LOVE IS NOT BOND TO ANY MAN"

LOVE is not bond to any man,
　Nor slave of woman, howso fair.
Love knows no architect nor plan,
　　　She is a lawless wanderer,
　　　She hath no master over her,
　　　And loveth not her worshiper.

But tho' she knoweth law nor plan, —
　Tho' she is free as light and air, —
Love was a slave since time began.
　　　Lo, now, behold a wondrous thing:
　　　Tho' from stone walls she taketh wing,
　　　Love may be led by a silken string.

XVII — "HE KNOWS NOT THE PATH OF DUTY"

HE knows not the path of duty
　Who says that the way is sweet;
But he who is blind to the beauty,
　And finds but thorns for his feet.

He alone is the perfect giver
　Who swears that his gift is naught;
And he is the sure receiver
　Who gains what he never sought.

Heaven from the hopeless doubter
    The true believer makes;
Against the darkness outer
    The light God's likeness takes.

Like the pale, cold moon above her
    With its heart of the heart of fire,
My Love is the one true lover,
    And hers is the soul of desire.

AFTER–SONG

THROUGH love to light! O, wonderful the way
That leads from darkness to the perfect day!
From darkness and from sorrow of the night
To morning that comes singing o'er the sea.
Through love to light! Through light, O God, to Thee,
Who art the love of love, the eternal light of light!

THE CELESTIAL PASSION

THE CELESTIAL PASSION

PRELUDE

O WHITE and midnight sky! O starry bath!
  Wash me in thy pure, heavenly, crystal flood;
  Cleanse me, ye stars, from earthly soil and scath;
  Let not one taint remain in spirit or blood!
Receive my soul, ye burning, awful deeps;
  Touch and baptize me with the mighty power
  That in ye thrills, while the dark planet sleeps;
  Make me all yours for one blest, secret hour!
O glittering host! O high angelic choir!
  Silence each tone that with thy music jars;
  Fill me even as an urn with thy white fire
Till all I am is kindred to the stars!
  Make me thy child, thou infinite, holy night —
  So shall my days be steeped in heavenly light!

PART I

ART AND LIFE

SAID the Poet unto the Seer:
How shall I learn to tell
What I know of Heaven and Hell?
I speak, but to ashes turn
The passions that in me burn.
I shout to the skies, but I hear
No answer from man or God.

Shall I cast my lyre to the sod,
Rest, and give over the strife,
And sink in a voiceless life?
 Said the Seer to the Poet: Arise
And give to the seas and the skies
The message that in thee burns.
Thrice speak, tho' the blue sky turns
Deaf ears, and the ocean spurns
Thy call. Tho' men despise
The word that from out thy heart
Flameth; do thou thy part.
Thrice speak it, aloud, I say,
Then go, released, on thy way;
Live thou deeply and wise;
Suffer as never before;
Know joy, till it cuts to the quick;
Eat the apple, Life, to the core.
Be thou curst
By them thou hast blest, by the sick
Whom thou in thy weakness nursed.
With thy strength the faint endue;
Be praised when 't were better to blame;
In the home of thy spirit be true,
Tho' the voice of the street cry shame.
Be silent till all is done,
Then return, in the light of the sun,
And once more sing.
O, then fling
Into music thy soul! Tell the seas
Again all thy thought; O, be strong
Thy voice as the voice of the waves, as the voice of the
    trees!
Tell the blast,
That shall shudder as onward it flies

With thy word, with thy song;
Tell the skies,
And the world, that shall listen at last!

THE POET AND HIS MASTER

ONE day the poet's harp lay on the ground,
Tho' from it rose a strange and trembling sound
What time the wind swept over with a moan,
Or, now and then, a faint and tinkling tone
When a dead leaf fell shuddering from a tree
And shook the silent wires all tremulously;
And near it, dumb with sorrow, and alone
The poet sat. His heart was like a stone.

Then one drew near him who was robed in white:
It was the poet's master; he had given
To him that harp, once in a happy night
When every silver star that shone in heaven
Made music ne'er before was heard by mortal wight.
And thus the master spoke: —

                              "Why is thy voice
Silent, O poet? Why upon the grass
Lies thy still harp? The fitful breezes pass
And stir the wires, but the skilled player's hand
Moves not upon them. Poet, wake! Rejoice!
Sing and arouse the melancholy land!"

"Master, forbear. I may not sing to-day;
My nearest friend, the brother of my heart,
This day is stricken with sorrow; he must part
From her who loves him. Can I sing, and play
Upon the joyous harp, and mock his woe?"

"Alas, and hast thou then so soon forgot
 The bond that with thy gift of song did go —
 Severe as fate, fixt and unchangeable?
 Even tho' his heart be sounding its own knell,
 Dost thou not know this is the poet's lot:
 'Mid sounds of war, in halcyon times of peace,
 To strike the ringing wire and not to cease;
 In hours of general happiness to swell
 The common joy; and when the people cry
 With piteous voice loud to the pitiless sky,
 'T is his to frame the universal prayer
 And breathe the balm of song upon the accursèd air?"

"But 't is not, O my master! that I borrow
 The robe of grief to deck my brother's sorrow —
 Mine eyes have seen beyond the veil of youth;
 I know what Life is, have caught sight of Truth;
 My heart is dead within me; a thick pall
 Darkens the midday sun."

                              "And dost thou call
 This sorrow? Call this knowledge? O thou blind
 And ignorant! Know, then, thou yet shalt find,
 Ere thy full days are numbered 'neath the sun,
 Thou, in thy shallow youth, hadst but begun
 To guess what knowledge is, what grief may be,
 And all the infinite sum of human misery;
 Shalt find that for each drop of perfect good
 Thou payest, at last, a threefold price in blood;
 What is most noble in thee, — every thought
 Highest and best, — crusht, spat upon, and brought
 To an open shame; thy natural ignorance
 Counted thy crime; the world all ruled by chance,
 Save that the good most suffer; but above

These ills another, cruel, monstrous, worse
Than all before — thy pure and passionate love
Shall bring the old, immitigable curse."

"And thou, who tell'st me this, dost bid me sing?"

"I bid thee sing, even tho' I have not told
All the deep flood of anguish shall be rolled
Across thy breast. Nor, Poet, shalt thou bring
From out those depths thy grief! Tell to the wind
Thy private woes, but not to human ear,
Save in the shape of comfort for thy kind.
But never hush thy song, dare not to cease
While life is thine. Haply, 'mid those who hear,
Thy music to one soul shall murmur peace,
Tho' for thyself it hath no power to cheer.

"Then shall thy still unbroken spirit grow
Strong in its silent suffering and more wise;
And, — as the drenched and thunder-shaken skies
Pass into golden sunset, — thou shalt know
An end of calm, when evening breezes blow;
And, looking on thy life with vision fine,
Shalt see the shadow of a hand divine."

MORS TRIUMPHALIS

I

In the hall of the king the loud mocking of many at one;
While lo! with his hand on his harp the old bard is undone!
One false note, then he stammers, he sobs like a child, he
    is failing,
And the song that so bravely began ends in discord and
    wailing.

II

Can it be it is they who make merry, 't is they taunting
　　him?
Shall the sun, then, be scorned by the planets, the tree
　　by the limb!
These bardlings, these mimics, these echoes, these shad-
　　ows at play,
While he only is real; — they shine but as motes in his
　　day!

III

All that in them is best is from him; all they know he has
　　taught;
But one secret he never could teach, and they never have
　　caught —
The soul of his songs, that goes sighing like wind through
　　the reeds,
And thrills men, and moves them to terror, to prayer,
　　and to deeds.

IV

Has the old poet failed, then — the singer forgotten his
　　art?
Why, 't was he who once startled the world with a cry
　　from his heart;
And he held it entranced in a life-song, all music, all love;
If now it grow faint and grow still, they have called him
　　above.

V

Ah, never again shall we hear such fierce music and
　　sweet —
Surely never from you, ye who mock, for his footstool
　　unmeet;

E'en his song left unsung had more power than the note
  ye prolong,
And one sweep of his harp-strings outpassioned the
  hight of your song.

VI

But a sound like the voice of the pine, like the roar of the
  sea
Arises. He breathes now; he sings; O, again he is
  free.
He has flung from his flesh, from his spirit, their shackles
  accurst,
And he pours all his heart, all his life, in one passionate
  burst.

VII

And now as he chants those who listen turn pale, are
  afraid;
For he sings of a God that made all, and is all that was
  made;
Who is maker of love, and of hate, and of peace, and of
  strife;
Smiles a heaven into being; frowns a hell, that yet
  thrills with His life.

VIII

And he sings of the time that shall be when the earth is
  grown old;
Of the day when the sun shall be withered, and shrunken,
  and cold;
When the stars, and the moon, and the sun, — all their
  glory o'erpast, —
Like apples that shrivel and rot, shall drop into the
  Vast.

IX

And onward and out soars his song on its journey sublime,
'Mid systems that vanish or live in the lilt of his rhyme;
And through making and marring of races, and worlds,
  still he sings
One theme, that o'er all and through all his wild music
  outrings —

X

This one theme: that whate'er be the fate that has hurt
  us or joyed;
Whatever the face that is turned to us out of the void;
Be it cursing or blessing; or night, or the light of the
  sun;
Be it ill, be it good; be it life, be it death, it is ONE; —

XI

One thought, and one law, and one awful and infinite
  power;
In atom, and world; in the bursting of fruit and of
  flower;
The laughter of children, and roar of the lion untamed;
And the stars in their courses — one name that can never
  be named.

XII

But sudden a silence has fallen, the music has fled;
Tho' he leans with his hand on his harp, now indeed
  he is dead;
But the swan-song he sang shall for ever and ever abide
In the heart of the world, with the winds and the murmur-
  ing tide.

THE MASTER-POETS

He the great World-Musician at whose stroke
The stars of morning into music broke;
He from whose Being Infinite are caught
All harmonies of light, and sound, and thought —
Once in each age, to keep the world in tune,
He strikes a note sublime. Nor late, nor soon,
A godlike soul, — music and passion's birth, —
Vibrates across the discord of the earth
And sets the world aright.
                    O, these are they
Who on men's hearts with mightiest power can play —
The master-poets of humanity,
From heaven sent down to lift men to the sky.

PART II

A CHRISTMAS HYMN

I

Tell me what is this innumerable throng
Singing in the heavens a loud angelic song?
These are they who come with swift and shining feet
From round about the throne of God the Lord of Light
    to greet.

II

O, who are these that hasten beneath the starry sky,
As if with joyful tidings that through the world shall fly?
The faithful shepherds these, who greatly were afeared
When, as they watched their flocks by night, the heav-
    enly host appeared.

III

Who are these that follow across the hills of night
A star that westward hurries along the fields of light?
*Three wise men from the east who myrrh and treasure
    bring*
*To lay them at the feet of him their Lord and Christ
    and King.*

IV

What babe new-born is this that in a manger cries?
Near on her bed of pain his happy mother lies.
*O, see ! the air is shaken with white and heavenly
    wings —*
*This is the Lord of all the earth, this is the King of
    Kings.*

V

Tell me, how may I join in this holy feast
With all the kneeling world, and I of all the least?
*Fear not, O faithful heart, but bring what most is
    meet :*
*Bring love alone, true love alone, and lay it at his
    feet.*

EASTER

I

When in the starry gloom
They sought the Lord Christ's tomb,
Two angels stood in sight,
All drest in burning white,
Who unto the women said:
"Why seek ye the living among the dead?"

II

His life, his hope, his heart,
With death they had no part;
For this those words of scorn
First heard that holy morn,
When the waiting angels said:
"Why seek ye the living among the dead?"

III

O, ye of this latter day,
Who journey the selfsame way —
Through morning's twilight gloom
Back to the shadowy tomb;
To you, as to them, was it said:
"Why seek ye the living among the dead?"

IV

The Lord is risen indeed,
He is here for your love, for your need —
Not in the grave, nor the sky,
But here where men live and die;
And true the word that was said:
"Why seek ye the living among the dead?"

V

Wherever are tears and sighs,
Wherever are children's eyes,
Where man calls man his brother,
And loves as himself another,
Christ lives! The angels said:
"Why seek ye the living among the dead?"

A MADONNA OF FRA LIPPO LIPPI

No heavenly maid we here behold,
Tho' round her brow a ring of gold;
This baby, solemn-eyed and sweet,
Is human all from head to feet.

Together close her palms are prest
In worship of that godly guest;
But glad her heart and unafraid
While on her neck his hand is laid.

Two children, happy, laughing, gay,
Uphold the little child in play;
Not flying angels these, what tho'
Four wings from their four shoulders grow.

Fra Lippo, we have learned from thee
A lesson of humanity;
To every mother's heart forlorn,
In every house the Christ is born.

COST

BECAUSE Heaven's cost is Hell, and perfect joy
　Hurts as hurts sorrow; and because we win
　Some boon of grace with the dread cost of sin,
　Or suffering born of sin; because the alloy
Of blood but makes the bliss of victory brighter;
　Because true worth hath surest proof herein,
　That it should be reproached, and called akin
　To evil things — black making white the whiter;
Because no cost seems great near this — that He

Should pay the ransom wherewith we were priced;
And none could name a darker infamy
Than that a god was spit upon, — enticed
By those he came to save, to the accursèd tree, —
For this I know that Christ indeed is Christ.

THE SONG OF A HEATHEN

(SOJOURNING IN GALILEE, A. D. 32)

I

IF Jesus Christ is a man, —
  And only a man, — I say
That of all mankind I cleave to him,
  And to him will I cleave alway.

II

If Jesus Christ is a God, —
  And the only God, — I swear
I will follow Him through heaven and hell,
  The earth, the sea, and the air!

HOLY LAND

THIS is the earth he walked on; not alone
  That Asian country keeps the sacred stain;
  Ah, not alone the far Judæan plain,
  Mountain and river! Lo, the sun that shone
On him, shines now on us; when day is gone
  The moon of Galilee comes forth again
  And lights our path as his; an endless chain
  Of years and sorrows makes the round world one.
The air we breathe, he breathed — the very air
  That took the mold and music of his high
  And godlike speech. Since then shall mortal dare

With base thought front the ever-sacred sky —
　Soil with foul deed the ground whereon he laid
　In holy death his pale, immortal head!

ON A PORTRAIT OF SERVETUS

THOU grim and haggard wanderer, who dost look
　With haunting eyes forth from the narrow page!
　I know what fires consumed with inward rage
　Thy broken frame, what tempests chilled and shook.
Ah, could not thy remorseless foeman brook
　Time's sure devourment, but must needs assuage
　His anger in thy blood, and blot the age
　With that dark crime which virtue's semblance took!
Servetus! that which slew thee lives to-day,
　Tho' in new forms it taints our modern air;
　Still in heaven's name the deeds of hell are done;
Still on the high-road, 'neath the noonday sun,
　The fires of hate are lit for them who dare
　Follow their Lord along the untrodden way.

"DESPISE NOT THOU"

DESPISE not thou thy father's ancient creed;
　Of his pure life it was the golden thread
　Whereon bright days were gathered, bead by bead,
　Till death laid low that dear and reverend head.
From olden faith how many a glorious deed
　Hath lit the world; its blood-stained banner led
　The martyrs heavenward; yea, it was the seed
　Of knowledge, whence our modern freedom spread.
Not always has man's *credo* proved a snare —
　But a deliverance, a sign, a flame
　To purify the dense and pestilent air,

Writing on pitiless heavens one pitying name;
  And 'neath the shadow of the dread eclipse
  It shines on dying eyes and pallid lips.

"TO REST FROM WEARY WORK"

To REST from weary work one day of seven;
  One day to turn our backs upon the world,
  Its soil wash from us, and strive on to Heaven —
  Whereto we daily climb, but quick are hurled
Down to the pit of human pride and sin.
  Help me, ye powers celestial! to come nigh;
  Ah, let me catch one little glimpse within
  The heavenly city, lest my spirit die.
These be my guides, my messengers, my friends:
  Books of wise poets; the musician's art;
  The ocean whose deep music never ends;
The silence of the forest's shadowy heart;
  Not less the brooding organ's solemn blare,
  And kneeling multitudes' low-murmuring prayer.

PART III

RECOGNITION

I

IN darkness of the visionary night
This I beheld: Wide space and therein God,
God who in dual nature doth abide —
Love, and the Loved One, Power and Beauty's self;
Him even the spirit's eye might not transfix
But sidelong gazed, fainting before the light.
And forth from God did come, — with dreadful thrill,
And starry music like to million wires

That shiver with the breathings of the dawn, —
Creation, boundless, bodiless, unformed,
And white with trembling fire and light intense,
And outward pulsings like the boreal flame.
One mighty cloud it seemed, nor star, nor earth,
Or like a nameless growth of the under-seas;
Creation dumb, unconscious, yet alive
With some deep, inward passion unexprest,
And swift, concentric, never-ceasing urge —
Resolving gradual to one disk of fire.
And as I looked, behold! the flying rim
Grew separate from the center; this again
Divided, and the whole still swift revolved,
Ring within ring, and fiery wheel in wheel;
Till, sudden or slow as chanced, the outmost edge
Whirled into fragments, each a separate sun,
With lesser globes attendant on its flight.
These while I gazed turned dark with smoldering fire
And, slow contracting, grew to solid orbs.
Then knew I that this planetary world,
Cradled in light, and curtained with the dawn
And starry eve, was born; tho' in itself
Complete and perfect all, yet but a part
And atom of the living universe.

II

Unconscious still the child of the conscious God —
Creation, born of Beauty and of Love,
Beauty the womb and mother of all worlds.
But soon with breathless speed the new-made earth
Swept near me where I watched the birth of things,
Its greatening bulk eclipsing, star by star,
Half the bright heavens. Then I beheld crawl forth
Upon the earth's cool crust most wondrous forms

Wherein were hid, in transmutation strange,
Sparks of the ancient, never-ending fire;
Shapes moved not solely by exterior law
But having will and motion of their own —
First sluggish and minute, then by degrees
Monstrous, enorm. Then other forms more fine
Streamed ceaseless on my sight, until at last,
Rising and turning its slow gaze about
Across the abysmal void, the mighty child
Of the supreme, divine Omnipotence —
Creation, born of God, by Him begot,
Conscious in MAN, no longer blind and dumb,
Beheld and knew its father and its God.

HYMN

SUNG AT THE PRESENTATION OF THE OBELISK TO THE
CITY OF NEW YORK, FEBRUARY 22, 1881

I

GREAT God, to whom since time began
  The world has prayed and striven;
Maker of stars, and earth, and man,
  To Thee our praise is given.
      Here, by this ancient Sign
      Of Thine own Light divine,
      We lift to Thee our eyes,
      Thou Dweller of the Skies;
    Hear us, O God in Heaven!

II

Older than Nilus' mighty flood
  Into the Mid-Sea pouring,
Or than the sea, Thou God hast stood —
  Thou God of our adoring!

Waters and stormy blast
Haste when Thou bid'st them haste;
Silent, and hid, and still,
Thou sendest good and ill;
Thy ways are past exploring.

III

In myriad forms, by myriad names,
  Men seek to bind and mold Thee;
But Thou dost melt, like wax in flames,
  The cords that would enfold Thee.
    Who madest life and light,
    Bring'st morning after night,
    Who all things didst create —
    No majesty, nor state,
Nor word, nor world can hold Thee!

IV

Great God, to whom since time began
  The world has prayed and striven;
Maker of stars, and earth, and man,
  To Thee our praise is given.
    Of suns Thou art the Sun,
    Eternal, holy One;
    Who us can help save Thou?
    To Thee alone we bow!
Hear us, O God in heaven!

A THOUGHT

ONCE, looking from a window on a land
That lay in silence underneath the sun, —
A land of broad, green meadows, through which
    poured

Two rivers, slowly widening to the sea, —
Thus as I looked, I know not how nor whence,
Was born into my unexpectant soul
That thought, late learned by anxious-witted man,
The infinite patience of the Eternal Mind.

THE VOICE OF THE PINE

'T IS night upon the lake. Our bed of boughs
Is built where, high above, the pine-tree soughs.
'T is still — and yet what woody noises loom
Against the background of the silent gloom!
One well might hear the opening of a flower
If day were husht as this. A mimic shower
Just shaken from a branch, how large it sounded,
As 'gainst our canvas roof its three drops bounded!
Across the rumpling waves the hoot-owl's bark
Tolls forth the midnight hour upon the dark.
What mellow booming from the hills doth come? —
The mountain quarry strikes its mighty drum.

Long had we lain beside our pine-wood fire,
From things of sport our talk had risen higher.
How frank and intimate the words of men
When tented lonely in some forest glen!
No dallying now with masks, from whence emerges
Scarce one true feature forth. The night-wind urges
To straight and simple speech. So was our thought
Audible ; secrets to the light were brought.
The hid and spiritual hopes, the wild,
Unreasoned longings that, from child to child,
Mortals still cherish (tho' with modern shame) —
To these, and things like these, we gave a name;
And as we talked, the intense and resinous fire

Lit up the towering boles, till nigh and nigher
They gathered round, a ghostly company,
Like beasts who seek to know what men may be.

Then to our hemlock beds, but not to sleep —
For listening to the stealthy steps that creep
About the tent, or falling branch, but most
A noise was like the rustling of a host,
Or like the sea that breaks upon the shore —
It was the pine-tree's murmur. More and more
It took a human sound. These words I felt
Into the skyey darkness float and melt: —

"Heardst thou these wanderers reasoning of a time
When men more near the Eternal One shall climb?
How like the new-born child, who cannot tell
A mother's arm that wraps it warm and well!
Leaves of His rose; drops in His sea that flow, —
Are they, alas, so blind they may not know
Here, in this breathing world of joy and fear,
We can no nearer get to God than here."

MORNING, NOON, AND NIGHT

THE mountain that the morn doth kiss
    Glad greets its shining neighbor;
Lord! heed the homage of our bliss,
    The incense of our labor.

Sharp smites the sun like burning rain,
    And field and flower languish;
Hear, Lord! the pleading of our pain,
    The passion of our anguish.

Now the long shadows eastward creep,
    The golden sun is setting;
Take, Lord! the worship of our sleep,
    The praise of our forgetting.

"DAY UNTO DAY UTTERETH SPEECH"

THE speech that day doth utter, and the night,
    Full oft to mortal ears it hath no sound;
    Dull are our eyes to read upon the ground
    What's written there; and stars are hid by light.
So when the dark doth fall, awhile our sight
    Kens the unwonted orbs that circle round,
    Then quick in sleep our human sense is bound —
    Speechless for us the starry heavens and bright.
But when the day doth close there is one word
    That's writ amid the sunset's golden embers;
    And one at morn; by them our hearts are stirred:
Splendor of Dawn, and Evening that remembers;
    These are the rhymes of God; thus, line on line,
    Our souls are moved to thoughts that are divine.

PART IV

THE SOUL

THREE messengers to me from heaven came
    And said: "There is a deathless human soul;
    It is not lost, as is the fiery flame
    That dies into the undistinguished whole.
Ah, no; it separate is, distinct as God —
    Nor any more than He can it be killed;
    Then fearless give thy body to the clod,
    For naught can quench the light that once it filled!"

Three messengers — the first was human Love;
   The second voice came crying in the night
   With strange and awful music from above;
None who have heard that voice forget it quite;
   Birth is it named; the third, O, turn not pale!
   'T was Death to the undying soul cried, Hail!

"WHEN LOVE DAWNED"

When love dawned on that world which is my mind,
   Then did the outer world wherein I went
   Suffer a sudden, strange transfigurement;
   It was as if new sight were given the blind.
Then where the shore to the wide sea inclined
   I watched with new eyes the new sun's ascent;
   My heart was stirred within me as I leant
   And listened to a voice in every wind.
O purple sea! O joy beyond control!
   O land of love and youth! O happy throng!
   Were ye then real, or did ye only seem?
Dear is that morning twilight of the soul, —
   The mystery, the waking voice of song, —
   For now I know it was not all a dream.

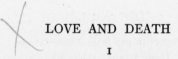

LOVE AND DEATH

I

Now who can take from us what we have known —
   We that have looked into each other's eyes?
   Tho' sudden night should blacken all the skies,
   The day is ours, and what the day has shown.
What we have seen and been, hath not this grown
   Part of our very selves? We, made love-wise,

What power shall slay our living memories,
 And who shall take from us what is our own?
So, when a shade of the last parting fell,
 This thought gave peace, as he deep comfort hath
 Who, thirsting, drinks cool waters from a well.
But soon I felt more near that fatal breath;
 More near he drew, till I his face could tell,
 Till then unseen, unknown — I looked on Death.

II

We know not where they tarry who have died;
 The gate wherein they entered is made fast;
 No living mortal hath seen one who past
Hither, from out that darkness deep and wide.
We lean on Faith; and some less wise have cried:
 "Behold the butterfly, the seed that's cast!"
 Vain hopes that fall like flowers before the blast!
What man can look on Death unterrified? —
Who love can never die! They are a part
 Of all that lives beneath the summer sky;
 With the world's living soul their souls are one;
Nor shall they in vast nature be undone
 And lost in the general life. Each separate heart
 Shall live, and find its own, and never die.

FATHER AND CHILD

BENEATH the deep and solemn midnight sky,
 At this last verge and boundary of time
 I stand, and listen to the starry chime
That sounds to the inward ear, and will not die.
Now do the thoughts that daily hidden lie
 Arise, and live in a celestial clime, —
 Unutterable thoughts, most high, sublime, —
Crossed by one dread that frights mortality.

Thus, as I muse, I hear my little child
  Sob in its sleep within the cottage near —
  My own dear child! Gone is that mortal doubt!
The Power that drew our lives forth from the wild
  Our Father is; we shall to Him be dear,
  Nor from His universe be blotted out!

"BEYOND THE BRANCHES OF THE PINE"

BEYOND the branches of the pine
The golden sun no more doth shine,
  But still the solemn afterglow
Floods the deep heavens with light divine.

The night-wind stirs the corn-field near,
The gray moon turns to silver clear,
  And one by one the glimmering stars
In the blue dome of heaven appear.

Now do the mighty hosts of light
Across the darkness take their flight;
  They rise above the eastern hill
And silent journey through the night.

And there beneath the starry zone,
In the deep, narrow grave, alone,
  Rests all that mortal was of her,
The purest spirit I have known.

AN AUTUMN MEDITATION

As the long day of cloud and storm and sun
Declines into the dark and silent night,
So past the old man's life from human gaze;

But not till sunset, full of lovely light
And color that the day might not reveal,
Bathed in soft gloom the landscape.

                         Thus, kind Heaven,
Let me, too, die when Autumn holds the year, —
Serene, with tender hues and bracing airs, —
And near me those I love; with no black thoughts,
Nor dread of what may come! Yea, when I die
Let me not miss from nature the cool rush
Of northern winds; let Autumn sunset skies
Be golden; let the cold, clear blue of night
Whiten with stars as now! then shall I fade
From life to life — pass on the year's full tide
Into the swell and vast of the outer sea
Beyond this narrow world.

                         For Autumn days
To me not melancholy are, but full
Of joy and hope, mysterious and high;
And with strange promise rife. Then it meseems
Not failing is the year, but gathering fire
Even as the cold increases.

                         Grows a weed
More richly here beside our mellow seas
That is the Autumn's harbinger and pride.
When fades the cardinal-flower, whose heart-red bloom
Glows like a living coal upon the green
Of the midsummer meadows, then how bright,
How deepening bright, like mounting flame doth burn
The goldenrod upon a thousand hills!
This is the Autumn's flower, and to my soul
A token fresh of beauty and of life,
And life's supreme delight.

                    When I am gone,
Something of me I would might subtly pass
Within these flowers twain of all the year;
So might my spirit send a sudden stir
Into the hearts of those who love these hills,
These woods, these waves, and meadows by the sea.

"CALL ME NOT DEAD"

CALL me not dead when I, indeed, have gone
  Into the company of the everliving
  High and most glorious poets! Let thanksgiving
  Rather be made. Say: "He at last hath won
Rest and release, converse supreme and wise,
  Music and song and light of immortal faces;
  To-day, perhaps, wandering in starry places,
  He hath met Keats, and known him by his eyes.
To-morrow (who can say?) Shakespeare may pass,
  And our lost friend just catch one syllable
  Of that three-centuried wit that kept so well;
Or Milton; or Dante, looking on the grass
  Thinking of Beatrice, and listening still
  To chanted hymns that sound from the heavenly hill."

"EACH MOMENT HOLY IS"

  EACH moment holy is, for out from God
  Each moment flashes forth a human soul.
  Holy each moment is, for back to Him
  Some wandering soul each moment home returns.

"WHEN TO SLEEP I MUST"

        WHEN to sleep I must
        Where my fathers sleep;

When fulfilled the trust,
And the mourners weep;
When, tho' free from rust,
Sword hath lost its worth —
Let me bring to earth
No dishonored dust.

TO A DEPARTED FRIEND

DEAR friend, who lovedst well this pleasant life!
  One year ago it is this very day
  Since thou didst take thy uncompanioned way
  Into the silent land, from out the strife
And joyful tumult of the world. The knife
  Wherewith that sorrow cut us still doth stay,
  And we, to whom thou daily didst betray
  Thy gentle soul, with faith and worship rife,
Love thee not less but more — as time doth go
  And we too hasten toward that land unknown
  Where those most dear are gathering one by one.
The power divine that here did touch thy heart —
  Hath this withdrawn from thee, where now thou art?
  Would thou indeed couldst tell what thou dost know!

"THE EVENING STAR"

THE evening star trembles and hides from him
  Who fain would hold it with imperious stare;
  Yet, to the averted eye, lo! unaware
  .It shines serene, no longer shy and dim.
O, slow and sweet, its chalice to the brim
  Fills the leaf-shadowed grape with rich and rare
  Cool sunshine, caught from the white circling air!
  Home from his journey to the round world's rim, —

Through lonely lands, through cloudy seas and vext, —
  At last the Holy Grail met Launfal's sight.
  So when my friend lost him who was her next
Of soul, — life of her life, — all day the fight
  Raged with a dumb and pitiless God. Perplext
  She slept. Heaven sent its comfort in the night.

LIFE

I

GREAT Universe — what dost thou with thy dead!
  Now thinking on the myriads that have gone
  Into a seeming blank oblivion,
  With here and there a most resplendent head, —
Eyes of such trancing sweetness, or so dread,
  That made the soul to quake who looked thereon, —
  All utterly wiped out, dismissed, and done;
  Lost, speechless, viewless, and forever fled!
Myriad on myriad, past the power to count; —
  Where are they, thou dumb Nature? Do they shine,
  Released from separate life, in summer airs,
On moony seas, in dawns? — or up the stairs
  Of spiritual being slowly mount
  And by degrees grow more and more divine?

II

Ah, thou wilt never answer to our call,
  Thou Voiceless One — naught in thee can be stirred,
  What tho' the soul, like to a frightened bird,
  Dash itself wildly 'gainst thy mountain-wall.
From Nature comes no answer, tho' we fall
  In utmost anguish praying to be heard,
  Or peer below, or our brave spirits gird
  For steep and starry flight; 't is silent all.

In vain to question — save the heart of man,
  The throbbing human heart, that still doth keep
  Its truth, love, hope, its high and quenchless faith.
By day, by night, when all else faints in sleep,
   "Naught is but Life," it cries; "there is no death;
  Life, Life doth only live, since Life began."

THE FREED SPIRIT

BROTHER of sorrow and mortality!
  Not always shall we chide the failing flesh
  That lets the netted soul to silence fly,
  Like a wild bird that breaks the treacherous mesh;
Not always shall men curse in stormy sky
  The laughter and the fury of a Power
  That sees its chance-born children sink and die —
  Hurling or death or life for dole or dower.
Who deep his spirit searches can deny
  O nevermore, that life doth leave a trace
  Of something not all heavenly; tho' we try
Daily to turn toward Heaven a stedfast face.
  Even grief doth soil us with its poisonous breath —
  Then free our spirits utterly, pure Death!

UNDYING LIGHT

I

WHEN in the golden western summer skies
  A flaming glory starts, and slowly fades
  Through crimson tone on tone to deeper shades,
  There falls a silence, while the daylight dies
Lingering — but not with human agonies
  That tear the soul, or terror that degrades;
  A holy peace the failing world pervades,
  Nor any fear of that which onward lies.

For well, ah well, the darkened vale recalls
  A thousand times ten thousand vanished suns;
  Ten thousand sunsets from whose blackened walls
Reflamed the white and living day that runs,
  In light which brings all beauty to the birth,
  Deathless forever round the ancient earth.

II

O Thou the Lord and Maker of life and light!
  Full heavy are the burdens that do weigh
  Our spirits earthward, as through twilight gray
  We journey to the end and rest of night;
Tho' well we know to the deep inward sight
  Darkness is but Thy shadow, and the day
  Where Thou art never dies, but sends its ray
  Through the wide universe with restless might.
O Lord of Light, steep Thou our souls in Thee!
  That when the daylight trembles into shade,
  And falls the silence of mortality,
And all is done, we shall not be afraid,
  But pass from light to light; from earth's dull gleam
  Into the very heart and heaven of our dream.

LYRICS

LYRICS

PART I

ODE

I

I AM the spirit of the morning sea;
I am the awakening and the glad surprise;
I fill the skies
With laughter and with light.
Not tears, but jollity
At birth of day brim the strong man-child's eyes.
Behold the white
Wide threefold beams that from the hidden sun
Rise swift and far —
One where Orion keeps
His armèd watch, and one
That to the midmost starry heaven upleaps;
The third blots out the firm-fixt Northern Star.

I am the wind that shakes the glittering wave,
Hurries the snowy spume along the shore
And dies at last in some far, murmuring cave.
My voice thou hearest in the breaker's roar —
That sound which never failed since time began,
And first around the world the shining tumult ran.

II

I light the sea and wake the sleeping land.
My footsteps on the hills make music, and my hand
Plays like a harper's on the wind-swept pines.

With the wind and the day
I follow round the world — away! away!
Wide over lake and plain my sunlight shines
And every wave and every blade of grass
Doth know me as I pass;
And me the western sloping mountains know, and me
The far-off, golden sea.

O sea, whereon the passing sun doth lie!
O man, who watchest by that golden sea!
Grieve not, O, grieve not thou, but lift thine eye
And see me glorious in the sunset sky!

III

I love not the night
Save when the stars are bright,
Or when the moon
Fills the white air with silence like a tune.
Yea, even the night is mine
When the Northern Lights outshine,
And all the wild heavens throb in ecstasy divine; —
Yea, mine deep midnight, tho' the black sky lowers,
When the sea burns white and breaks on the shore in
      starry showers.

IV

I am the laughter of the new-born child
On whose soft-breathing sleep an angel smiled.
And I all sweet first things that are:
First songs of birds, not perfect as at last, —
Broken and incomplete, —
But sweet, O, sweet!
And I the first faint glimmer of a star
To the wreckt ship that tells the storm is past;
The first keen smells and stirrings of the Spring;

First snowflakes, and first May-flowers after snow;
The silver glow
Of the new moon's ethereal ring;
The song the morning stars together made,
And the first kiss of lovers under the first June shade.

V

My sword is quick, my arm is strong to smite
In the dread joy and fury of the fight.
I am with those who win, not those who fly;
With those who live I am, not those who die.
Who die? Nay, nay, that word
Where I am is unheard;
For I am the spirit of youth that cannot change,
Nor cease, nor suffer woe;
And I am the spirit of beauty that doth range
Through natural forms and motions, and each show
Of outward loveliness. With me have birth
All gentleness and joy in all the earth.
Raphael knew me, and showed the world my face;
Me Homer knew, and all the singing race —
For I am the spirit of light, and life, and mirth.

A SONG OF EARLY SUMMER

NOT yet the orchard lifted
  Its cloudy bloom to the sky,
Nor through the dim twilight drifted
  The whippoorwill's low cry;

The gray rock had not made
  Of the vine its glistening kirtle;
Nor shook in the locust shade
  The purple bells of the "myrtle."

Not yet up the chimney-hollow
  Was heard in the darkling night
The boom and whir of the swallow,
  And the twitter that follows the flight;

Before the foamy whitening
  Of the water below the mill;
Ere yet the summer lightning
  Shone red at the edge of the hill;

In the time of sun and showers,
  Of skies half black, half clear;
'Twixt melting snows and flowers;
  At the poise of the flying year;

When woods flusht pink and yellow
  In dreams of leafy June;
And days were keen or mellow
  Like tones in a changing tune;

Before the birds had broken
  Forth in their song divine,
O, then the word was spoken
  That made my darling mine.

A MIDSUMMER SONG

O, father's gone to market-town, he was up before the
    day,
And Jamie's after robins, and the man is making hay,
And whistling down the hollow goes the boy that minds
    the mill,
While mother from the kitchen-door is calling with a will:
      "Polly! — Polly! — The cows are in the corn!
        O, where's Polly?"

From all the misty morning air there comes a summer
    sound —
A murmur as of waters from skies and trees and ground.
The birds they sing upon the wing, the pigeons bill and
    coo,
And over hill and hollow rings again the loud halloo:
      "Polly! — Polly! — The cows are in the corn!
      O, where's Polly?"

Above the trees the honey-bees swarm by with buzz and
    boom,
And in the field and garden a thousand blossoms bloom.
Within the farmer's meadow a brown-eyed daisy blows,
And down at the edge of the hollow a red and thorny
    rose.
      But Polly! — Polly! — The cows are in the corn!
      O, where's Polly?

How strange at such a time of day the mill should stop
    its clatter!
The farmer's wife is listening now and wonders what's
    the matter.
O, wild the birds are singing in the wood and on the hill,
While whistling up the hollow goes the boy that minds
    the mill.
      But Polly! — Polly! — The cows are in the corn!
      O, where's Polly?

"ON THE WILD ROSE TREE"

On the wild rose tree
Many buds there be,
Yet each sunny hour
Hath but one perfect flower.

Thou who wouldst be wise
Open wide thine eyes;
In each sunny hour
Pluck the one perfect flower!

"BEYOND ALL BEAUTY IS THE UNKNOWN GRACE"

BEYOND all beauty is the unknown grace;
  Above all bliss a higher; and above
  The lovingest is a more loving love
  That shows not the still anguish of its face.
Than death there is a deathlier. Brief space
  Behind despair the blacker shadows rove;
  Beneath all life a deeper life doth move:
  So, friends of mine, when empty is my place,—
For me no more grass grows, dead leaves are stirred,—
  And still the songs that once you loved to hear;
  True friends whom well I thank for every word
Of heart-help,— praise or blame,— as you draw near
  I pray that 'mid your tears this may be heard:
  "For what he never did he is most dear."

THE VIOLET

A VIOLET lay in the grass,
A tear in its golden eye;
And it said: "Alas and alas!
The night is over and gone,
Another day is anigh,
And I am alone, alone!
There is none to care if I die,
There is none to be glad that I live;
The lovers they pass me by

And never a glance they give.
And I could love so well, so well!
If one would but tarry and tell
A tale that was told to me only: —
My lover might go his ways,
But through all the nights and the days
I should never again be lonely!"

Then sudden there fell a look
Into that violet's heart.
It lifted its face with a start;
It arose; it trembled and shook.
"At last, O, at last!" it cried;
Down drooped its head, and it died.

Is God in Heaven! Is the light
Of the moons, and the stars, and the suns,
His — or the Evil One's,
Is He cruel, or mad, or right!

The lily that grew by the wall,
Its heart was heavy with bliss.
In the night it heard a call;
It listened, it felt a kiss;
Then a loving Wind did fall
On its breast, and shiver with gladness:
The morning brought love's madness
To light, — and the lover fled.
But the eyes that burned in his head
Shot love through each and all,
For the lily that bloomed by the wall
Shone sweet in every place, —
In the earth, and the sky above,
And the lover saw never the face
Of the flower that died of love.

Hush! Hush! Let no sorrow be spoken!
Tho' it perish, no pity shall flout it.
Better to die heart-broken
Of love than to live without it!

THE YOUNG POET

I

WHEN I am dead and buried, then
There will be mourning among men.
I hear one musing on my dust:
"How hard he fought to win his crust."
And one, "He was too sensitive
In this cold-wintered world to live."
Another, weeping, "Ah, how few
So gentle-hearted and so true."
"I saw him only once, and yet
I think I never shall forget
The strange, sad look in those young eyes,"
Another says, and then with wise
And solemn-shaking head — "No doubt
The hot heart burned that frail frame out."

II

Good friends, a discount on your grief!
A little present help were worth
More than a sorrow-stricken earth
When I am but a withered leaf.
An outstretched hand were better to me
Than your glib graveyard sympathy.
You need not pity and rhyme and paint me,
You need not weep for, and sigh for, and saint me
After you've starved me — driven me dead.
Friends! do you hear? What I want is bread!

A SONG OF EARLY AUTUMN

WHEN late in summer the streams run yellow,
   Burst the bridges and spread into bays;
When berries are black and peaches are mellow,
   And hills are hidden by rainy haze;

When the goldenrod is golden still,
   But the heart of the sunflower is darker and sadder;
When the corn is in stacks on the slope of the hill,
   And slides o'er the path the stripèd adder;

When butterflies flutter from clover to thicket,
   Or wave their wings on the drooping leaf;
When the breeze comes shrill with the call of the cricket,
   Grasshoppers' rasp, and rustle of sheaf;

When high in the field the fern-leaves wrinkle,
   And brown is the grass where the mowers have mown;
When low in the meadow the cow-bells tinkle,
   And small brooks crinkle o'er stock and stone.

When heavy and hollow the robin's whistle
   And shadows are deep in the heat of noon;
When the air is white with the down o' the thistle,
   And the sky is red with the harvest moon;

O, then be chary, young Robert and Mary,
   No time let slip, not a moment wait!
      If the fiddle would play it must stop its tuning,
      And they who would wed must be done with their
         mooning;
So, let the churn rattle, see well to the cattle,
   And pile the wood by the barn-yard gate!

THE BUILDING OF THE CHIMNEY

I

My chimney is builded
On a hill by the sea,
At the edge of a wood
That the sunset has gilded
Since time was begun
And the earth first was done:
For mine and for me
And for you, John Burroughs,
My friend old and good,
At the edge of a wood
On a hill by the sea
My chimney is builded.

II

My chimney gives forth
All its heat to the north,
While its right arm it reaches
Toward the meadows and beaches,
And its left it extends
To its pine-tree friends.
All its heat to the north
My chimney gives forth.

III

My chimney is builded
Of red and gray granite:
Of great split boulders
Are its thighs and its shoulders;
Its mouth — try to span it.

'T is a nine-foot block —
The shelf that hangs over

The stout hearth-rock.
Then the lines they upswell
Like a huge church-bell,
Or a bellying sail
In a stiff south gale
When the ship rolls well,
With a blue sky above her.

IV

My chimney — come view it,
And I'll tell you, John Burroughs,
What is built all through it:
First the derrick's shrill creak,
That perturbed the still air
With a cry of despair.
The lone traveler who past
At the fall of the night
If he saw not its mast
Stood still with affright
At a sudden strange sound —
Hark! a woman's wild shriek?
Or the baying of a hound?

Then the stone-hammer's clink
And the drill's sharp tinkle,
And bird-songs that sprinkle
Their notes through the wood
(With pine odors scented),
On the swift way to drink
At the spring cold and good
That bubbles 'neath the stone
Where the red chieftain tented
In the days that are gone.

Yes, 'twixt granite and mortar
Many songs, long or shorter,
Are imprisoned in the wall;
And when red leaves shall fall, —
Coming home, all in herds,
From the air to the earth, —
When I have my heart's desire,
And we sit by the hearth
In the glow of the fire,
You and I, John of Birds,
We shall hear as they call
From the gray granite wall;
You shall name one and all.

There's the crow's caw-cawing
From the pine-tree's hight,
And the cat-bird's sawing,
The hissing of the adder
That climbed the rock ladder,
And the song of Bob White;
The robin's loud clatter,
The chipmunk's chatter,
And the mellow-voiced bell
That the cuckoo strikes well;
Yes, betwixt the stones and in
There is built a merry din.

But not all bright and gay
Are the songs we shall hear;
For as day turns to gray
Comes a voice low and clear —
Whippoorwill sounds his wail
Over hill, over dale,
Till the soul fills with fright.

'T is the bird that was heard
On the fields drenched with blood
By the dark southern flood
When they died in the night.

V

But you cannot split granite
Howsoe'er you may plan it,
Without bringing blood;
(There's a drop of mine there
On that block four-square).
Certain oaths, I'm aware,
Sudden, hot, and not good
(May Heaven cleanse the guilt!)
In these stone walls are built; —
With the wind through the pine-wood blowing,
The creak of tree on tree,
Child-laughter, and the lowing
Of the homeward-driven cattle,
The sound of wild birds singing,
Of steel on granite ringing,
The memory of battle,
And tales of the roaring sea.

VI

For my chimney was builded
By a Plymouth County sailor,
An old North Sea whaler.
In the warm noon spell
'T was good to hear him tell
Of the great September blow
A dozen years ago: —
How at dawn of the day
The wind began to play,

Till it cut the waves flat
Like the brim of your hat.
There was no sea about,
But it blew straight out
Till the ship lurcht over;
But 't was quick to recover,
When, all of a stroke,
The hurricane broke.
Great heavens! how it roared,
And how the rain poured;
The thirty-fathom chain
Dragged out all in vain.
"What next?" the captain cried
To the mate by his side;
Then Tip Ryder he replied:
"Fetch the ax — no delay —
Cut the mainmast away;
If you want to save the ship
Let the mainmast rip!"
But another said, "Wait!"
And they did — till too late.
On her beam-ends she blew,
In the sea half the crew —
Struggling back through the wrack,
There to cling day and night.
Not a sail heaves in sight;
And, the worst, one in thirst
(Knows no better, the poor lad!)
Drinks salt water and goes mad.

Eighty hours blown and tost,
Five good sailors drowned and lost,
And the rest brought to shore;
— Some to sail as before;

"Not Tip Ryder, if he starves
Building chimneys, building wharves."

VII

Now this was the manner
Of the building of the chimney.
('T is a good old-timer,
As you, friend John, will own.)
Old man Vail cut the stone;
William Ryder was the builder;
Stanford White was the planner;
And the owner and rhymer
Is Richard Watson Gilder.

"A WORD SAID IN THE DARK"

A WORD said in the dark
And hands prest, for a token;
"Now, little maiden, mark
The word that you have spoken;
Be not your promise broken!"

His lips upon her cheek
Felt tears among their kisses;
"O, pardon I bespeak
If for my doubting this is!
Now all my doubting ceases."

A RIDDLE OF LOVERS

OF my fair lady's lovers there were two
Who loved her more than all; nor she, nor they
Guessed which of these loved better, for one way
This had of loving, that another knew.

One round her neck brave arms of empire threw
   And covered her with kisses where she lay;
   The other sat apart, nor did betray
   Sweet sorrow at that sight; but rather drew
His pleasure of his lady through the soul
   And sense of this one. So there truly ran
   Two separate loves through one embrace; the whole
This lady had of both, when one began
   To clasp her close, and win her dear lips' goal.
   Now read my lovers' riddle if you can.

THE DARK ROOM

(A PARABLE)

I

A MAIDEN sought her love in a dark room, —
   So early had she yearned from yearning sleep,
   So hard it was from her true love to keep, —
   And blind she went through that all-silent gloom,
Like one who wanders weeping in a tomb.
   Heavy her heart, but her light fingers leap
   With restless grasp and question in that deep
   Unanswering void. Now when a hand did loom
At last, how swift her warm impassioned face
   Prest 'gainst the black and solemn-yielding air,
   As near more near she groped to that bright place,
And seized the hand, and drowned it with her hair,
   And bent her body to his fierce embrace,
   And knew what joy was in the darkness there.

II

Great God! the arms wherein that maiden fell
   Were not her lover's; I am her lover — I,

Who sat here in the shadows silently,
  Thinking — at last the longed-for miracle!
Thinking to me she moved, and all was well.
  She saw me not, yet dimly could descry
  That beautiful hand of his, and with a sigh
  Sank on his fair and treacherous breast. The spell
Of the Evil One was on me. All in vain
  I strove to speak — my parchèd lips were dumb.
  See! see! the wan and whitening window-pane!
See, in the night, the awful morning bloom!
  Too late she will know all! Heaven! send thy rain
  Of death, nor let the sun of wakening come!

BEFORE SUNRISE

THE winds of morning move and sing;
The western stars are lingering;
In the pale east one planet still
Shines large above King Philip's hill; —

And near, in gold against the blue,
The old moon, in its arms the new.
Lo, the deep waters of the bay
Stir with the breath of hurrying day.

Wake, loved one, wake and look with me
Across the narrow, dawn-lit sea!
Such beauty is not wholly mine
Till thou, dear heart, hast made it thine.

"THE WOODS THAT BRING THE SUNSET NEAR"

THE wind from out the west is blowing;
The homeward-wandering cows are lowing;

Dark grow the pine-woods, dark and drear —
The woods that bring the sunset near.

When o'er wide seas the sun declines,
Far off its fading glory shines, —
Far off, sublime, and full of fear, —
The pine-woods bring the sunset near.

This house that looks to east, to west,
This, dear one, is our home, our rest;
Yonder the stormy sea, and here
The woods that bring the sunset near.

SUNSET FROM THE TRAIN

I

But then the sunset smiled,
Smiled once and turned toward dark,
Above the distant, wavering line of trees that filed
Along the horizon's edge;
Like hooded monks that hark
Through evening air
The call to prayer; —
Smiled once, and faded slow, slow, slow away;
When, like a changing dream, the long cloud-wedge,
Brown-gray,
Grew saffron underneath and, ere I knew,
The interspace, green-blue —
The whole, illimitable, western, skyey shore,
The tender, human, silent sunset smiled once more.

II

Thee, absent loved one, did I think on now,
Wondering if thy deep brow

In dreams of me were lifted to the skies,
Where, by our far sea-home, the sunlight dies;
If thou didst stand, alone,
Watching the day pass slowly, slow, as here,
But closer and more dear,
Beyond the meadow and the long, familiar line
Of blackening pine;
When lo! that second smile; — dear heart, it was thine
   own.

"AFTER SORROW'S NIGHT"

AFTER sorrow's night
Dawned the morning bright.
In dewy woods I heard
A golden-throated bird,
   And "Love, love, love," it sang,
   And "Love, love, love."

Evening shadows fell
In our happy dell.
From glimmering woods I heard
A golden-throated bird,
   And "Love, love, love," it sang,
   And "Love, love, love."

O, the summer night
Starry was and bright.
In the dark woods I heard
A golden-throated bird,
   And "Love, love, love," it sang,
   And "Love, love, love."

A NOVEMBER CHILD

November winds, blow mild
On this new-born child!
Spirit of the autumn wood,
Make her gentle, make her good!
Still attend her,
And befriend her,
Fill her days with warmth and color;
Keep her safe from winter's dolor.

On thy bosom
Hide this blossom
Safe from summer's rain and thunder!
When those eyes of light and wonder
Tire at last of earthly places —
Full of years and full of graces,
Then, O, then
Take her back to heaven again!

AT NIGHT

The sky is dark, and dark the bay below
Save where the midnight city's pallid glow
　　　Lies like a lily white
　　　On the black pool of night.

O rushing steamer, hurry on thy way
Across the swirling Kills and gusty bay,
　　　To where the eddying tide
　　　Strikes hard the city's side!

For there, between the river and the sea,
Beneath that glow, — the lily's heart to me, —
　　　A sleeping mother mild,
　　　And by her breast a child!

CRADLE SONG

In the embers shining bright
A garden grows for thy delight,
With roses yellow, red, and white.

But, O my child, beware, beware!
Touch not the blossoms blowing there,
For every rose a thorn doth bear.

"NINE YEARS"

Nine years to heaven had flown,
    And June came, with June's token —
The wild rose that had known
    A maiden's silence broken.

'T was thus the lover spoke,
    And thus she leaned and listened
(Below, the billows broke,
    The blue sea shook and glistened): —

"We have been happy, Love,
    Through bright and stormy weather,
Happy all hope above,
    For we have been together.

"To meet, to love, to wed, —
    Joy without stint or measure, —
This was our lot," he said,
    "To find untouched our treasure;

"But had some blindfold fate
    Bound each unto another —
To turn from Heaven's gate,
    Each heart-throb hide and smother!

"O dear and faithful heart,
   If thus had we been fated;
To meet, to know, to part —
   Too early, falsely, mated!

"Were this our bitter plight,
   Ah, could we have dissembled?"
Her cheek turned pale with fright;
   She hid her face, and trembled.

"BACK FROM THE DARKNESS TO THE LIGHT AGAIN"

"BACK from the darkness to the light again!" —
Not from the darkness, Love, for hadst thou lain
Within the shadowy portal of the tomb,
Thy light had warmed the darkness into bloom.

PART II

FATE

I FLUNG a stone into a grassy field; —
How many tiny creatures there may yield
(I thought) their petty lives through that rude shock!
To me a pebble, 't is to them a rock —
Gigantic, cruel, fraught with sudden death.
Perhaps it crusht an ant, perhaps its breath
Alone tore down a white and glittering palace,
And the small spider damns the giant's malice
Who wrought the wreck — blasted his pretty art!

Who knows what day some saunterer, light of heart,
An idle wanderer through the fields of space,
Large-limbed, big-brained, to whom our puny race

Seems small as insects, — one whose footstep jars
On some vast world-orb islanded by stars, —
May fling a stone and crush our earth to bits,
And all that men have builded by their wits?

"Ah, what a loss!" you say; "our bodies go,
But not our temples, statues, and the glow
Of glorious canvases; and not the pages
Our poets have illumed through myriad ages.
What boots the insect's loss? Another day
Will see the selfsame ant-hill and the play
Of light on dainty web the same. But blot
All human art from this terrestrial plot,
Something indeed would pass that nevermore
Would light the universe as once before!"

The spider's work is not original, —
You hold, — but what of ours? I fear that all
We do is just the same thing over and over.
Take Life: you have the woman and her lover;
'T is old as Eden; naught is new in that!
Take Building, and you reach ere long the flat
Nile desert sands, by way of France, Rome, Greece.
And there is poetry — our bards increase
In numbers, not in sweetness, not in force,
Since he, sublimest poet of this globe,
Forgotten now, poured forth the chant of Job —
Where Man with the Eternal holds discourse.
No, no! The forms may change, but even they
Come round again. Could we but truly scan it,
We'd find in the heavens some little, busy planet,
Whence all we are was borrowed. If to-day
The imagined giant flung his ponderous stone,
And we and all our far-stretched schemes were done,
His were a scant remorse and short-lived trouble,
Like mine for those small creatures in the stubble.

"WE MET UPON THE CROWDED WAY"

I

WE met upon the crowded way;
We spoke and past. How bright the day
Turned from that moment, for a light
Did shine from her to make it bright!
And then I asked: Can such as she
From life be blotted utterly?
The thoughts from those clear eyes that dawn —
Down to the ground can they be drawn?

II

Among the mighty who can find
One that hath a perfect mind?
Angry, jealous, curst by feuds,
They own the sway of fatal moods;
But thou dost perfect seem to me
In thy divine simplicity.
Tho' from the heavens the stars be wrenched,
Thy light, dear maid, shall not be quenched.
Gentle, and true, and pure, and free —
The gods will not abandon thee!

THE WHITE AND THE RED ROSE

I

IN Heaven's happy bowers
There blossom two flowers,
One with fiery glow
And one as white as snow;
While lo! before them stands,
With pale and trembling hands,
A spirit who must choose
One, and one refuse.

II

O, tell me of these flowers
That bloom in heavenly bowers,
One with fiery glow,
And one as white as snow!
And tell me who is this
In Heaven's holy bliss
Who trembles and who cries
Like a mortal soul that dies!

III

These blossoms two,
Wet with heavenly dew —
The Gentle Heart is one,
And one is Beauty's own;
And the spirit here that stands,
With pale and trembling hands,
Before to-morrow's morn
Will be a child new-born,
Will be a mortal maiden
With earthly sorrows laden;
But of these shining flowers
That bloom in heavenly bowers,
To-day she still may choose
One, and one refuse.

IV

Will she pluck the crimson flower
And win Beauty's dower?
Will she choose the better part
And gain the Gentle Heart?
Awhile she weeping waits
Within those pearly gates;
Alas! the mortal maiden

With earthly sorrow laden;
Her tears afresh they start —
She has chosen the Gentle Heart.

v

And now the spirit goes,
In her breast the snow-white rose.
When hark! a voice that calls
Within the garden walls:
"Thou didst choose the better part,
Thou hast won the Gentle Heart —
Lo, now to thee is given
The red rose of Heaven."

A WOMAN'S THOUGHT

I AM a woman — therefore I may not
Call to him, cry to him,
Fly to him,
Bid him delay not!

Then when he comes to me, I must sit quiet;
Still as a stone —
All silent and cold.
If my heart riot —
Crush and defy it!
Should I grow bold,
Say one dear thing to him,
All my life fling to him,
Cling to him —
What to atone
Is enough for my sinning!
This were the cost to me,
This were my winning —
That he were lost to me.

Not as a lover
At last if he part from me,
Tearing my heart from me,
Hurt beyond cure —
Calm and demure
Then must I hold me,
In myself fold me,
Lest he discover;
Showing no sign to him
By look of mine to him
What he has been to me —
How my heart turns to him,
Follows him, yearns to him,
Prays him to love me.

Pity me, lean to me,
Thou God above me!

THE RIVER INN

THE night was black and drear
Of the last day of the year.
Two guests to the river inn
Came, from the wide world's bound —
One with clangor and din,
The other without a sound.

"Now hurry, servants and host!
Get the best that your cellars boast.
White be the sheets and fine,
And the fire on the hearthstone bright;
Pile the wood, and spare not the wine,
And call him at morning-light."

"But where is the silent guest?
In what chamber shall she rest?
In this! Should she not go higher?
'T is damp, and the fire is gone."

"You need not kindle the fire,
You need not call her at dawn."

Next morn he sallied forth
On his journey to the North.
O, bright the sunlight shone
Through boughs that the breezes stir;
But for her was lifted a stone
Under the churchyard fir.

THE HOMESTEAD

I

HERE stays the house, here stay the selfsame places,
Here the white lilacs and the buttonwoods;
Here the dark pine-groves, there the river-floods,
And there the threading brook that interlaces
Green meadow-bank with meadow-bank the same.
The melancholy nightly chorus came
Long, long ago from the same pool, and yonder
Stark poplars lift in the same twilight air
Their ancient lonelinesses; nearer, fonder,
The black-heart cherry-tree's gaunt branches bare
Rasp on the same old window where I ponder.

II

And we, the only living, only pass;
We come and go, whither and whence we know not.
From birth to bound the same house keeps, alas!
New lives as gently as the old; there show not

Among the haunts that each had thought his own
The looks that partings bring to human faces.
The black-heart there, that heard my earliest moan,
And yet shall hear my last, like all these places
I love so well, unloving lives from child
To child; from morning joy to evening sorrow —
Untouched by joy, by anguish undefiled;
All one the generations gone, and new;
All one dark yesterday and bright to-morrow;
To the old tree's insensate sympathy
All one the morning and the evening dew —
My far, forgotten ancestor and I.

AT FOUR SCORE

THIS is the house she was born in, full four-score years
    ago,
And here she is living still, bowed and ailing, but clinging
Still to this wonted life — like an ancient and blasted oak-
    tree,
Whose dying roots yet clasp the earth with an iron hold.

This is the house she was born in, and yonder across the
    bay
Is the home her lover builded, for her and for him and
    their children;
Daily she watched it grow, from dawn to the evening
    twilight,
As it rose on the orchard hill, 'mid the springtime showers
    and bloom.

There is the village church, its steeple over the trees
Rises and shows the clock she has watched since the day
    it was started —

O, many a year ago, how many she cannot remember.
Now solemnly over the water rings out the evening hour.

And there in that very church, — tho', alas, how bediz-
        ened, and changed!
They've painted it up, she says, in their queer, new,
        modern fashion, —
There on a morning in June, she gave her hand to her
        husband;
Her heart it was his (she told him) long years and years
        before.

Now here she sits at the window, gazing out on steeple
        and hill;
All but the houses are gone, — the church, and the trees,
        and the houses; —
All, all have gone long since, parents, and husband, and
        children;
And herself — she thinks, at times, she too has vanished
        and gone.

No, it cannot be she who stood in the church that morn-
        ing in June,
Nor she who felt at her breast the lips of a child in the
        darkness;
But hark in the gathering dusk comes a low, quick moan
        of anguish —
Ah, it is she indeed, who has lived, who has loved, and
        lost.

For she thinks of a wintry night, when her last was taken
        away,
Forty years this very month, the last, the fairest, the
        dearest;

All gone — ah, yes, it is she who has loved, who has
    lost, and suffered,
She and none other it is, left alone in her sorrow and pain.

Still with its sapless roots, that stay tho' the branches
    have dropt —
Have withered, and fallen, and gone, their strength and
    their glory forgotten;
Still with the life that remains, silent, and faithful, and
    stedfast,
Through sunshine and bending storm clings the oak to
    its mother-earth.

JOHN CARMAN

I

John Carman of Carmeltown
    Worked hard through the livelong day;
He drove his awl and he snapt his thread
    And he had but little to say.

He had but little to say
    Except to a neighbor's child;
Three summers old she was, and her eyes
    Had a look that was deep and wild.

Her hair was heavy and brown
    Like clouds in a starry night.
She came and sat by the cobbler's bench
    And his soul was filled with delight.

No kith nor kin had he
    And he never went gadding about;
A strange, shy man, the people said;
    They could not make him out.

And some of them shook their heads
  And would never tell what they'd heard.
But he drove his awl and snapt his thread —
  And he always kept his word;

And the little child that knew him
  Better than all the rest,
She threw her arms around his neck
  And went to sleep on his breast.

One day in that dreadful summer
  When children died by the score,
John Carman glanced from his work and saw
  Her mother there at the door.

He knew by the look on her face —
  And his own turned deathly white;
He rose from his bench and followed her out
  And watched by the child that night.

He tended her day and night;
  He watched by her night and day.
He saw the cruel pain in her eyes;
  He saw her lips turn gray.

II

The day that the child was buried
  John Carman went back to his last,
And the neighbors said that for weeks and weeks
  Not a word his clencht lips past.

"He takes it hard," they gossiped,
  "Poor man, he's lacking in wit";
"I'll drop in to-day," said Deacon Gray,
  "And comfort him up a bit."

So Deacon Gray dropt in
　　With a kind and neighborly air,
And before he left he knelt on the floor
　　And wrestled with God in prayer.

And he said: "O Lord, Thou hast stricken
　　This soul in its babyhood;
In Thy own way, we beseech and pray,
　　Bring forth from evil good."

III

That night the fire-bells rang
　　And the flames shot up to the sky,
And into the street as pale as a sheet
　　The town-folk flock and cry.

The bells ring loud and long,
　　The flames leap high and higher,
The rattling engines come too late —
　　The old First Church is on fire!

And lo and behold in the crimson glare
　　They see John Carman stand —
A look of mirth on his iron lips
　　And a blazing torch in his hand.

"You say it was He who killed her"
　　(His voice had a fearful sound):
"I'd have you know, who love Him so,
　　I've burned His house to the ground."

.　　.　　.　　.　　.　　.　　.　　.

John Carman died in prison,
　　In the madman's cell, they say;
And from his crime, that I've told in rhyme,
　　Heaven cleanse his soul, I pray.

DRINKING SONG

THOU who lov'st and art forsaken,
Didst believe and wert mistaken,
From thy dream thou wilt not waken
    When Death thee shall call.
Like are infidel, believer,
The deceived, and the deceiver,
    When the grave hides all.

What if thou be saint or sinner,
Crooked graybeard, straight beginner, —
Empty paunch, or jolly dinner, —
    When Death thee shall call.
All alike are rich and richer,
King with crown, and cross-legged stitcher,
    When the grave hides all.

Hope not thou to live hereafter
In men's memories and laughter,
When, 'twixt hearth and ringing rafter,
    Death thee shall call.
For we both shall be forgotten,
Friend, when thou and I are rotten
    And the grave hides all.

THE VOYAGER

I

"FRIEND, why goest thou forth
  When ice-hills drift from the north
    And crush together?"

"The Voice that me doth call
  Heeds not the ice-hill's fall,
    Nor wind, nor weather."

II

"But, friend, the night is black;
Behold the driving rack
   And wild seas under!"

"My straight and narrow bark
Fears not the threatening dark,
   Nor storm, nor thunder."

III

"But O, thy children dear!
Thy wife, — she is not here, —
   I haste to bring her!"

"No, no, it is too late!
Hush, hush! I may not wait,
   Nor weep, nor linger."

IV

"Hark! Who is he that knocks
With slow and dreadful shocks
   The walls to sever?"

"It is my Master's call,
I go, whate'er befall;
   Farewell forever."

A LAMENT

FOR THE DEAD OF THE JEANNETTE BROUGHT HOME ON THE FRISIA

I

O GATES of ice! long have ye held our loved ones.
Ye Cruel! how could ye keep from us them for whom
our hearts yearned — our dear ones, our fathers, our
children, our brothers, our lovers?

Cold and Sleet, Darkness and Ice! hard have ye held them; ye would not let them go.

Their hands ye have bound fast; their feet ye have detained; and well have ye laid hold upon the hearts of our loved ones.

O silent Arctic Night! thou hast wooed them from us.

O Secret of the white and unknown world! too strong hast thou been for us; we were as nothing to thee; thou hast drawn them from us; thou wouldst not let them go.

The long day past; thou wouldst not let them go.

The long, long night came and went; thou wouldst not let them go.

O thou insatiate! What to thee are youth, and life, and hope, and love?

For thou art Death, not Life; thou art Despair, not Hope.

Naught to thee the rush of youthful blood; naught to thee the beauty and strength of our loved ones.

The breath of their bodies was not sweet to thee; they loved thee, and thou lovedst not them.

They followed thee, thou didst not look upon them; but still, O thou inviolate! still did they follow thee.

Thee did they follow through storm, through perils of the ice, and of the unknown darkness.*

The sharp spears of the frost they feared not; the terrors of death they feared not. For thee, for thee, for thee, not for us; only that they might look upon thy face!

All these they endured for thee; the thought of us whom yet they loved, this also they endured for thee.

For thou art beautiful, beyond the beauty of woman. In thy hair are the stars of night. Thou wrappest about thee garments of fire that burn not, and are never quenched;

When thou movest they are moved; when thou breathest they tremble.

Yea, awful art thou in thy beauty; with white fingers beckoning in mists and shadows of the frozen sea; drawing to thee the hearts of heroes.

II

Long, long have they tarried in thy gates, O North!

But now thou hast given them up. Lo, they come to us once more — our belovèd, our only ones!

O dearest, why have ye stayed so long?

With ye, night and day have come and gone, but with us there was night only.

But no, we will not reproach ye, hearts of our hearts, dearest and best; our fathers, our children, our brothers, our lovers!

Come back to us! Behold our arms are open for you; ye are ours; ye have returned unto us; ye shall never go hence again.

But why are ye silent, why do ye not stir, why do ye not speak to us, O belovèd ones?

White are your cheeks like snow; your eyes they do not look upon us.

So long ye have been gone, and is this your joy to see us once more?

Lo! do we not welcome ye? Are not our souls glad? Do not our tears, long kept, fall upon your faces?

Or do ye but sleep well, after those hard and weary labors? O, now awaken, for ye shall take rest and pleasure; here are your homes and kindred!

Listen, belovèd: here is your sister, here is your brother, here is your lover!

III

They will not hearken to our voices.

They are still; their eyes look not upon us.

O insatiate! O Secret of the white and unknown world, cruel indeed thou art!

Thou hast sent back to us our best belovèd; their bodies thou hast rendered up, but their spirits thou hast taken away from us forever.

In life thou didst hold them from us — and in death, in death they are thine.

NEW YORK, February 20, 1884.

ILL TIDINGS

(THE STUDIO CONCERT)

IN the long studio from whose towering walls
Greek Phidias beams, and Angelo appalls,
Eager the listening, downcast faces throng
While violins their piercing tones prolong.
At times I know not if I see, or hear,
Yon statue's smile, or some not sorrowing tear
Down-falling on the surface of the stream
That music pours across my waking dream.
Ah, is it then a dream that while repeat
Those chords, like strokes of silver-shod light feet,
And the great Master's music marches on —
I hear the horses of the Parthenon?

. . . .

But all to-day seems vague, unreal, far,
With fear and discord in the dearest strain,
For 'neath yon slowly-sinking western star
One that I love lies on her bed of pain.

A NEW WORLD

"I KNOW," he said,
"The thunder and the lightning have past by
And all the earth is black, and burned, and dead;

But, friend, the grass will grow again, the flowers
Again will bloom, the summer birds will sing,
And the all-healing sun will shine once more."
"Blind prophecy," she answered in her woe.
Yet still, as time wore on, the prophet's words
Came true, — but not all true. (So shall it be
With all who here may suffer mortal loss.)
Ere long the grass, the flowers, the birds, the sun
Once more made bright the bleak and desolate earth;
They came once more, those joys of other days;
She felt them, moved among them, and was glad.

Glad — glad! O mocking word! They came once more,
But not the same to her. Familiar they
As a remembered dream, and beautiful —
But changed, all changed, the whole world changed for-
ever.

PART III

CONGRESS: 1878

'T WAS in the year when mutterings, loud and deep,
Were heard in all the dark, distracted land;
And grave men questioned: "Can the State withstand
The shock and strain to come? O, will she keep
Firm her four walls, should the wild creature leap
To ruin and ravish? Will her pillars planned
By the great dead, tremble to either hand?
The dead! would heaven they might awake from sleep!"
Haply (I thought) our Congress still may hold
One voice of power — when lo! upon the blast
A sound like jackals ravening to and fro.
Great God! And has it come to this at last?
Such noise, such shame, where once, not long ago,
The pure and wise their living thoughts outrolled.

THE CITY

Come, Spirit of Song! true, faithful friend of mine!
　Oft hast thou served me in life's warfare rough;
　No knight of old found lance more keen or tough
　At tourney or in dreadful battle-line:
Come, tho' they own thee not, the Muses Nine;
　Strike one more blow, — the past is not enough, —
　Not now for Love's sake, nor in Fate's rebuff,
　Nor for Provence and all its golden wine:
But be one iron scorn for this huge town
　Where love of God has turned to lust of gold,
　And civic pride in private greed grows cold;
Where speculation stains the judge's gown,
　And where, in new-born broods, foul beasts of prey
　Ravage the treasure-house by night and day.

REFORM

I

O, how shall I help to right the world that is going wrong!
And what can I do to hurry the promised time of peace!
The day of work is short and the night of sleep is long;
And whether to pray or preach, or whether to sing a
　　　song,
To plow in my neighbor's field, or to seek the golden fleece,
Or to sit with my hands in my lap, and wish that ill
　　　would cease!

II

I think, sometimes, it were best just to let the Lord alone;
I am sure some people forget He was here before they
　　　came;
Tho' they say it is all for His glory, 't is a good deal
　　　more for their own,

That they peddle their petty schemes, and blate and
   babble and groan.
I sometimes think it were best, and a man were little to
   blame,
Should he pass on his silent way nor mix with the noisy
   shame.

AT GARFIELD'S GRAVE

(SEPTEMBER, 1881)

ALL summer long the people knelt
   And listened at the sick man's door:
Each pang which that pale sufferer felt
   Throbbed through the land from shore to shore;

And as the all-dreaded hour drew nigh,
   What breathless watching, night and day!
What tears, what prayers! Great God on high!
   Have we forgotten how to pray!

O broken-hearted, widowed one,
   Forgive us if we press too near!
Dead is our husband, father, son,
   For we are all one household here.

And not alone here by the sea,
   And not in his own land alone,
Are tears of anguish shed with thee —
   In this one loss the world is one.

EPITAPH

A man not perfect, but of heart
   So high, of such heroic rage,
That even his hopes became a part
   Of earth's eternal heritage.

MEMORIAL DAY

I

SHE saw the bayonets flashing in the sun,
The flags that proudly waved; she heard the bugles call-
        ing;
She saw the tattered banners falling
About the broken staffs, as one by one
The remnant of the mighty army past;
And at the last
Flowers for the graves of those whose fight was done.

II

She heard the tramping of ten thousand feet
As the long line swept round the crowded square;
She heard the incessant hum
That filled the warm and blossom-scented air —
The shrilling fife, the roll and throb of drum,
The happy laugh, the cheer. O, glorious and meet
To honor thus the dead,
Who chose the better part,
Who for their country bled!
— The dead! Great God! she stood there in the street,
Living, yet dead in soul and mind and heart —
While far away
His grave was deckt with flowers by strangers' hands
        to-day.

THE NORTH TO THE SOUTH

LAND of the South, — whose stricken heart and brow
    Bring grief to eyes that erewhile only knew
For their own loss to sorrow, — spurn not thou
    These tribute tears; ah, we have suffered too.
NEW ORLEANS, 1885.

THE BURIAL OF GRANT

(NEW YORK, AUGUST 8, 1885)

I

YE living soldiers of the mighty war,
    Once more from roaring cannon and the drums
    And bugles blown at morn, the summons comes;
Forget the halting limb, each wound and scar;
        Once more your Captain calls to you;
        Come to his last review!

II

And come ye, too, bright spirits of the dead,
    Ye who flamed heavenward from the embattled field;
    And ye whose harder fate it was to yield
Life from the loathful prison or anguished bed;
        Dear ghosts! come join your comrades here
        Beside this sacred bier.

III

Nor be ye absent, ye immortal band, —
    Warriors of ages past, and our own age, —
    Who drew the sword for right, and not in rage,
Made war that peace might live in all the land,
        Nor ever struck one vengeful blow,
        But helped the fallen foe.

IV

And fail not ye, — but, ah, ye falter not
    To join his army of the dead and living, —
    Ye who once felt his might, and his forgiving;
Brothers, whom more in love than hate he smote.
        For all his countrymen make room
        By our great hero's tomb!

V

Come, soldiers — not to battle as of yore,
  But come to weep; ay, shed your noblest tears;
  For lo, the stubborn chief, who knew not fears,
Lies cold at last, ye shall not see him more.
    How long grim Death he fought and well,
    That poor, lean frame doth tell.

VI

All's over now; here let our Captain rest,
  Silent amid the blare of praise and blame;
  Here let him rest, while never rests his fame;
Here in the city's heart he loved the best,
    And where our sons his tomb may see
    To make them brave as he; —

VII

As brave as he — he on whose iron arm
  Our Greatest leaned, our gentlest and most wise;
  Leaned when all other help seemed mocking lies,
While this one soldier checked the tide of harm,
    And they together saved the state,
    And made it free and great.

THE DEAD COMRADE

At the burial of Grant, a bugler stood forth and sounded " taps."

I

    Come, soldiers, arouse ye!
    Another has gone;
    Let us bury our comrade,
    His battles are done.
      His sun it is set;
    He was true, he was brave,
    He feared not the grave,
    There is naught to regret.

II

Bring music and banners
And wreaths for his bier —
No fault of the fighter
That Death conquered here.
Bring him home ne'er to rove,
Bear him home to his rest,
And over his breast
Fold the flag of his love.

III

Great Captain of battles,
We leave him with Thee!
What was wrong, O, forgive it;
His spirit make free.
Sound taps, and away!
Out lights, and to bed!
Farewell, soldier dead!
Farewell — for a day.

ON THE LIFE-MASK OF ABRAHAM
LINCOLN

This bronze doth keep the very form and mold
Of our great martyr's face. Yes, this is he:
That brow all wisdom, all benignity;
That human, humorous mouth; those cheeks that hold
Like some harsh landscape all the summer's gold;
That spirit fit for sorrow, as the sea
For storms to beat on; the lone agony
Those silent, patient lips too well foretold.
Yes, this is he who ruled a world of men
As might some prophet of the elder day —
Brooding above the tempest and the fray

With deep-eyed thought and more than mortal ken.
A power was his beyond the touch of art
Or armèd strength — his pure and mighty heart.

THE PRESIDENT

(WRITTEN DURING THE FIRST ADMINISTRATION OF PRESIDENT CLEVELAND)

NOT his to guide the ship while tempests blow,
War's billows burst, and glorious thunders beat;
Not his the joy to see an alien foe
Fly down the dreadful valley of defeat;
Not his the fame of that great soul and tried,
Who conquered civil peace by arms and love;
Nor his the emprize of one who lately died
Hand-claspt with foes, who weep his tomb above.
But this his task, — all passionless, unsplendid, —
To teach, in public place, a nobler creed;
To build a wall, — alone or well befriended, —
'Gainst the base partizan's ignoble greed.
Or will he fail, or triumph? History lays
A moment down her pen. A nation waits — and prays.

PART IV

ESSIPOFF

I

WHAT is her playing like?
I ask — while dreaming here under her music's power.
'T is like the leaves of the dark passion-flower
Which grows on a strong vine whose roots, O, deep they
sink,
Deep in the ground, that flower's pure life to drink.

II

What is her playing like?
'T is like a bird
Who, singing in a wild wood, never knows
That its lone melody is heard
By wandering mortal, who forgets his heavy woes.

ADELE AUS DER OHE

(LISZT)

I

WHAT is her playing like?
'T is like the wind in wintry northern valleys.
A dream-pause; — then it rallies
And once more bends the pine-tops, suddenly shatters
The ice-crags, whitely scatters
The spray along the paths of avalanches,
Startles the blood, and every visage blanches.

II

Half-sleeps the wind above a swirling pool
That holds the trembling shadow of the trees;
Where waves too wildly rush to freeze
Tho' all the air is cool;
And hear, O, hear, while musically call
With nearer tinkling sounds, or distant roar,
Voices of fall on fall;
And now a swelling blast, that dies; and now — no more,
     no more.

(CHOPIN)

AH, what celestial art!
And can sweet thoughts become pure tone and float,
All music, note by note,
Into the trancèd mind and quivering heart!

Her hand scarce stirs the singing, wiry metal —
Hear from the wild-rose fall each perfect petal!

And can we have, on earth, of heaven the whole,
Or be to heaven upcaught,
Hearing the soul of inexpressible thought,
Roses of sound
That strew melodious leaves upon the silent ground;
And music that is music's very soul,
Without one touch of earth,
Too tender, even, for sorrow, and too bright for mirth!

MODJESKA

THERE are four sisters known to mortals well,
  Whose names are Joy and Sorrow, Death and Love;
  This last it was who did my footsteps move
  To where the other deep-eyed sisters dwell.
To-night, or ere yon painted curtain fell,
  These, one by one, before my eyes did rove
  Through the brave mimic world that Shakespeare wove.
  Lady! thy art, thy passion were the spell
That held me, and still holds; for thou dost show,
  With those most high each in his sovereign art, —
  Shakespeare supreme, and Tuscan Angelo, —
Great art and passion are one. Thine too the part
  To prove, that still for him the laurels grow
  Who reaches through the mind to pluck the heart.

THE DRAMA

(SUPPOSED TO BE FROM THE POLISH)

I SAT in the crowded theater. The first notes of the
orchestra wandered in the air; then the full harmony burst
forth; then ceased.

The conductor, secretly pleased with the loud applause, waited a moment, then played again; but as he struck upon his desk for the third time, the bell sounded, the just-beginning tones of the wind-instruments and the violins husht suddenly, and the curtain was rolled to the ceiling.

Then appeared a wonderful vision, which shall not soon be forgotten by me.

For know that I am one who loves all things beautiful. Did you find the figure of a man lying solitary upon the wind-fashioned hills of sand, watching the large sun rise from the ocean? That was I.

It was I who, lonely, walked at evening through the woods of autumn, beholding the sun's level light strike through the unfallen red and golden foliage, —

Whose heart trembled when he saw the fire that rapidly consumed the dead leaves lying upon the hillside, and spread a robe of black that throbbed with crimson jewels under the wind of the rushing flame.

Know, also, that the august forms wrought in marble by the ancient sculptors have power upon me, also the imaginative works of the incomparable painters; and that the voices of the early poets are modern and familiar to me.

What vision was it, then, that I beheld; what art was it that made my heart tremble and filled me with joy that was like pain?

Was it the art of the poet; was it of a truth poetry made visible in human attitudes and motions?

Was it the art of the painter — which Raphael knew so well when he created those most gracious shapes that yet live on the walls of the Vatican?

Or was it the severe and marvelous art of the sculptor, in which antique Phidias excelled, and which Michael Angelo indued with new and mighty power?

Or, haply, it was that enchanting myth, made real before our eyes — of the insensate marble warmed to life beneath the passionate gaze of the sculptor!

No, no; it was not this miracle, of which the bards have so often sung; nor was it the art of the poet, nor of the painter, nor of the musician (tho' often I thought of music), nor of the sculptor. It was none of these that moved my heart, and the hearts of all who beheld, and yet it was all of these,

For it was the ancient and noble art of the drama, — that art which includes all other arts, — and she who was the mistress of it was the divine Modjeska.

FOR AN ALBUM

(TO BE READ ONE HUNDRED YEARS AFTER)

A CENTURY'S summer breezes shook
  The maple shadows on the grass
Since she who owned this ancient book
  From the green world to heaven did pass.

Beside a northern lake she grew,
  A wild-flower on its craggy walls;
Her eyes were mingled gray and blue,
  Like waves where summer sunlight falls.

Cheerful from morn to evening-close,
  No humblest work, no prayer forgot!
Yet who of woman born but knows
  The sorrows of our mortal lot!

And she too suffered, tho' the wound
  Was hidden from the general gaze,
And most from those who thus had found
  An added burden for their days.

She had no special grace, nor art;
　　Her riches not in banks were kept;
Her treasure was a gentle heart;
　　Her skill to comfort those who wept.

Not without foes her days were past,
　　For quick her burning scorn was fanned.
Her friends were many — least and last,
　　A poet from a distant land.

PORTO FINO

I KNOW a girl — she is a poet's daughter,
　　And many-mooded as a poet's day,
And changing as the Mediterranean water;
　　We walked together by an emerald bay,

So deep, so green, so promontory-hidden
　　That the lost mariner might peer in vain
Through storms, to find where he erewhile had ridden,
　　Safe-sheltered from the wild and windy main.

Down the high stairs we clambered just to rest a
　　Cool moment in the church's antique shade.
How gay the aisles and altars! 'T was the festa
　　Of brave Saint George who the old dragon laid.

How bright the little port! The red flags fluttered,
　　Loud clanged the bells, and loud the children's glee;
What tho' some distant, unseen storm-cloud muttered,
　　And waves breathed big along the weedy quay.

We climbed the hill whose rising cleaves asunder
　　Green bay and blue immeasurable sea;
We heard the breakers at its bases thunder;
　　We heard the priests' harsh chant soar wild and free.

Then through the graveyard's straight and narrow
    portal
  Our journey led. How dark the place! How strange
Its steep, black mountain wall — as if the immortal
  Spirit could thus be stayed its skyward range!

Beyond, the smoky olives clothed the mountains
  In green that grew through many a moonlit night.
Below, down cleft and chasm leapt snowy fountains;
  Above, the sky was warm, and blue, and bright;

When, sudden, from out a fair and smiling heaven
  Burst forth the rain, quick as a trumpet-blare;
Yet still the Italian sun each drop did leaven,
  And turned the rain to diamonds in the air.

So past the day in shade, and shower, and sun,
  Like thine own moods, thou sweet and changeful
    maiden!
Great Heaven! deal kindly with this gentle one,
  Nor let her soul too heavily be laden.

IMPROMPTUS

I — TO F. F. C. ON THE PANSY, HER CLASS FLOWER

  THIS is the flower of thought;
  Take it, thou empress of a land
  Of true hearts, from a loyal subject's hand;
  And with it naught,
  O, naught beneath life's ever-brightening dome
  Of sad remembrance! May it bring
  Dreams of joy only, and of happy days
  Backward and still to come;

Of birds that sang last eve, and still shall sing
In dawns of morrows only joyful lays.
  Or yet, if thou shouldst go
Not utterly unscathed of mortal woe —
Thy blackest hour be touched by memory's gold,
As is this flower's leaf. Then shalt thou hold
Ever a young heart in thee, ever as now
A look of quenchless youth beneath thy peerless brow.

II — ART

FOLLOWING the sun, westward the march of power!
  The Rose of Might blooms in our new-world mart:
But see, just bursting forth from bud to flower, —
  A late, slow growth, — the fairer Rose of Art.

III — TO A SOUTHERN GIRL

SWEET rose that bloomed on the red field of war,
  Think not too sadly of the dreadful Past!
  Are not old foes new friends — not least, tho' last,
One whose far home lies 'neath yon Northern star?

IV — FOR A FAN

EACH of us answers to a call;
Master or mistress have we all.
I belong to lovely Anne;
Dost thou not wish *thou* wert a fan?
Thus to be treasured, thus to be prest,
Pleasuring thus, and thus carest?

V — TO T. B. A.

IN ACKNOWLEDGMENT OF A BOOK OF PROSE

YOUR pretty book doth please me,
Of carks and cares doth ease me;
But don't forget, my boy,

Verse is your true employ.
And surely, Thomas Bailey,
In all this new-world mêlée
Too seldom comes the poet,
And when he does we know it!
Yes, no one else can do
The work that's play to you.
So spend your precious time in
Your master art of rhymin',
Then shall you keep the praise
Of these and future days.

1893.

VI — A THEME

"GIVE me a theme," the little poet cried,
  "And I will do my part."
"'T is not a theme you need," the world replied,
  "You need a heart."

VII — THE CHRISTMAS TREE IN THE NURSERY

(FOR F. AND R.)

WITH wild surprise
Four great eyes
In two small heads
From neighboring beds
Looked out — and winkt —
And glittered and blinkt
At a very queer sight
In the dim dawn-light.
As plain as can be
A fairy tree
Flashes and glimmers
And shakes and shimmers.
Red, green, and blue

Meet their view;
Silver and gold
Sharp eyes behold;
Small moons, big stars;
And jams in jars,
And cakes and honey
And thimbles and money;
Pink dogs, blue cats,
Little squeaking rats,
And candles and dolls
And crackers and polls,
A real bird that sings,
And tokens and favors,
And all sorts of things
For the little shavers.

Four black eyes
Grow big with surprise,
And then grow bigger
When a tiny little figure
Jaunty and airy,
A fairy! a fairy!
From the tree-top cries:
"Open wide! Black Eyes!
Come, children, wake now!
Your joys you may take now."

Quick as you can think
Twenty small toes
In four pretty rows,
Like little piggies pink,
All kick in the air —
And before you can wink
The tree stands bare!

PART V

MUSIC AND WORDS

I

THIS day I heard such music that I thought:
Hath human speech the power thus to be wrought,
Into such melody,—pure, sensuous sound, —
Into such mellow, murmuring mazes caught;
Can words (I said), when these keen tones are bound
(Silent, except in memory of this hour) —
Can human words alone usurp the power
Of trembling strings that thrill to the very soul,
And of this ecstasy bring back the whole?

II

Ah, no ('t was answered in my inmost heart),
Unto itself sufficient is each art,
And each doth utter what none other can —
Some hidden mood of the large soul of man.
Ah, think not thou with words well interweaved
To wake the tones wherein the viol grieved
With its most heavy burden; think not thou,
Adventurous, to push thy shallop's prow
Into that surge of well-remembered tones,
Striving to match each wandering wind that moans,
Each bell that tolls, and every bugle's blowing
With some most fitting word, some verse bestowing
A never-shifting form on that which past
Swift as a bird that glimmers down the blast.

III

So, still unworded, save in memory mute,
Rest thou sweet hour of viol and of lute;

Of thoughts that never, never can be spoken,
Too frail for the rough usage of men's words —
Thoughts that shall keep their silence all unbroken
Till music once more stirs them; — then like birds
That in the night-time slumber, they shall wake,
While all the leaves of all the forest shake.
O, hark! I hear it now, that tender strain
Fulfilled with all of sorrow save its pain.

THE POET'S FAME

MANY the songs of power the poet wrought
To shake the hearts of men. Yea, he had caught
The inarticulate and murmuring sound
That comes at midnight from the darkened ground
When the earth sleeps; for this he framed a word
Of human speech, and hearts were strangely stirred
That listened. And for him the evening dew
Fell with a sound of music, and the blue
Of the deep, starry sky he had the art
To put in language that did seem a part
Of the great scope and progeny of nature.
In woods, or waves, or winds, there was no creature
Mysterious to him. He was too wise
Either to fear, or follow, or despise
Whom men call Science — for he knew full well
All she had told, or still might live to tell,
Was known to him before her very birth;
Yea, that there was no secret of the earth,
Nor of the waters under, nor the skies,
That had been hidden from the poet's eyes;
By him there was no ocean unexplored,
Nor any savage coast that had not roared
Its music in his ears.

He loved the town —
Not less he loved the ever-deepening brown
Of summer twilights on the enchanted hills;
And long would listen to the starts and thrills
Of birds that sang and rustled in the trees,
Or watch the footsteps of the wandering breeze
And the quick, wingèd shadows flashing by,
Or birds that slowly wheeled across the unclouded sky.

All these were written on the poet's soul;
But he knew, too, the utmost, distant goal
Of the human mind. His fiery thought did run
To Time's beginning, ere yon central sun
Had warmed to life the swarming broods of men.
In waking dreams, his many-visioned ken
Clutcht the large, final destiny of things.
He heard the starry music, and the wings
Of beings unfelt by others thrilled the air
About him. Yet the loud and angry blare
Of tempests found an echo in his verse,
And it was here that lovers did rehearse
The ditties they would sing when, not too soon,
Came the warm night; — shadows, and stars, and moon.

Who heard his songs were filled with noble rage,
And wars took fire from his prophetic page —
Most righteous wars, wherein, 'midst blood and tears,
The world rushed onward through a thousand years.
And still he made the gentle sounds of peace
Heroic; bade the nation's anger cease!
Bitter his songs of grief for those who fell —
And for all this the people loved him well.

They loved him well and therefore, on a day,
They said with one accord: "Behold how gray

Our poet's head hath grown! Ere 't is too late
Come, let us crown him in our Hall of State;
Ring loud the bells, give to the winds his praise,
And urge his fame to other lands and days!"
    So was it done, and deep his joy therein.
But passing home at night, from out the din
Of the loud Hall, the poet, unaware,
Moved through a lonely and dim-lighted square —
There was the smell of lilacs in the air
And then the sudden singing of a bird,
Startled by his slow tread. What memory stirred
Within his brain he told not. Yet this night, —
Lone lingering when the eastern heavens were bright, —
He wove a song of such immortal art
That there lives not in all the world one heart —
One human heart unmoved by it. Long! long!
The laurel-crown has failed, but not that song
Born of the night and sorrow. Where he lies
At rest beneath the ever-shifting skies,
Age after age, from far-off lands they come,
With tears and flowers, to seek the poet's tomb.

THE POET'S PROTEST

O MAN with your rule and measure,
    Your tests and analyses!
You may take your empty pleasure,
    May kill the pine, if you please;
You may count the rings and the seasons,
    May hold the sap to the sun,
You may guess at the ways and the reasons
    Till your little day is done.

But for me the golden crest
    That shakes in the wind and launches

Its spear toward the reddening West!
  For me the bough and the breeze,
The sap unseen, and the glint
  Of light on the dew-wet branches,
The hiding shadows, the hint
  Of the soul of mysteries.

You may sound the sources of life,
  And prate of its aim and scope;
You may search with your chilly knife
  Through the broken heart of hope.
But for me the love-sweet breath,
  And the warm, white bosom heaving,
And never a thought of death,
  And only the bliss of living.

TO A YOUNG POET

In the morning of the skies
I heard a lark arise.
On the first day of the year
A wood-flower did appear.

Like a violet, like a lark,
Like the dawn that kills the dark,
Like a dewdrop, trembling, clinging,
Is the poet's first sweet singing.

"WHEN THE TRUE POET COMES"

"When the true poet comes, how shall we know him?
  By what clear token; manners, language, dress?
Or will a voice from heaven speak and show him —
  Him the swift healer of the earth's distress?

Tell us, that when the long-expected comes
　　At last, with mirth and melody and singing,
We him may greet with banners, beat of drums,
　　Welcome of men and maids and joybells ringing;
　　　　And, for this poet of ours,
　　　　Laurels and flowers."

Thus shall ye know him, this shall be his token —
　　Manners like other men, an unstrange gear;
His speech not musical, but harsh and broken
　　Will sound at first, each line a driven spear.
For he will sing as in the centuries olden,
　　Before mankind its earliest fire forgot —
Yet whoso listens long hears music golden.
　　How shall ye know him? Ye shall know him not
　　　　Till, ended hate and scorn,
　　　　To the grave he's borne.

YOUTH AND AGE

　　"I LIKE your book, my boy,
　　'T is full of youth and joy,
　　And love that sings and dreams.
　　Yet it puzzles me," he said;
　　"A string of pearls it seems,
　　But I cannot find the thread."

　　"O friend of olden days!
　　Dear to me is your praise,
　　But, many and many a year
　　You must go back, I fear;
　　You must journey back," I said,
　　"To find that golden thread!"

THE SONNET

WHAT is a sonnet? 'T is the pearly shell
  That murmurs of the far-off murmuring sea;
  A precious jewel carved most curiously;
  It is a little picture painted well.
What is a sonnet? 'T is the tear that fell
  From a great poet's hidden ecstasy;
  A two-edged sword, a star, a song — ah me!
  Sometimes a heavy-tolling funeral bell.
This was the flame that shook with Dante's breath;
  The solemn organ whereon Milton played,
  And the clear glass where Shakespeare's shadow falls:
A sea this is — beware who ventureth!
  For like a fiord the narrow floor is laid
  Mid-ocean deep sheer to the mountain walls.

A SONNET OF DANTE

("*Tanto gentile e tanto onesta pare*")

So fair, so pure my lady as she doth go
  Upon her way, and others doth salute,
  That every tongue becometh trembling-mute,
  And every eye is troubled by that glow.
Her praise she hears as on she moveth slow,
  Clothed with humility as with a suit;
  She seems a thing that came (without dispute)
  From heaven to earth a miracle to show.
Through eyes that gaze on her benignity
  There passes to the heart a sense so sweet
  That none can understand who may not prove;
And from her countenance there seems to move
  A gentle spirit, with all love replete,
  That to the soul comes, saying, "Sigh, O, sigh!"

THE NEW TROUBADOURS

(AVIGNON, 1879)

THEY said that all the troubadours had flown —
 No bird to flash a wing or swell a throat!
 But as we journeyed down the rushing Rhone
 To Avignon, what joyful note on note
Burst forth beneath thy shadow, O Ventour!
 Whose eastward forehead takes the dawn divine; —
 Ah, dear Provence! ah, happy troubadour,
 And that sweet, mellow, antique song of thine!
First, Roumanille, the leader of the choir,
 Then graceful Matthieu, tender, sighing, glowing,
 Then Wyse all fancy, Aubanel all fire,
And Mistral, mighty as the north-wind's blowing;
 And youthful Gras, and lo! among the rest
 A mother-bird who sang above her nest.

KEATS

TOUCH not with dark regret his perfect fame,
 Sighing, "Had he but lived he had done so";
 Or, "Were his heart not eaten out with woe
 John Keats had won a prouder, mightier name!"
Take him for what he was and did — nor blame
 Blind fate for all he suffered. Thou shouldst know
 Souls such as his escape no mortal blow —
 No agony of joy, or sorrow, or shame!
"Whose name was writ in water!" What large laughter
 Among the immortals when that word was brought!
 Then when his fiery spirit rose flaming after
High toward the topmost heaven of heavens up-caught!
 "All hail! our younger brother!" Shakespeare said,
 And Dante nodded his imperial head.

AN INSCRIPTION IN ROME

(PIAZZA DI SPAGNA)

SOMETHING there is in Death not all unkind;
  He hath a gentler aspect, looking back;
  For flowers may bloom in the dread thunder's track,
  And even the cloud that struck with light was lined.
Thus, when the heart is silent, speaks the mind;
  But there are moments when comes rushing, black
  And fierce upon us, the old, awful lack,
  And Death once more is cruel, senseless, blind.
So when I saw beside a Roman portal
  "In this house died John Keats"—for tears that sprung
  I could no further read. O bard immortal!
Not for thy fame's sake — but so young, so young;
  Such beauty vanished; spilled such heavenly wine;
  All quenched that power of deathless song divine!

DESECRATION

THE poet died last night;
    Outworn his mortal frame.
He hath fought well the fight,
    And won a deathless name.

Bring laurel for his bier,
    And flowers to deck the hearse.
The tribute of a tear
    To his immortal verse.

Husht is that piercing strain —
    Who heard, for pleasure wept.
His were our joy and pain;
    He sang — our sorrow slept.

Yes, weep for him; no more
　　Shall such high songs have birth;
Gone is the harp he bore
　　Forever from the earth.

Weep, weep, and scatter flowers
　　Above his precious dust;
Child of the heavenly powers —
　　Divine, and pure, and just.

Weep, weep — for when to-night
　　Shall hoot the hornèd owl,
Beneath the pale moon's light
　　The human ghouls will prowl.

What creatures those will throng
　　Within the sacred gloom,
To do our poet wrong —
　　To break the sealèd tomb?

Not the great world and gay
　　That pities not, nor halts
By thoughtless night or day,
　　But, — O more sordid-false! —

His trusted friend and near,
　　To whom his spirit moved;
The brother he held dear;
　　The woman that he loved.

"JOCOSERIA"

MEN grow old before their time,
　　With the journey half before them;
In languid rhyme
　　They deplore them.

Life up-gathers carks and cares,
   So good-by to maid and lover!
Find three gray hairs,
   And cry, "All 's over!"

Look at Browning! How he keeps
   In the seventies still a heart
That never sleeps —
   Still an art

Full of youth's own grit and power,
   Thoughts we deemed to boys belonging;
The springtime's flower —
   Love-and-longing.

TO AN ENGLISH FRIEND

WITH EMERSON'S "POEMS"

EDMUND, in this book you'll find
Music from a prophet's mind.
Even when harsh the numbers be,
There's an inward melody;
And when sound is one with sense,
'T is a bird's song, sweet, intense.
Chide me not the book is small,
For in it lies our all in all.
We who in El Dorado live
Have no better gift to give.
When no more is silver mill,
Golden stream, or iron hill —
Search the New World from pole to pole,
Here you'll find its singing soul!

OUR ELDER POETS

(1878)

HE is gone! We shall not see again
    That reverend form, those silver locks;
Silent at last the iron pen
    And words that poured like molten rocks.

He is gone, and we who thought him cold
    Miss from our lives a generous heat,
And know that stolid form did hold
    A fire that burned, a heart that beat.

He is gone, but other bards remain —
    Our gray old prophet, young at heart;
Our scholar-poet's patriot strain;
    And he of the wise and mellow art.

And he who first to Science sought,
    But to the Merry Muses after;
Who learned a secret never taught —
    The knowledge of men's tears and laughter.

He also in whose music rude
    Our peopled hills and prairies speak,
Resounding, in his modern mood,
    The tragic fury of the Greek.

And he, too, lingers round about
    The darling city of his birth —
The bard whose gray eyes looking out
    Find scarce one peer in all the earth.

LONGFELLOW'S "BOOK OF SONNETS"

'T was Sunday evening as I wandered down
   The central highway of this swarming place,
   And felt a pleasant stillness — not a trace
   Of Saturday's harsh turmoil in the town;
Then as a gentle breeze just stirs a gown,
   Yet almost motionless, or as the face
   Of silence smiles, I heard the chimes of "Grace"
   Sound murmuring through the autumn evening's
      brown.
To-day, again, I past along Broadway
   In the fierce tumult and mid-noise of noon,
   While 'neath my feet the solid pavement shook;
When lo! it seemed that bells began to play
   Upon a Sabbath eve a silver tune —
   For as I walked I read the poet's book.

"H. H."

I would that in the verse she loved some word,
   Not all unfit, I to her praise might frame —
   Some word wherein the memory of her name
   Should through long years its incense still afford.
But no, her spirit smote with its own sword;
   Herself has lit the fire whose blood-red flame
   Shall not be quenched — this is her living fame
   Who struck so well the sonnet's subtile chord.
None who e'er knew her can believe her dead;
   Tho' should she die they deem it well might be
   Her spirit took its everlasting flight
In summer's glory, by the sunset sea —
   That onward through the Golden Gate it fled.
   Ah, where that bright soul is cannot be night.

THE MODERN RHYMER

I

Now you who rhyme, and I who rhyme,
Have not we sworn it, many a time,
That we no more our verse would scrawl,
For Shakespeare he has sung it all!
And yet, whatever others see,
The earth is fresh to you and me;
And birds that sing, and winds that blow,
And blooms that make the country glow,
And lusty swains, and maidens bright,
And clouds by day, and stars by night,
And all the pictures in the skies
That moved before Will Shakespeare's eyes;
Love, hate, and scorn; frost, fire, and flower;
On us as well as him have power.
Go to! our spirits shall not be laid,
Silenced and smothered by a shade.
Avon is not the only stream
Can make a poet sing and dream;
Nor are those castles, queens, and kings
The hight of sublunary things.

II

Beneath the false moon's pallid glare,
By the cool fountain in the square
(This gray-green dusty square they set
Where two gigantic highways met)
We hear a music rare and new,
Sweet Shakespeare was not known to you!
You saw the New World's sun arise;
High up it shines in our own skies.
You saw the ocean from the shore;

Through mid-seas now our ship doth roar —
A wild, new, teeming world of men
That wakens in the poet's brain
Thoughts, that were never thought before,
Of hope, and longing, and despair,
Wherein man's never-resting race
Westward, still westward, on doth fare,
Doth still subdue, and still aspire,
Or turning on itself doth face
Its own indomitable fire; —
O million-centuried thoughts that make
The Past seem but a shallop's wake!

TWO WORLDS

AND OTHER POEMS

TWO WORLDS
AND OTHER POEMS

PART I

TWO WORLDS

I — THE VENUS OF MILO

GRACE, majesty, and the calm bliss of life;
  No conscious war 'twixt human will and duty;
Here breathes, forever free from pain and strife,
  The old, untroubled pagan world of beauty.

II — MICHAEL ANGELO'S SLAVE

OF life, of death the mystery and woe,
  Witness in this mute, carven stone the whole.
That suffering smile were never fashioned so
  Before the world had wakened to a soul.

PART II

THE STAR IN THE CITY

As down the city street
I pass at the twilight hour,
'Mid the noise of wheels and hoofs
That grind on the stones, and beat; —
Upward, by spire and tower,
Over the chimneys and roofs
Climbs my glance to the skies,

And I see, with a glad surprise,
A mist with a core of light.
    Slowly, as grows the night, —
As the sky turns blue from gray, —
Slowly it beams more bright,
And keeps with me on my way.
    Soul of the twilight star
That leads me from afar,
Spirit that keener glows
As the daylight darker grows;
That leaps the chasm of blue
Where the cross-street thunders through,
And follows o'er roof and spire,
In the night-time soaring higher;
I know thee, and only I,
Thou comrade of the sky —
Star of the poet's heart,
The light and soul of his art.

MOONLIGHT

I

'T IS twelve o' the clock.
    The town is still;
As gray as a rock
    From gable to sill
Each cottage is standing.
    The narrow street
    (Where the tree-tops meet),
From the woods to the landing,
Is black with shadows;
    The roofs are white,
And white are the meadows;
    The harbor is bright.
    Can this be night?

II

'T is twelve o' the clock.
  The town is still;
As still as a stock
  From harbor to hill.
The moon's broad marge
  Has no stars near,
  Far off how clear
They shine, how large!
Something is strange
  In the air, in the light;
Come forth! Let us range
  In the black, in the white,
  Through the day-like night.

III

In the elm-trees all
  No flutter, no twitter;
From the granite wall
  The small stars glitter.
A filmy thread
  My forehead brushes;
  A meteor rushes
From green to red.
Naught is but the bliss
  Of this dark, of this white,
Of these stars — of this kiss,
  O my Love and my Light
  In the day and the night.

"I CARE NOT IF THE SKIES ARE WHITE"

I CARE not if the skies are white,
  Nor if the fields are gold;

I care not whether 't is black or bright,
　Or winds blow soft or cold;
　　　But O the dark, dark woods,
　　　For thee, and me — and love.

Let all but us at last depart,
　The great world say farewell!
This is the kingdom of the heart,
　Where only two may dwell;
　　　And O the dark, dark woods,
　　　For thee, and me — and love.

CONTRASTS

Thunder in the north sky,
　Sunshine in the south;
Frowning eyes and forehead
　And a smiling mouth.

Maiden in the morning —
　Love her? Yes, but fear her!
In the moony shadows —
　Nearer, nearer, nearer!

SERENADE

(for music)

Deep in the ocean of night
　A pearl through the darkness shines;
Asleep in the garden of night
　A lily's head reclines;
Afar in the forest of night
　Dreams the nightingale;
Clouds in the sky of night
　Make one bright star grow pale.

O thou, sweet soul of my love,
   Art my pearl, my lily-flower;
Thou, hiding heart of my love,
   Art my bird, in thy maiden bower;
Heart of my only love
   That shin'st in the heavens afar —
Thou, in the night of love,
   Art my one, dear, trembling star.

Let me draw thee to the light,
   Pearl of the shadowy sea!
Awake, thou lily of light,
   Turn thy face divine on me!
Arouse thee, bird of the night,
   Let thy voice to my voice reply!
Star of thy lover's night,
   Shine forth or I die — I die!

LARGESS

Sweet mouth, dark eyes, deep heart —
   All of beauty, all of glamor heaven could fashion
With its divinest art;
   A woman's life and love, a woman's passion:

But these, at last, to win,
   Land, or sea, or hell, or heaven might well be ravished
At price of any sin —
   Yet freely all she on her lover lavished.

INDOORS, AT NIGHT

The window's white, the candle's red,
Show evening falleth overhead;
The candle's red, the window's black,
And earth is close in midnight's sack;

The candle fades,
The midnight shades
Turn suddenly a starry blue —
And now to dreams, my soul, of you!

THE ABSENT LOVER

THE purple of the summer fields, the dark
Of forests, and the upward mountain sweep —
Broken by crag, and scar of avalanche;
The trembling of the tops of million trees;
A world of sunlight thrilled with winds of dawn;
All these I feel, I breathe, all these I am
When with closed eyes I bring thy presence near,
And touch thy spirit with my spirit's love.

"TO-NIGHT THE MUSIC DOTH A BURDEN BEAR"

TO-NIGHT the music doth a burden bear —
One word that moans and murmurs; doth exhale
Tremulously as perfume on the air
From out a rose blood-red, or lily pale.
The burden is thy name, dear soul of me,
Which the rapt melodist unknowing all
Still doth repeat through fugue and reverie;
Thy name, to him unknown, to me doth call,
And weeps my heart at every music-fall.

SANCTUM SANCTORUM

I

I THOUGHT I knew the mountain's every mood,
Gray, black with storms, or lit by lightening dawn;
But once in evening twilight came a spell

Upon its brow, that held me with new power;
A look of unknown beauty, a deep mood
Touched with a sorrow as of human kind.

II

I thought I knew full well my comrade's face,
But a new face it was to me this day.
She sat among the worshipers and heard
The preacher's voice, yet listened not, but leaned
Her head unto a tone whose accents fell
On her sweet spirit only. Deep the awe
Struck then upon me, for my friend no more
Seemed to be near, as with forgetting gaze,
And piteous features steeped in tenderness,
She thought on things unspeakable — unknown
To all the world beside.

III

　　　　　When forth doth pass,
In holy pilgrimage and awful quest,
The soul of thy soul's comrade, thou must stand
In silence by, and let it move alone
And unattended far to the inner shrine;
Thou canst but wait, and bow thine head, and pray;
And well for thee if thou may'st prove so pure, —
Ended that hour, — thy comrade thou regain'st,
Thine as before, or even more deeply thine.

THE GIFT

I

LIFE came to me and spoke:
"A palace for thee I have built
Wherein to take thy pleasure;
I have filled it with priceless treasure;

Seven days shalt thou dwell therein;
Thy joy shall be keener than sin,
Without the stain of guilt —
Enter the door of oak!"

II

I entered the oaken door;
Within, no ray of light,
I saw no golden store,
My heart stood still with fright;
To curse Life was I fain;
Then one unseen before
Laid in my own her hand,
And said: "Come thou and know
This is the House of Woe;
I am Life's sister, Pain."

III

Through many a breathless way,
In dark, on dizzying hight,
She led me through the day
And into the dreadful night.
My soul was sore distrest
And wildly I longed for rest;
Till a chamber met my sight,
Far off, and hid, and still,
With diamonds all bedight
And every precious thing;
Not even a god might will
More beauty there to bring.

IV

Then spoke Life's sister, Pain:
"Here thou as a king shalt reign,
Here shalt thou take thy pleasure,
This is the priceless treasure,

The chamber of thy delight
Through endless day and night;
Rejoice, this is the end —
Thou hast found the heart of a friend."

"AH, TIME, GO NOT SO SOON"

AH, Time, go not so soon;
I would not thus be used, I would forego that boon;
Turn back, swift Time, and let
Me many a year forget;
Let her be strange once more — an unfamiliar tune,
An unimagined flower,
Not known till that mute, wondrous hour
When first we met!

"THE YEARS ARE ANGELS"

THE years are angels that bring down from Heaven
Gifts of the gods. What has the angel given
Who last night vanished up the heavenly wall?
He gave a friend — the gods' best gift of all.

"IN HER YOUNG EYES"

IN her young eyes the children looked and found
Their happy comrade. Summer souls false-bound
In age's frosty winter,— without ruth,—
Lived once again in her their long-lost youth.

"YESTERDAY, WHEN WE WERE FRIENDS"

I

YESTERDAY, when we were friends,
We were scarcely friends at all;
Now we have been friends so long,
Now our love has grown so strong.

II

When to-morrow's eve shall fall
　We shall say, as night descends,
　　Again shall say: Ah, yesterday
Scarcely were we friends at all —
　　Now we have been friends so long;
　　　Our love has grown so deep, so strong.

A NIGHT SONG

(FOR THE GUITAR)

THE leaves are dark and large, Love,
'T is blue at every marge, Love;

The stars hang in the tree, Love,
I 'll pluck them all for thee, Love;

The crescent moon is curled, Love,
Down at the edge of the world, Love;

I 'll run and bring it now, Love,
To crown thy gentle brow, Love;

For in my song,
　　　　　　The summer long,

The stars, and moon, and night, Love,
Are but for thy delight, Love!

LEO

I

OVER the roofs of the houses I hear the barking of Leo —
Leo the shaggy, the lustrous, the giant, the gentle New-
　　foundland.
Dark are his eyes as the night, and black is his hair as the
　　midnight;

Large and slow is his tread till he sees his master returning,
Then how he leaps in the air, with motion ponderous,
    frightening!
Now, as I pass to my work, I hear o'er the roar of the
    city —
Far over the roofs of the houses, I hear the barking of Leo;
For me he is moaning and crying, for me in measure
    sonorous
He raises his marvelous voice, for me he is wailing and
    calling.

II

None can assuage his grief, tho' but for a day is the
    parting,
Tho' morn after morn 't is the same, tho' home every
    night comes his master,
Still will he grieve when we sever, and wild will be his
    rejoicing
When at night his master returns and lays but a hand on
    his forehead.
No lack will there be in the world of faith, of love, and
    devotion,
No lack for me and for mine, while Leo alone is living —
While over the roofs of the houses I hear the barking of
    Leo.

PART III

BROTHERS

PASSION is a wayward child,
Art his brother firm and mild.
Lonely each
Doth fail to reach
Hight of music, song, or speech.

If hand in hand they sally forth,
East or west, or south or north,
Naught can stay them
Nor delay them.
Slaves not they of space or time
In their journeyings sublime.

LOVE, ART, AND TIME

ON A PICTURE ENTITLED "THE PORTRAIT,"
BY WILL H. LOW

SWEET Grecian girl who on the sunbright wall
  Tracest the outline of thy lover's shade,
  While, on the dial near, Time's hand is laid
  With silent motion — fearest thou, then, all?
How that one day the light shall cease to fall
  On him who is thy light; how lost, dismayed, —
  By Time, and Time's pale comrade Death, be-
      trayed, —
  Thou shalt breathe on beneath the all-shadowing
      pall!
Love, Art, and Time, these are the triple powers
  That rule the world, and shall for many a morrow —
Love that beseecheth Art to conquer Time!
Bright is the picture, but, O fading flowers!
  O youth that passes! love that bringeth sorrow! —
Bright is the picture; sad the poet's rhyme.

THE DANCERS

ON A PICTURE ENTITLED "SUMMER," BY T. W. DEWING

BEHOLD these maidens in a row
Against the birches' freshening green;
Their lines like music sway and flow;
They move before the emerald screen

Like broidered figures dimly seen
On woven cloths, in moony glow —
Gracious, and graceful, and serene.
They hear the harp; its lovely tones
Each maiden in each motion owns,
As if she were a living note
Which from that curvèd harp doth float.

THE TWENTY-THIRD OF APRIL

A LITTLE English earth and breathèd air
  Made Shakespeare, the divine; so is his verse
  The broidered soil of every blossom fair;
  So doth his song all sweet bird-songs rehearse.
But tell me, then, what wondrous stuff did fashion
  That part of him which took those wilding flights
  Among imagined worlds; whence the white passion
  That burned three centuries through the days and
      nights!
Not heaven's four winds could make, nor the round earth,
  The soul wherefrom the soul of Hamlet flamed;
  Nor anything of merely mortal birth
Could lighten as when Shakespeare's name is named.
  How was his body bred we know full well,
  But that high soul's engendering who may tell!

EMMA LAZARUS

WHEN on thy bed of pain thou layest low,
  Daily we saw thy body fade away,
  Nor could the love wherewith we loved thee stay
  For one dear hour the flesh borne down by woe;
But as the mortal sank, with what white glow
  Flamed thy eternal spirit, night and day;

Untouched, unwasted, tho' the crumbling clay
Lay wreckt and ruined! Ah, is it not so,
Dear poet-comrade, who from sight hast gone;
Is it not so that spirit hath a life
Death may not conquer? But, O dauntless one!
Still must we sorrow. Heavy is the strife
And thou not with us; thou of the old race
That with Jehovah parleyed, face to face.

THE TWELFTH OF DECEMBER

On this day Browning died?
Say, rather: On the tide
That throbs against those glorious palace walls;
That rises — pauses — falls
With melody and myriad-tinted gleams;
On that enchanted tide,
Half real, and half poured from lovely dreams,
A soul of Beauty, — a white, rhythmic flame, —
Past singing forth into the Eternal Beauty whence it came.

PART IV

SHERIDAN

I

Quietly, like a child
That sinks in slumber mild,
No pain or troubled thought his well-earned peace to mar,
Sank into endless rest our thunderbolt of war.

II

Tho' his the power to smite
Quick as the lightning's light, —
His single arm an army, his very name a host, —
Not his the love of blood, the warrior's cruel boast.

III

But in the battle's flame
How glorious he came! —
Even like a white-combed wave that breaks and tears the
shore,
While wreck lies strewn behind, and terror flies before.

IV

'T was he, — his voice, his might, —
Could stay the panic-flight,
Alone shame back the headlong, many leagued retreat,
And turn to evening triumph morning's foul defeat.

V

He was our modern Mars;
Yet firm his faith that wars
Ere long would cease to vex the sad, ensanguined earth,
And peace forever reign, as at Christ's holy birth.

VI

Blest land, in whose dark hour
Arise to loftiest power
No dazzlers of the sword to play the tyrant's part,
But patriot-soldiers, true and pure and high of heart!

VII

Of such our chief of all;
And he who broke the wall
Of civil strife in twain, no more to build or mend;
And he who hath this day made Death his faithful friend.

VIII

And now above his tomb
From out the eternal gloom
"Welcome!" his chieftain's voice sounds o'er the can-
non's knell;
And of the three one only stays to say "Farewell!"

SHERMAN

I

GLORY and honor and fame and everlasting laudation
For our captains who loved not war, but fought for the life
of the nation;
Who knew that, in all the land, one slave meant strife,
not peace;
Who fought for freedom, not glory; made war that war
might cease.

II

Glory and honor and fame; the beating of muffled drums;
The wailing funeral dirge, as the flag-wrapt coffin
comes.
Fame and honor and glory, and joy for a noble soul;
For a full and splendid life, and laureled rest at the goal.

III

Glory and honor and fame; the pomp that a soldier
prizes;
The league-long waving line as the marching falls and
rises;
Rumbling of caissons and guns; the clatter of horses' feet,
And a million awe-struck faces far down the waiting
street.

IV

But better than martial woe, and the pageant of civic sorrow;
Better than praise of to-day, or the statue we build
to-morrow;
Better than honor and glory, and History's iron pen,
Was the thought of duty done and the love of his fellow-
men.

PRO PATRIA

IN MEMORY OF A FAITHFUL CHAPLAIN [1]

I

EREWHILE I sang the praise of them whose lustrous names
  Flashed in war's dreadful flames;
Who rose in glory, and in splendor, and in might
  To fame's sequestered hight.

II

Honor to all, for each his honors meekly carried,
  Nor e'er the conquered harried;
All honor, for they sought alone to serve the state —
  Not merely to be great.

III

Yes, while the glorious past our grateful memory craves,
  And while yon bright flag waves,
Lincoln, Grant, Sherman, Sheridan, the peerless four,
  Shall live for evermore;

IV

Shall shine the eternal stars of stern and loyal love,
  All other stars above;
The imperial nation they made one, at last, and free,
  Their monument shall be.

V

Ah, yes! but ne'er may we forget the praise to sound
  Of the brave souls that found
Death in the myriad ranks, 'mid blood, and groans, and
    stenches —
  Tombs in the abhorrèd trenches.

[1] Chaplain William Henry Gilder, of the 40th New York Volunteers, died at Brandy Station, Virginia, in April, 1864, of smallpox caught while in attendance upon the regimental hospital.

VI

Comrades! To-day a tear-wet garland I would bring —
    But one song let me sing,
For one sole hero of my heart and desolate home;
    Come with me, Comrades, come!

VII

Bring your glad flowers, your flags, for this one humble
    grave;
    For, Soldiers, he was brave!
Tho' fell not he before the cannon's thunderous breath,
    Yet noble was his death.

VIII

True soldier of his country and the sacred cross —
    He counted gain, not loss,
Perils and nameless horrors of the embattled field,
    While he had help to yield.

IX

But not where 'mid wild cheers the awful battle broke, —
    A hell of fire and smoke, —
He to heroic death went forth with soul elate;
    Harder his lonely fate.

X

There in the pest-house died he; stricken he fearless
    fell,
    Knowing that all was well;
The high, mysterious Power whereof mankind has
    dreamed
    To him not distant seemed.

XI

Yet life to him was O, most dear, — home, children,
    wife, —
    But, dearer still than life,

Duty — that passion of the soul which from the sod
    Alone lifts man to God.

XII

So nobly past this unknown hero of the war;
    And heroes, near and far,
Sleep now in graves like his unfamed in song or story —
    But theirs is more than glory!

TO THE SPIRIT OF ABRAHAM LINCOLN

(REUNION AT GETTYSBURG TWENTY-FIVE YEARS AFTER THE BATTLE)

SHADE of our greatest, O look down to-day!
    Here the long, dread midsummer battle roared,
    And brother in brother plunged the accursèd sword; —
    Here foe meets foe once more in proud array,
Yet not as once to harry and to slay,
    But to strike hands, and with sublime accord
    Weep tears heroic for the souls that soared
    Quick from earth's carnage to the starry way.
Each fought for what he deemed the people's good,
    And proved his bravery by his offered life,
    And sealed his honor with his outpoured blood;
But the Eternal did direct the strife,
    And on this sacred field one patriot host
    Now calls thee father — dear, majestic ghost!

FAILURE AND SUCCESS

(G. C., 1888)

He fails who climbs to power and place
Up the pathway of disgrace.
He fails not who makes truth his cause,
Nor bends to win the crowd's applause.

He fails not, he who stakes his all
Upon the right, and dares to fall; —
What tho' the living bless or blame,
For him the long success of fame.

J. R. L.

ON HIS BIRTHDAY

NAVIES nor armies can exalt the state;
  Millions of men, nor coinèd wealth untold;
  Down to the pit may sink a land of gold;
But one great name can make a country great.

NAPOLEON

A SOUL inhuman? No, but human all,
  If human is each passion man has known:
  Scorn, hate, and love; the lust of empire, grown
To such a hight as did the world appall; —
If the same human soul may soar and crawl
  As soared his and as crawled; if to be shown
  The utmost heaven and hell; if to atone
For power consummate by colossal fall; —
If human 't is to see friend, partizan,
  Turn, dastardly, the imperial hand to tear
  That fed them; if through gnawing years to plan
Vengeance, and space to breathe the unfettered air —
  No alien from his kind but very man
  Slow perished on that island of despair.

THE WHITE CZAR'S PEOPLE

PART I

THE White Czar's people cry:
    "Thou God of the heat and the cold,
    Of storm and of lightning,

Of darkness, and dawn's red brightening;
　Hold, Lord God, hold,
Hold Thy hand lest we curse Thee and die."

The White Czar's people pray:
　"Thou God of the South and the North,
We are crusht, we are bleeding;
'T is Christ, 't is Thy Son interceding;
　Forth, Lord, come forth!
Bid the slayer no longer slay."

The White Czar's people call
　Aloud to the skies of lead:
"We are slaves, not freemen;
Ourselves, our children, our women —
　Dead, we are dead,
Tho' we breathe, we are dead men all.

"Blame not if we misprize Thee
　Who can, but will not draw near.
'T is Thou who hast made us —
Not Thou, dread God, to upbraid us.
　Hear, Lord God, hear!
Lest we whom Thou madest despise Thee."

PART II

Then answered the Most High God,
　Lord of the heat and the cold,
Of storm and of lightning,
Of darkness, and dawn's red brightening:
　"Bold, yea, too bold,
Whom I wrought from the air and the clod!

"Hast thou forgotten from me
　Are those ears so quick to hear

The passion and anguish
Of your sisters, your children who languish
  Near? Ah, not near —
Far off by the uttermost sea!

"Who gave ye your brains to plan —
    Your hearts to suffer and bleed?
Why call ye on heaven —
'T is the earth that to you is given!
    Plead, ye may plead,
But for man I work through man.

"Who gave ye a voice to utter
    Your tale to the wind and the sea?
One word well spoken
And the iron gates are broken!
    From me, yea, from me
The word that ye will not mutter.

"I love not murder but ruth.
    Begone from my sight ye who take
The knife of the coward —
Even ye who by heaven were dowered!
    Wake ye, O wake,
And strike with the sword of Truth!

"Fear ye lest I misprize ye —
    I who fashioned not brutes, but men.
After the lightning
And darkness — the dawn's red brightening!
    Men! Be ye men!
Lest I who made ye despise ye!"

PART III
(January 22, 1905)

The great word is uttered, at last!
   White Czar! O, where hast thou fled?
Thy children, heart-broken,
To thee their sorrows have spoken!
   To thee it is said —
That WORD on the wings of the blast!

For the word is their fearful cry,
   And the word is their innocent blood.
O, red is the chalice
Lifted up to thy empty palace!
   Blood, crimson blood,
On the snows where the murdered lie!

Their shed blood is the word! It is winning
   Its way swift from zone unto zone;
Through the world it has thrilled
And the heart of the nations stilled.
   Alone, thou alone!
Art thou deaf to the voice and the meaning?

Lo, it swells like the sound of the sea.
   Dull monarch! yet, yet, shalt thou hear it.
For, once 'neath the sun
By the brave it is spoken — all's done!
   Hear it — and fear it;
For "Freedom" it cries, "We are free!"

CHARLESTON
1886

Is this the price of beauty! Fairest, thou,
   Of all the cities of the sunrise sea,

Yet thrice art stricken. First, war harried thee;
Then the dread circling tempest drove its plow
Right through thy palaces; and now, O now!
A sound of terror, and thy children flee
Into the night and death. O Deity!
Thou God of war and whirlwind, whose dark brow,
Frowning, makes tremble sea and solid land!
These are Thy creatures who to heaven cry
While hell roars 'neath them, and its portals ope;
To Thee they call, — O Thou who bidst them die,
Who hast forgotten to withhold Thy hand, —
For thou, Destroyer, art man's only Hope!

PART V

HIDE NOT THY HEART

I

THIS is my creed,
This be my deed:
"Hide not thy heart!"
Soon we depart;
Mortals are all;
A breath, then the pall;
A flash on the dark —
All's done — stiff and stark.
No time for a lie;
The truth, and then die.
Hide not thy heart!

II

Forth with thy thought!
Soon 't will be naught,
And thou in thy tomb.
Now is air, now is room.

Down with false shame;
Reck not of fame;
Dread not man's spite;
Quench not thy light.
This be thy creed,
This be thy deed:
"Hide not thy heart!"

III

If God is, He made
Sunshine and shade,
Heaven and hell;
This we know well.
Dost thou believe?
Do not deceive;
Scorn not thy faith —
If 't is a wraith,
Soon it will fly.
Thou, who must die,
Hide not thy heart!

IV

This is my creed;
This be my deed:
Faith, or a doubt,
I shall speak out
And hide not my heart.

"THE POET FROM HIS OWN SORROW"

THE poet from his own sorrow
    Poured forth a love-sad song.
A stranger, on the morrow,
    Drew near, with a look of wrong,

And said: "Beneath its pall
  I have hidden my heart in vain —
To the world thou hast sung it all!
  Who told thee my secret pain?"

"WHITE, PILLARED NECK"

WHITE, pillared neck; a brow to make men quake;
  A woman's perfect form;
Like some cool marble, should that wake,
  Breathe, and be warm.

A shape, a mind, a heart,
  Of womanhood the whole:
Her breath, her smile, her touch, her art,
  All — save her soul.

"GREAT NATURE IS AN ARMY GAY"

GREAT nature is an army gay,
Resistless marching on its way;
I hear the bugles clear and sweet,
I hear the tread of million feet.
  Across the plain I see it pour;
It tramples down the waving grass;
Within the echoing mountain-pass
I hear a thousand cannon roar.
  It swarms within my garden gate;
My deepest well it drinketh dry.
It doth not rest; it doth not wait;
By night and day it sweepeth by;
Ceaseless it marcheth by my door;
It heeds me not, tho' I implore.
I know not whence it comes, nor where
It goes. For me it doth not care —

Whether I starve, or eat, or sleep,
Or live, or die, or sing, or weep.
And now the banners all are bright,
Now torn and blackened by the fight.
Sometimes its laughter shakes the sky,
Sometimes the groans of those who die.
Still through the night and through the livelong day
The infinite army marches on its remorseless way.

"LIFE IS THE COST"

I

LIFE is the cost.
Behold yon tower,
That heavenward lifts
To the cloudy drifts —
Like a flame, like a flower!
What lightness, what grace,
What a dream of power!
One last endeavor
One stone to place —
And it stands forever.

II

A slip, a fall;
A cry, a call;
Turn away, all's done.
Stands the tower in the sun
Forever and a day.
On the pavement below
The crimson stain
Will be worn away
In the ebb and flow;
The tower will remain.
Life is the cost.

THE PRISONER'S THOUGHT

I

Is 't I for whom the law's brute penalty
Was made; to whom the law once seemed a power
Far off and not to be concerned withal?
Am I indeed this rank and noisome thing
Fit for such handling; to be pushed aside
Into a human, foul receptacle, —
A fetid compost of dull, festering crime —
Even not meet for nutriment of earth,
But only here to rot in memories
Of my own shame, and shame of other men?
    Here let me rot, then — there's a taste one has
For just the best of all things, even of sin.
He's a poor devil who in deepest hell
Knows no keen relish for the worst that is, —
The very acme of intensest pain, —
Nor smacks charred lips at thoughts of some dear crime,
The sweetest, deadliest, damnablest of all.
Sometimes I hug that hellish happiness;
And then a loathing falls upon my soul
For what I was, and am, and still must be.

II

And this same I — there comes to me a time,
And often comes, when all this slips away;
Stays not one stain, nor scar, nor fatal hurt.
Perhaps it is a sort of waking dream;
But if I dream, I'm breathing audibly,
I feel my pulse beat, hear the talk and tread
Down these long corridors; see the barred blue
Of the cell's window, hear a singing bird —
Yes, O my God, I hear a singing bird,
Such as I heard in childhood. Now, you think,

I dream I am a child once more. Not so;
I am just what I am: a man in prison —
(Damn them! I'm innocent of what they swore
And proved — with cant, and well-paid perjury;
Tho' other crimes, they know not of, I did) —
But suddenly my soul is pure as yours;
My thought as clean; my spirit is as free
As any man's, or any purest woman's.
I think as justly, as for instance, sir,
You think; as circumspectly, wisely, freely,
As does my jolly keeper, or the smith
Who enters once a day to try the bars
That shut my body out from freedom! Not
My soul. Why, this my soul has thoughts that strike
Into the very hights and depths of Heaven.
You'll think it passing strange, good friend, no doubt.
'T is strange; but here's a further mystery:
Think you that in some other living state
After what we call death, — or in this life, —
The thinking part of us we name the soul
Can ever get away from its old self;
Can wash the earth all off from it, that so
It really will be, what I sometimes seem —
As sinless as a little child at birth,
With all a woman's love for all things pure,
And all a grown man's strength to do the right?

THE CONDEMNED

Thou art not fit to die? — Why not?
The fairest body ripes to rot.
Thy soul? O, why not let it go
Free from the flesh that drags it low!
To die! Poor wretch, do not deceive
Thyself — who art not fit to live.

"SOW THOU SORROW"

Sow thou sorrow and thou shalt reap it;
Sow thou joy and thou shalt keep it.

TEMPTATION

Not alone in pain and gloom,
Does the abhorrèd tempter come;
Not in light alone and pleasure
Proffers he the poisoned measure.
   When the soul doth rise
Nearest to its native skies,
There the exalted spirit finds
Borne upon the heavenly winds
Satan, in an angel's guise,
With voice divine and innocent eyes.

A MIDSUMMER MEDITATION

I

Face once the thought: This piled up sky of cloud,
Blue vastness, and white vastness steept in light, —
Struck through with light, that centers in the sun, —
This blue of waves below that meets blue sky;
But a white, trembling shore between, that sweeps
The circle of the bay; this green of woods,
And keener green of new-mown, grassy fields;
This ceaseless, leaf-like rustle of the waves;
These shining, billowy tree-tops; songs of birds;
Strong scent of seaweed, mixt with smell of pines;
Face once this thought: Thy spirit that looks forth,
That breathes the light, and life, and joy of all,
Shall cease, but not the things that pleasure thee;

They shall endure for eyes like thine, but not
For thine own eyes; for human hearts like thine,
But not for thine own heart, all dust and dead.

II

Face it, O Spirit, then look up once more,
Brave conqueror of dull mortality!
Look up and be a part of all thou seest.
Ocean and earth and miracle of sky,
All that thou seest, thou art, and without thee
Were nothing. Thou, a god, dost recreate
The whole; breathing thy soul in all, till all
Is one wide world made perfect at thy touch.
And know that thou, who darest a world create,
Art one with the Almighty, son to sire —
Of His eternity a quenchless spark.

AS DOTH THE BIRD"

As doth the bird, on outstretched pinions, dare
The dread abysm's viewless air,
Take thou, my soul, thy fearless flight
Into the void and dark of death's eternal night.

VISIONS

I

Cast into the pit
Of lonely sorrow,
The suffering soul,
Looking aloft,
Sees with amaze
In the daytime sky
The shine of stars.

II

Came to him once
In the seething town
A form of beauty,
Innocent brow,
And soul of youth;
Deep, sweet eyes,
An angel's gaze,
And rose-leaf lips
That murmured low:
"I, lost, forgotten,
Long left, long dead,
I am thy sin."

III

With full-toned beat
Of the happy heart,
In a day of peace,
In an hour of joy,
Once in my life
And only once,
Of a sudden, I saw,
The end of all!
— Death!

WITH A CROSS OF IMMORTELLES

WHEN Christ cried: "It is done!"
The face of a small red flower,
Looking up to the suffering One,
Turned pale with love and pain,
And never shone red again.
In memory of that hour

Which holds the secret of bliss;
  And the darker secret of sorrow
  That shall come to each, to-morrow;
Sweet friend, I send you this.

THE PASSING OF CHRIST

I

O mAN of light and lore!
Do you mean that in our day
The Christ hath past away;
That nothing now is divine
In the fierce rays that shine
Through every cranny and thought;
That Christ as he once was taught
Shall be the Christ no more?
That the Hope and Savior of men
Shall be seen no more again;
That, miracles being done,
Gone is the Holy One?
And thus, you hold, this Christ
For the past alone sufficed;
From the throne of the hearts of the world
The Son of God shall be hurled,
And henceforth must be sought
New prophets and kings of thought;
That the tenderest, truest word
The heart of sorrow hath heard
Shall sound no more upon earth;
That he who hath made of birth
A dread and sacred rite;
Who hath brought to the eyes of death
A vision of heavenly light,
Shall fade with our failing faith; —

He who saw in children's eyes
Eternal paradise;
Who made the poor man's lowly
Labor a service holy,
And sweat of work more sweet
Than incense at God's feet;
Who turned the God of Fear
To a father, bending near;
Who looked through shame and sin
At the sanctity within;
Whose memory, since he died,
The earth hath sanctified —
Hath been the stay and the hold
Of millions of lives untold,
And the world on its upward path
Hath led from crime and wrath; —
You say that this Christ hath past
And we cannot hold him fast?

II

Ah, no! If the Christ you mean
Shall pass from this time, this scene,
These hearts, these lives of ours,
'T is but as the summer flowers
Pass, but return again,
To gladden a world of men.
For he, — the only, the true, —
In each age, in each waiting heart,
Leaps into life anew;
Tho' he pass, he shall not depart.

Behold him now where he comes!
Not the Christ of our subtile creeds,
But the lord of our hearts, of our homes,

Of our hopes, our prayers, our needs;
The brother of want and blame,
The lover of women and men,
With a love that puts to shame
All passions of mortal ken; —
Yet of all of woman born
His is the scorn of scorn;
Before whose face do fly
Lies, and the love of a lie;
Who from the temple of God
And the sacred place of laws
Drives forth, with smiting rod,
The herds of ravening maws.

'T is he, as none other can,
Makes free the spirit of man,
And speaks, in darkest night,
One word of awful light
That strikes through the dreadful pain
Of life, a reason sane —
That word divine which brought
The universe from naught.

Ah, no, thou life of the heart,
Never shalt thou depart!
Not till the leaven of God
Shall lighten each human clod;
Not till the world shall climb
To thy hight serene, sublime,
Shall the Christ who enters our door
Pass to return no more.

CREDO

How easily my neighbor chants his creed,
Kneeling beside me in the House of God.
His "I believe" he chants, and "I believe,"
With cheerful iteration and consent —
Watching meantime the white, slow sunbeam move
Across the aisle, or listening to the bird
Whose free, wild song sounds through the open door.

Thou God supreme — I too, I too, believe!
But O, forgive, if this one human word,
Binding the deep and breathless thought of Thee
And my own conscience with an iron band,
Stick in my throat. I cannot say it, thus —
This "I believe" that doth Thyself obscure;
This rod to smite; this barrier; this blot
On Thy most unimaginable face
And soul of majesty.

                 'T is not man's faith
In Thee that he proclaims in echoed phrase,
But faith in man; faith not in Thine own Christ,
But in another man's dim thought of him.

Christ of Judea, look thou in my heart!
Do I not love thee, look to thee, in thee
Alone have faith of all the sons of men —
Faith deepening with the weight and woe of years.

Pure soul and tenderest of all that came
Into this world of sorrow, hear my prayer:

Lead me, yea, lead me deeper into life,
This suffering, human life wherein thou liv'st

And breathest still, and hold'st thy way divine.
'T is here, O pitying Christ, where thee I seek,
Here where the strife is fiercest; where the sun
Beats down upon the highway thronged with men,
And in the raging mart. O! deeper lead
My soul into the living world of souls
Where thou dost move.

      But lead me, Man Divine,
Where'er thou will'st, only that I may find
At the long journey's end thy image there,
And grow more like to it. For art not thou
The human shadow of the infinite Love
That made and fills the endless universe!
The very Word of Him, the unseen, unknown
Eternal Good that rules the summer flower
And all the worlds that people starry space!

NON SINE DOLORE

I

WHAT, then, is Life — what Death?
Thus the Answerer saith;
O faithless mortal, bend thy head and listen:

Down o'er the vibrant strings,
That thrill, and moan, and mourn, and glisten,
The Master draws his bow.
A voiceless pause; then upward, see, it springs,
Free as a bird with disimprisoned wings!
In twain the chord was cloven,
While, shaken with woe,
With breaks of instant joy all interwoven,
Piercing the heart with lyric knife,

On, on the ceaseless music sings,
Restless, intense, serene; —
Life is the downward stroke; the upward, Life;
Death but the pause between.

II

Then spake the Questioner: If 't were only this,
Ah, who could face the abyss
That plunges steep athwart each human breath?
If the new birth of Death
Meant only more of Life as mortals know it,
What priestly balm, what song of highest poet,
Could heal one sentient soul's immitigable pain?
All, all were vain!
If, having soared pure spirit at the last,
Free from the impertinence and warp of flesh,
We find half joy, half pain, on every blast;
Are caught again in closer-woven mesh —
Ah! who would care to die
From out these fields and hills, and this familiar sky;
These firm, sure hands that compass us, this dear human-
ity?

III

Again the Answerer saith:
O ye of little faith,
Shall, then, the spirit prove craven,
And Death's divine deliverance but give
A summer rest and haven?
By all most noble in us, by the light that streams
Into our waking dreams,
Ah, we who know what Life is, let us live!
Clearer and freer, who shall doubt?
Something of dust and darkness cast forever out;

But Life, still Life, that leads to higher Life,
Even tho' the highest be not free from the immortal
    strife.

The highest! Soul of man, O, be thou bold,
And to the brink of thought draw near, behold!
Where, on the earth's green sod,
Where, where in all the universe of God,
Hath strife forever ceased?
When hath not some great orb flashed into space
The terror of its doom? When hath no human face
Turned earthward in despair,
For that some horrid sin had stampt its image there?

If at our passing Life be Life increased,
And we ourselves flame pure unfettered soul,
Like the Eternal Power that made the whole
And lives in all He made
From shore of matter to the unknown spirit shore;
If, sire to son, and tree to limb,
Cycle on countless cycle more and more
We grow to be like Him;
If He lives on, serene and unafraid,
Through all His light, His love, His living thought,
One with the sufferer, be it soul or star;
If He escape not pain, what beings that are
Can e'er escape while Life leads on and up the unseen
    way and far?
If He escape not, by whom all was wrought,
Then shall not we, —
Whate'er of godlike solace still may be, —
For in all worlds there is no Life without a pang, and can
    be naught.
No Life without a pang! It were not Life,

If ended were the strife —
Man were not man, nor God were truly God!
  See from the sod
The lark thrill skyward in an arrow of song:
Even so from pain and wrong
Upsprings the exultant spirit, wild and free.
He knows not all the joy of liberty
Who never yet was crusht 'neath heavy woe.
He doth not know,
Nor can, the bliss of being brave
Who never hath faced death, nor with unquailing eye hath
      measured his own grave.
  Courage, and pity, and divinest scorn —
Self-scorn, self-pity, and high courage of the soul;
The passion for the goal;
The strength to never yield tho' all be lost —
All these are born
Of endless strife; this is the eternal cost
Of every lovely thought that through the portal
Of human minds doth pass with following light.
Blanch not, O trembling mortal!
But with extreme and terrible delight
Know thou the truth,
Nor let thy heart be heavy with false ruth.

  No passing burden is our earthly sorrow
That shall depart in some mysterious morrow.
'T is His one universe where'er we are —
One changeless law from sun to viewless star.
Were sorrow evil here, evil it were forever,
Beyond the scope and help of our most keen endeavor.
    God doth not dote,
His everlasting purpose shall not fail.
Here where our ears are weary with the wail

And weeping of the sufferers; there where the Pleiads
    float —
Here, there, forever, pain most dread and dire
Doth bring the intensest bliss, the dearest and most sure.
'T is not from Life aside, it doth endure
Deep in the secret heart of all existence.
It is the inward fire,
The heavenly urge, and the divine insistence.

   Uplift thine eyes, O Questioner, from the sod!
It were no longer Life,
If ended were the strife;
Man were not man, God were not truly God.

PART VI

ODE

Read before the Alpha Chapter of the Phi Beta Kappa Society, Harvard
University, June 26, 1890.

I

In the white midday's full, imperious show
    What glorious colors hide from human sight!
    But in the breathing pause 'twixt day and night
Forth stream those prisoned splendors, glow on glow;
        Like billows on they pour
        And beat against the shore
Of cloud-wrought cliffs high as the utmost dome,
To die in purple waves that break on dawns to come.

II

Divine, divine! O, breathe no earthlier word!
    Behold the western heavens how swift they flame
    With hues that bring to mortal language shame;

Swelling and pulsing like deep music heard
      On sacred summer eves
      When the loud organ grieves
And thrills with lyric life the incensed air,
While 'mid the pillared gloom the people bow in prayer.

III

Now is it some huge bird with monstrous vans
   That through the sunset plies its shadowy way,
   Catching on outstretched pinions the last play
Of failing tint celestial! See! it spans
      Darkly the fading west,
      And now its beamy crest
Follows from sight the glittering, golden sun;
And now one mighty wing-beat more, and all is done.

IV

But in those skyey spaces what dread change!
   Thus have we seen the mortal turn immortal;
   So doth the day's soul die, as through death's portal
The soul of man takes up its heavenward range.
      A million orbs endue
      The unfathomable blue —
Till, the long miracle of night withdrawn,
The world beholds once more the miracle of dawn.

V

Dawn, eve, and night, the iridescent seas,
   Bright moon, enlightening sun, and quivering stars,
   The midnight rose whose petals are the bars
Of Boreal lights, the pomp of autumn trees,
      The pearl of curvèd shells,
      The prismy bow that swells
'Gainst stormy skies — these witness, these are sign
Of thee, O spirit of Beauty, eternal and divine!

VI

And fairer still than all, — chief sign of all, —
  The naked loveliness in Eden's bower,
  Whose flesh blusht back the tint of fruit and flower;
Whose eye reflamed the starlight; who could call
      Father and friend the God
      That pluckt them from the sod;
The Almighty's image, and Creation's hight;
Whose deep souls mirrored clear the circling day and
    night.

VII

Spirit of Beauty! 'neath thy joyful spell
  Man hath been ever; therefore doth each breeze
  Bring to his trancèd ears glad melodies, —
Voices of birds, the brook's low, silvery bell, —
      Wild music manifold,
      Which he hath power to hold
His own enchanted harmonies among,
That echo round the world the songs that nature sung.

VIII

And thus all Beautiful in Holiness
  Doth Israel stand before the Eternal One;
  Striking his harp with rapt, angelic tone,
Till tribes and nations the Unseen God confess;
      Knowing that only where
      His face makes white the air
Could such seraphic song have mortal birth,
One saving faith sublime to keep alive on earth.

IX

And therefore with most passionate desire
  And longing, man yearned ever to express
  Thy majesty, and light, and loveliness,

O Spirit of Beauty, unconsuming fire!
     Therefore by ancient Nile
     Rose the vast columned aisle,
And on the Athenian Hill the wonder white
Whose shattered glory is the world's supreme delight.

X

So is it that to thy imperial shore,
  Bright Italy! the generations fly,
   Even but once to breathe, or e'er they die,
Where did a godlike race its soul outpour;
     Its birth divine revealing
     On glorious wall and ceiling,
While dome and rhythmic statue, Beauty-wrought,
Declare all human art is but what Heaven hath taught.

XI

Fair Italy! whose dread and peerless hight
  The song is of the awful Ghibelline!
  Poet! who 'mid the threefold dream divine
Didst follow Art and Love to the Central Light!
     Tell us, O Dante! tell
     What thou dost know so well,
That horror and death are but the shade and foil
Of Beauty, deathless, godlike, with never scathe or soil.

XII

Spirit divine! man falls upon the sod
  In awe of thee, in worship and amaze: —
  Thou older than the mountains, or the blaze
Of sunsets, or the sun; thou old as God;
     As God who did create
     Long ere man reached his state
All shapes of natural Beauty that men see,
And His wide universe did dedicate to thee.

XIII

Ye who bear on the torch of living art
  In this new world, saved for some wondrous fate,
  Deem not that ye have come, alas, too late,
But haste right forward with unfailing heart!
      Ye shall not rest forlorn;
      Behold, even now, the morn
Rises in splendor from the orient sea,
And the new world shall greet a new divinity.

XIV

Shall greet, ah, who can say! a nobler face
  Than from the foam of Cytherean seas:
  Loveliness lovelier; mightier harmonies
Of song and color; an intenser grace;
      Beauty that shall endure
      Like Charis, heavenly-pure;
A Spirit solemn as the starry night,
And full as the triumphant dawn of golden light.

AFTER–SONG

TO ROSAMOND

Rose of the world,
Bloom of the year,
Birth of the dawn!
By morn's one star
Lighted to life! —
Thou and my songs
Come to the day
Hand claspt in hand.

Flung on this page
May the glow of thy name
Back through each song
Shine with the light
Drawn from the skies —
Thou birth of the dawn,
Flower of the morn,
Rose of the world!

THE GREAT REMEMBRANCE

AND OTHER POEMS

THE GREAT REMEMBRANCE

AND OTHER POEMS

PART I

THE GREAT REMEMBRANCE

Read at the Annual Reunion of the Society of the Army of the Potomac,
Faneuil Hall, Boston, June 27, 1893.

COMRADES, the circle narrows, heads grow white,
As once more by the camp-fire's flaring light
We gather and clasp hands, as we have done
These many, many years. So long ago
A part we were of all that glorious show, —
Stood, side by side, 'neath the red battle-sun, —
So long ago we breathed war's thunderous breath,
Knew the white fury of that life-in-death,
So long ago that troubled joy, it seems
The valorous pageant might resolve to splendid dreams.

But no! Too deep 't is burned into the brain!
As well were lightning-scar by summer rain
Washed clean away, when stroke on blinding stroke
Hath torn the rock, and riven the blackened oak.

How oft as down these peaceful streets we pass
All vanishes save, lo! the rutted grass,
Wreckt caissons, frightened beasts, and, merciful God!
The piteous burden of the ensanguined sod!

Yet not all terror doth the memory save
From war's emblazonry and open grave:
In glimpses, flashing like a meteor's light,

A silent army marches through the night;
The guidons flutter in a golden valley
Where, at the noonday halt, the horsemen dally;
Or, look! a thousand tents gleam through the black;
Or, now, where quick-built camp-fires flame and crack,
From blaze to shade men stretch o'erwearied limbs,
Chant songs, or wake the hills with chorused hymns;
Or, ere the dawn makes pale the starry dark,
The fiery signals, spark on trailing spark,
Write on the silent sky their still command,
While the great army moves, drawn by a single hand.

So long ago it seems, so long ago,
Behold, our sons, grown men since those great days, —
Born since the last clear bugle ceased to blow
Its summons down the valley; since the bays
Shook with the roar of fort and answering fleet, —
Our very children look into our eyes
And find strange records, with a mute surprise;
As they some curious traveler might greet
Who kept far countries in his musing mind,
Beyond the weltering seas, the mountain-walls behind.
And yet it was this land and not another,
Where blazed war's flame and rolled the battle-cloud.
In all this land there was no home where brother,
Father, or son hurried not forth; where bowed
No broken-hearted woman when pale Death
Laid his cold finger on the loved one's breath.

Like to a drama did the scene unroll —
Some dark, majestic drama of the soul,
Wherein all strove as actors, hour by hour,
Yet breathless watched the whole swift, tragic play.
Faithful did each his little part essay,

Urged to an end unknown by one all-knowing Power;
While if the drama pauses, now and then,
On the huge stage, 't is for a moment only —
Here at the heart or in some vista lonely,
A single hero or a million men,
And with the tragic theme the world resounds again.

First, in the awful waiting came the shock,
The shame unbearable, the sacred flag assailed —
Assailed in freedom's name by those who freedom mock!
Ah, then the oath, to stand as stands the rock
'Gainst flood and tempest, lest that flag be trailed
And torn, or any star therefrom be lost —
The oath, murmured alone, or where the crowd,
As by a wind of heaven swept and tost,
Passioned its soul to God, and strong men wept aloud.

Then sweet farewell; O bitter-sweet farewell;
O brave farewell! Who were the bravest then,
Or they who went, or waited — women or men?
They who the cheers heard, or the funeral knell?
They who stept proudly to the rattling drum,
Inflamed by war's divine delirium,
Or they who knew no mad joy of the fight,
And yet breathed on through waiting day and weeping
        night?

Farewell and forward! O, to live it over,
The first wild heart-beat of heroic hours!
Forward, like mountain-torrents after showers!
Forward to death, as to his bride the lover!
Forward, till quick recoils the impetuous flood,
And ends the first dread scene in terror and in blood!
Onward once more, through sun and shivering storm, —
A monstrous length with wavering bulk enorm, —
Wounded or striking, bringing blood or bleeding,

Onward, still on, the agony unheeding!
Onward with failing heart, or courage high!
Onward through heat, and hunger, and dismay,
Turning the starry night to murderous day!
Onward, with hope appalled, once more to strike, and
     die!

So marched, so fought, so agonized, the hosts;
Battling through forests; rotting where slow crawls
The deathly swamp-stream; and like pallid ghosts
Haunting the hospitals, and loathèd prison-walls.
They knew what freedom was, and right to breathe
Clean air who burrowed from the filth and seethe
Of foulest pens, only that dogs might track,
And to the death-pit drag their living corpses back.
  O, would to Heaven some sights could fade from out
Clear memory's all too melancholy page —
Fade and be gone forever! Let the shout
Of victory only linger, and the rage
And glory of battle over land and sea,
And all that noblest is in war's fierce pageantry.
  Echoes of deeds immortal, O, awake!
Tremble to language, into music break,
Till lyric memory takes the old emotion,
And leaps from heart to heart the ancient thrill!
Tell of great deeds that yet the wide earth fill:
How first upon the amazèd waves of ocean
The black, infernal, deadly armored-ships
Together rushed, and all the world stood still,
While a new word of war burst from those iron lips;
How up the rivers thundered the strong fleets;
How the great captains 'gainst each other dashed
Gigantic armies. What wild welcome meets
Some well-loved chief who, ere those armies clashed,

Rides like a whirlwind the embattled line,
Kindling the stricken ranks to bravery divine!
And, hark, at set of sun, the cheer that greets
Victorious news from far-off armies, flashed
From camp to camp, with roar on answering roar,
Like bellowing waves that track the tempest down the
      shore.
  But chiefly tell of that one hour of all
When threatening war rolled highest its full tide,
Even to the perilous northern mountain-side
Where Heaven should bid our good cause rise or fall.
Tell of that hour, for never in all the world
Was braver army 'gainst a braver hurled.
To both the victory, all unawares,
Beyond all dreams of losing or of winning;
For the new land which now is ours and theirs,
Had on that topmost day its glorious beginning.
They who charged up that drenched and desperate slope
Were heroes all — and looked in heroes' eyes!
Ah! heroes never heroes did despise!
That day had Strife its bloodiest bourn and scope;
Above the shaken hills and sulphurous skies
Peace lifted up her mournful head and smiled on Hope.

  Rushed the great drama on its tragic way
Swift to the happy end from that tremendous day.
Happy, indeed, could memory lose her power
And yield to joy alone the glad, triumphant hour;
Happy if every aching heart could shun
Remembrance of the unreturning one;
If at the Grand Review, when mile on mile
And day on day the marching columns past,
Darkened not o'er the world the shadow vast
Of his foul murder — he the free from guile,

Sad-hearted, loving, and beloved, and wise,
Who ruled with sinewy hands and dreaming eyes.
What soul that lived then who remembers not
The hour, the landscape, ah! the very spot, —
Hateful for aye, — where news that he was slain
Struck like a hammer on the dazèd brain!

So long ago it was, so long ago,
All, all have past; the terror and the splendor
Have turned like yester-evening's stormy glow
Into a sunset memory strange and tender.
How beautiful it seems, what lordly sights,
What deeds sublime, what wondrous days and nights,
What love of comrades, ay, what quickened breath,
When first we knew that, startled, quailing, still
We too, even we, along the blazing hill,
We, with the best, could face and conquer death!

Glorious all these, but these all less than naught
To the one passion of those days divine,
Love of the land our own hearts' blood had bought —
Our country, our own country, yours and mine,
Then known, then sternly loved, first in our lives.
Ah! loved we not our children, sisters, wives?
But our own country, this was more than they, —
Our wives, our children, this, — our hope, our love
For all most dear, but more — the dawning day
Of freedom for the world, the hope above
All hope for the sad race of man. For where,
In what more lovely world, 'neath skies more fair,
If freedom here should fail, could it find soil and air?
In this one thought, one passion, — whate'er fate
Still may befall, — one moment we were great!
One moment in life's brief, perplexèd hour

We climbed the hight of being, and the power
That falls alone on those who love their kind
A moment made us one with the Eternal Mind.

One moment, ah! not so, dear Country! Thou
Art still our passion; still to thee we bow
In love supreme! Fairer than e'er before
Art thou to-day, from golden shore to shore
The home of freemen. Not one stain doth cling
Now to thy banner. Argosies of war
On thy imperial rivers bravely fling
Flags of the nations, but no message bring
Save of peace only; while, behold, from far
The Old World comes to greet thy natal star
That with the circling century returns,
And in the Western heavens with fourfold beauty burns.

Land that we love! Thou Future of the World!
Thou refuge of the noble heart opprest!
O, never be thy shining image hurled
From its high place in the adoring breast
Of him who worships thee with jealous love!
Keep thou thy starry forehead as the dove
All white, and to the eternal Dawn inclined!
Thou art not for thyself but for mankind,
And to despair of thee were to despair
Of man, of man's high destiny, of God!
Of thee should man despair, the journey trod
Upward, through unknown eons, stair on stair,
By this our race, with bleeding feet and slow,
Were but the pathway to a darker woe
Than yet was visioned by the heavy heart
Of prophet. To despair of thee! Ah, no!
For thou thyself art Hope, Hope of the World thou art!

Comrades belovèd, see, the fire burns low,
And darkness thickens. Soon shall our brief part
On earth forever end, and we shall go
To join the unseen ranks; nor will we swerve
Or fear, when to the silent, great reserve
At last we ordered are — as one by one
Our Captains have been called, their labors done,
To rest and wait in the Celestial Field.
Ay, year by year, we to the dead did yield
Our bravest. Them we followed to the tomb
Sorrowing; for they were worthy of our love —
High-souled and generous, loving peace above
War and its glories: therefore lives no gloom
In this our sorrow; rather pride, and praise,
And gratitude, and memory of old days.

A little while and these tired hands will cease
To lift obedient or in war or peace —
Faithful we trust in peace as once in war;
And on the scroll of peace some triumphs are
Noble as battles won; tho' less resounds
The fame, as deep and bitter are the wounds.

But now the fire burns low, and we must sleep
Erelong, while other eyes than ours the vigil keep.
And after we are gone, to other eyes
That watch below shall come, in starry skies,
A fairer dawn, whereon in fiery light
The Eternal Captain shall his signals write;
And shaken from rest, and gazing at that sign,
On shall the mighty Nation move, led by a hand divine.

PART II

"THE WHITE CITY"

(THE COLUMBIAN EXPOSITION)

I

GREECE was; Greece is no more.
Temple and town
Have crumbled down;
Time is the fire that hath consumed them all.
Statue and wall
In ruin strew the universal floor.

II

Greece lives, but Greece no more!
Its ashes breed
The undying seed
Blown westward till, in Rome's imperial towers,
Athens reflowers;
Still westward — lo, a veiled and virgin shore!

III

Say not, "Greece is no more."
Through the clear morn
On light winds borne
Her white-winged soul sinks on the New World's breast.
Ah! happy West —
Greece flowers anew, and all her temples soar!

IV

One bright hour, then no more
Shall to the skies
These columns rise.

But tho' art's flower shall fade, again the seed
Onward shall speed,
Quickening the land from lake to ocean's roar.

V

Art lives, tho' Greece may never
From the ancient mold
As once of old
Exhale to heaven the inimitable bloom;
Yet from that tomb
Beauty walks forth to light the world forever!

THE VANISHING CITY

I

ENRAPTURED memory, and all ye powers of being,
  To new life waken! Stamp the vision clear
On the soul's inmost substance. O, let seeing
  Be more than seeing; let the entrancèd ear
Take deep these surging sounds, inweaved with light
  Of unimagined radiance; let the intense
Illumined loveliness that thrills the night
  Strike in the human heart some deeper sense!
So shall these domes that meet heaven's curvèd blue,
  And yon long, white, imperial colonnade,
And many-columned peristyle, endue
  The mind with beauty that shall never fade;
Tho' all too soon to dark oblivion wending —
Reared in one happy hour to know as swift an ending.

II

Thou shalt of all the cities of the world
  Famed for their grandeur, evermore endure
Imperishably and all alone impearled
  In the world's living thought, the one most sure

Of love undying and of endless praise
   For beauty only — chief of all thy kind;
Immortal, even because of thy brief days;
   Thou cloud-built, fairy city of the mind!
Here man doth pluck from the full tree of life
   The latest, lordliest flower of earthly art;
This doth he breathe, while resting from his strife,
   This presses he against his weary heart;
Then, wakening from his dream within a dream,
He flings the faded flower on Time's down-rushing
     stream.

III

O, never as here in the eternal years
   Hath burst to bloom man's free and soaring spirit,
Joyous, untrammeled, all untouched by tears
   And the dark weight of woe it doth inherit.
Never so swift the mind's imaginings
   Caught sculptured form, and color. Never before,—
Save where the soul beats unembodied wings
   'Gainst viewless skies,—was such enchanted shore
Jeweled with ivory palaces like these:
   By day a miracle, a dream by night;
Yet real as beauty is, and as the seas
   Whose waves glance back keen lines of glittering light
When million lamps, and coronets of fire,
And fountains as of flame, to the bright stars aspire.

IV

Glide, magic boat, from out the green lagoon,
   'Neath the dark bridge, into this smiting glow
And unthought glory. Even the glistening moon
   Hangs in the nearer splendor. Let not go
The scene, my soul, till ever 't is thine own!
   This is Art's citadel and crown. How still

The innumerous multitudes from every zone,
    That watch and listen; while each eye doth fill
With joyous tears unwept. Now solemn strains
    Of brazen music give the waiting soul
Voice and a sigh — it other speech disdains,
    Here where the visual sense faints to its goal!
Ah, silent multitudes, ye are a part
Of the wise architect's supreme and glorious art!

V

O joy almost too high for saddened mortal!
    O ecstasy envisioned! Thou shouldst be
Lasting as thou art lovely; as immortal
    As through all time the matchless thought of thee!
Yet would we miss, then, the sweet, piercing pain
    Of thy inconstancy! Could we but banish
This haunting pang, ah, then thou wouldst not reign
    One with the golden sunset that doth vanish
Through myriad lingering tints down melting skies;
    Nor the pale mystery of the New World flower
That blooms once only, then forever dies —
    Pouring a century's wealth on one dear hour.
Then vanish, City of Dream, and be no more;
Soon shall this fair Earth's self be lost on the unknown
    shore.

THE TOWER OF FLAME

(THE COLUMBIAN EXPOSITION, JULY 10, 1893)

HERE for the world to see men brought their fairest,
    Whatever of beauty is in all the earth;
The priceless flower of art, the loveliest, rarest,
    Here by our inland ocean came to glorious birth.

Yet on this day of doom a strange new splendor
  Shed its celestial light on all men's eyes:
Flower of the hero-soul,— consummate, tender,—
  That from the tower of flame sprang to the eternal
    skies.

LOWELL

I

FROM the shade of the elms that murmured above thy
  birth
And the pines that sheltered thy life and shadowed the
  end,
'Neath the white-blue skies thee to thy rest we bore,—
'Neath the summer skies thou didst love, 'mid the songs
  of thy birds,
By thy childhood's stream, 'neath the grass and the
  flowers thou knewest,
Near the grave of the singer whose name with thine own
  is enlaureled,
By the side of the brave who live in thy deathless song,—
Here all that was mortal of thee we left, with our tears,
With our love, and our grief that could not be quenched
  or abated;
For even the part that was mortal, sweet friend and com-
  panion!
That face, and that figure of beauty, and flashing eye
Which in youth shone forth like a god's 'mid lesser men,
And in gray-haired, strenuous age still glowed and lus-
  tered,—
These, too, were dear to us,— blame us not, soaring spirit!
These, too, were dear, and now we shall never behold
  them,
Nor ever shall feel the quick clasp of thy welcoming hand.

II

But not for ourselves alone are we spent in grieving,
For the stricken Land we mourn whose light is darkened,
Whose soul in sorrow went forth in the night-time with
　　　thine.
Lover and laureate thou of the wide New World,
Whose pines, and prairies, and people, and teeming soil,
Where was shaken of old the seed of the freedom of men,
Thou didst love as a strong man loveth the maiden he
　　　woos,—
Not the woman he toys with, and sings to, and, passing,
　　　forgets,—
Whom he woos, whom he wins, whom he weds; his pas-
　　　sion, his pride;
Who no shadow of wrong shall suffer, who shall stand in
　　　his sight
Pure as the sky of the evil her foeman may threat,
Save by word or by thought of her own in her whiteness
　　　untouched
And wounded alone of the lightning her spirit engenders.

III

Take of thy grief new strength, new life, O Land!
Weep no more he is lost, but rejoice and be glad forever
That thy lover who died was born, for thy pleasure, thy
　　　glory —
While his love and his fame light ever thy climbing path.

August 14, 1891.

THE SILENCE OF TENNYSON

When that great shade into the silence vast
Through thinking silence past;
When he, our century's soul and voice, was husht,

We who, — appalled, bowed, crusht, —
Within the holy moonlight of his death
Waited the parting breath;
Ah, not in song
Might we our grief prolong.
Silence alone, O golden spirit fled!
Silence alone could mourn that silence dread.

ON THE DEATH OF A GREAT MAN

PHILLIPS BROOKS

WHEN from this mortal scene
A great soul passes to the vast unknown,
Let not in hopeless grief the spirit groan.
Death comes to all, the mighty and the mean.
If by that death the whole world suffer loss,
This be the proof (and lighter thus our cross),
That he for whom the world doth sorely grieve
Greatly hath blessed mankind in that he once did live.
Then, at the parting breath
Let men praise Life, nor idly blame dark Death.

A HERO OF PEACE

IN MEMORY OF ROBERT ROSS: SHOT MARCH 6, 1894

"No bugle on the blast
    Calls warriors face to face;
  Grim battle being forever past,
    Gone is the hero-race."

  Ah, no! there is no peace!
    If liberty shall live,
  Never may freemen dare to cease
    Their love, their life to give.

Unto the patriot's heart
  The silent summons comes;
Not braver he who does his part
  To the sound of beating drums.

And thou who gavest youth,
  And life, and all most dear;
Sweet soul, impassionate of truth,
  White on thy murdered bier! —

Thy deed, thy date, thy name
  Are wreathed with deathless flowers.
Thy fate shall be the guiding flame
  That lights to nobler hours.

WASHINGTON AT TRENTON

THE BATTLE MONUMENT, OCTOBER 19, 1893

Since ancient Time began,
  Ever on some great soul God laid an infinite burden —
The weight of all this world, the hopes of man.
  Conflict and pain, and fame immortal are his guerdon!

And this the unfaltering token
  Of him, the Deliverer — what tho' tempests beat,
Tho' all else fail, tho' bravest ranks be broken,
  He stands unscared, alone, nor ever knows defeat.

Such was that man of men;
  And if are praised all virtues, every fame
Most noble, highest, purest — then, ah! then,
  Upleaps in every heart the name none needs to name.

Ye who defeated, 'whelmed,
  Betray the sacred cause, let go the trust;

Sleep, weary, while the vessel drifts unhelmed;
  Here see in triumph rise the hero from the dust!

All ye who fight forlorn
  'Gainst fate and failure; ye who proudly cope
With evil high enthroned; all ye who scorn
  Life from Dishonor's hand, here take new heart of
    hope.

Here know how Victory borrows
  For the brave soul a front as of disaster,
And from the bannered East what glorious morrows
  For all the blackness of the night speed surer, faster.

Know by this pillared sign
  For what brief while the powers of earth and hell
Can war against the spirit of truth divine,
  Or can against the heroic heart of man prevail.

FAME

Fame is an honest thing,
  It is deceivèd not;
  It passes by the palace gates
  Where the crowned usurper waits,
  Enters the peasant-poet's cot
  And cries: "Thou art the king!"

A MONUMENT BY SAINT-GAUDENS

This is not Death, nor Sorrow, nor sad Hope;
Nor Rest that follows strife. But, O, more dread!
'T is Life, for all its agony serene;
Immortal, and unmournful, and content.

A MEMORY OF RUBINSTEIN

ʌᴇ of the ocean is, its thunderous waves
Echo his music; while far down the shore
Mad laughter hurries — a white, blowing spume.
I hear again in memory that wild storm;
The winds of heaven go rushing round the world,
And broods above the rage one sphinx-like face.

PADEREWSKI

I

Iꜰ songs were perfume, color, wild desire;
If poet's words were fire
That burned to blood in purple-pulsing veins;
If with a bird-like thrill the moments throbbed to hours;
If summer's rains
Turned drop by drop to shy, sweet, maiden flowers;
If God made flowers with light and music in them,
And saddened hearts could win them;
If loosened petals touched the ground
With a caressing sound;
  If love's eyes uttered word
No listening lover e'er before had heard;
If silent thoughts spake with a bugle's voice;
If flame passed into song and cried, "Rejoice! Rejoice!"
  If words could picture life's, hope's, heaven's eclipse
When the last kiss has fallen on dying eyes and lips;
If all of mortal woe
Struck on one heart with breathless blow on blow;
  If melody were tears, and tears were starry gleams
That shone in evening's amethystine dreams;
Ah, yes, if notes were stars, each star a different hue,
Trembling to earth in dew;

Or if the boreal pulsings, rose and white,
Made a majestic music in the night;
If all the orbs lost in the light of day
In the deep, silent blue began their harps to play;
  And when in frightening skies the lightnings flashed
And storm-clouds crashed,
If every stroke of light and sound were but excess of
     beauty;
If human syllables could e'er refashion
That fierce electric passion;
If other art could match (as were the poet's duty)
The grieving, and the rapture, and the thunder
Of that keen hour of wonder,—
That light as if of heaven, that blackness as of hell,—
How the great master plays then might I dare to tell.

II

  How the great master plays! And was it he
Or some disbodied spirit which had rushed
From silence into singing; and had crushed
Into one startled hour a life's felicity,
And highest bliss of knowledge — that all pain, grief,
     wrong,
Turn at the last to beauty and to song!

HANDEL'S LARGO

WHEN the great organs, answering each to each,
Joined with the violin's celestial speech,
Then did it seem that all the heavenly host
Gave praise to Father, Son, and Holy Ghost:
We saw the archangels through the ether winging;
We heard their souls go forth in solemn singing;
"Praise, praise to God," they sang, "through endless
     days,

Praise to the Eternal One, and naught but praise";
And as they sang the spirits of the dying
Were upward borne from lips that ceased their sighing;
And dying was not death, but deeper living —
Living, and prayer, and praising and thanksgiving!

THE STAIRWAY

By this stairway narrow, steep,
Thou shalt climb from song to sleep;
From sleep to dream and song once more; —
Sleep well, sweet friend, sleep well, dream deep!

THE ACTOR

GLORIOUS that ancient art! —
In thine own form to show the fire and fashion
Of every age and clime, of every passion
That dwells in man's deep heart!

Player, play well, not meanly,
Thy part in life, as on the mimic stage!
From highest thought is born art's noblest rage:
Live, act, end all, serenely!

THE STRICKEN PLAYER

WHEN at life's last the stricken player lies,
When throng before his darkened, dreaming eyes
His soul's companions, which more real then —
The human comrades, the live women and men
Of the large world he knew, or the ideal
Imagined creatures his own art made real;
Wherein he poured his spirit's very being,
His soul and body? Are those dim eyes seeing

Himself as one of Shakespeare's men? Are maids
And queens he wooed, the kings he was, or knew
Upon the tragic stage, are these the shades
That now his visionary hours pursue,
Attendant on his passing? Listen near!
What breathèd murmurs 'scape those pallid lips
To which the nations hearkened, ere the eclipse
Of all that brightness? Now lean close and hear;
Ah, see that look, sweeter than when he smiled
Upon the applauding world, while *she* draws near
And hears a dear voice whisper: "Child, my Child!"

AN AUTUMN DIRGE

(E. F. H.)

I

O EASE my heart, sad song, O ease my heart!
In all this autumn pageantry no part
Hath sorrow! Woods, and fields, and meadows glow
With jeweled colors. All alone I go
Amid the poignant beauty of the year,
Too heavy-hearted for one easeful tear.

For she who loved this autumn splendor,
These flaming marsh-flowers, oak-leaves rich and ten-
    der, —
And who in loving all, made all to me more dear, —
No more is here;
No more, no more is here!

Sad song, O, bring some thought
With music from some happy memory caught!
No light for me in all the lovely day
Those eyes being shut that first did lead the way
'Neath these great pines whose green vault hides the sky,
And down the rock-strewn shore where the white sea-
    birds cry!

II

All fades but those young, happy hours,
And in my soul once more the old joy flowers.
It flowers once more only to bring new pain;
For all in vain,
O song! thou singest in my grieving heart!
Thou hast no art
To bring again the smile I loved so well,
The voice that like a bell
Sounded all moods of sorrow and of laughter,
And the dear presence that in childhood's earliest
        thought,
And all the bright or darkened days thereafter,
Into my life a saddened sweetness brought —
Something of mother and of sister love,
A friendship far above
The ties that bind and loosen as we tread
The throngèd pleasures of life's later days.
  Sweet maiden soul, I cannot praise
But mourn thee, mourn thee, to the shadows fled.

III

Shadows, O nevermore!
For when past forth thy spirit it did seem
As if against the black a golden door
Were opened and a gleam
From the eternal Light fell on thy face
And made a visible glory in the place.
  Ah, well I know
Whatever be the source from whence we flow,
Whate'er the power begot these hearts of ours, —
As the great earth brings forth the summer flowers, —
That power is good, is God, and in her dying room
Humaned itself to sense and lightened all the gloom.

ELEONORA DUSE

IF ever flashed upon this mortal scene
A soul unsheathèd, a pale, trembling flame,
That suffered every gust, and yet did cling
With fire unquenchable — it is thine own,
Thou artist of the real! Unto thee
No mirth of life is secret; but, sweet soul,
With what sure art thou picturest human woe!
How natural tears to those Italian eyes —
Shadowing in untold depths whatever grief
Familiar is to mortals!

KELP ROCK

(E. C. S.)

ROCK's the song-soil, truly
(So sang one bard of power);
Therefore our poet duly
Built on this rock his tower;
And therefore in his singing
We breathe the salty morning;
We hear the storm-bell ringing,
The "siren's" piercing warning,
The sea-winds roaring, sighing,
The long waves rising, falling;
We hear the herons calling,
The clashing waves replying.

AT NIAGARA

I

THERE at the chasm's edge behold her lean
Trembling as, 'neath the charm,
A wild bird lifts no wing to 'scape from harm;

Her very soul drawn to the glittering, green,
Smooth, lustrous, awful, lovely curve of peril;
While far below the bending sea of beryl
Thunder and tumult — whence a billowy spray
Enclouds the day.

II

What dream is hers? No dream hath wrought that
      spell!
The long waves rise and sink;
Pity that virgin soul on passion's brink,
Confronting Fate, — swift, unescapable, —
Fate, which of nature is the intent and core,
And dark and strong as the steep river's pour,
Cruel as love, and wild as love's first kiss!
Ah, God! the abyss!

THE CHILD-GARDEN

In the child-garden buds and blows
A blossom lovelier than the rose.

If all the flowers of all the earth
In one garden broke to birth,

Not the fairest of the fair
Could with this sweet bloom compare;

Nor would all their shining be
Peer to its lone bravery.

Fairer than the rose, I say?
Fairer than the sun-bright day

In whose rays all glories show,
All beauty is, all blossoms blow;

While beside it deeply shine
Blooms that take its light divine:

The perilous sweet flower of Hope
Here its hiding eyes doth ope,

And Gentleness doth near uphold
Its healing leaves and heart of gold;

Here tender fingers push the seed
Of Knowledge; pluck the poisonous weed;

Here blossoms Joy one singing hour,
And here of Love the immortal flower.

What this blossom, fragrant, tender,
That outbeams the rose's splendor —

Purer is, more tinct with light
Than the lily's flame of white?

Of beauty hath this flower the whole,
And its name — the Human Soul!

THE CHRIST-CHILD

A PICTURE BY FRANK VINCENT DU MOND

DONE is the day of care.
Into the shadowy room
Flows the pure evening light,
To stem the gathering gloom,
The lily's flame illume,
And the bowed heads make bright
The heads bowed low in prayer.

See how the level rays
Through the white garments pour
Of the holy child, who stands,
With bending brow, to implore
Grace on the toilers' store;
O, see those sinless hands!
Behold, the Christ-child prays!

Wait, wait, ye lingering rays,
Stand still, O Earth and Sun,
Draw near, thou Soul of God —
This is the suffering one!
Already the way is begun
The piercèd Savior trod;
And now the Christ-child prays,
The holy Christ-child prays.

A CHILD

HER voice was like the song of birds;
    Her eyes were like the stars;
Her little waving hands were like
    Bird's wings that beat the bars.

And when those waving hands were still, —
    Her soul had fled away, —
The music faded from the air,
    The color from the day.

TWO VALLEYS

YES, 'tis a glorious sight,
This valley, that mountain hight.

The river plunges and roars
Like the loud sea on its shores

What time in waves enorm
Breaks the gigantic storm.

The wooded mount doth climb
To a thought intense, sublime.

The glory of all I feel;
But my heart, my heart, will steal

Down the journey of years,
Through the lands of laughter and tears,

Far back to the least of valleys
Where a slow brook curves and dallies,

Where a boy, in the twilight gleam,
Walks alone with his dream.

ON THE BAY

THIS watery vague how vast! This misty globe,
Seen from this center where the ferry plies, —
It plies, but seems to poise in middle air, —
Soft gray below gray heavens, and in the west
A rose-gray memory of the sunken sun;
And, where gray water touches grayer sky,
A band of darker gray prickt out with lights —·
A diamond-twinkling circlet bounding all;
And where the statue looms, a quenchless star;
And where the lighthouse, a red, pulsing flame;
While the great bridge its starry diadem
Lifts through the gray, itself in grayness lost!

WASHINGTON SQUARE

THIS is the end of the town that I love the best.
O, lovely the hour of light from the burning west —

Of light that lingers and fades in the shadowy square
Where the solemn fountain lifts a shaft in the air
To catch the skyey colors, and fling them down
In a wild-wood torrent that drowns the noise of the
    town.
And lovely the hour of the still and dreamy night
When, lifted against the blue, stands the arch of white
With one clear planet above; and the sickle moon,
In curve reversed from the arch's marble round,
Silvers the sapphire sky. Now soon, ah, soon,
Shall the city square be turned to holy ground,
Through the light of the moon and the stars and the
    glowing flower,—
The Cross of Light,— that looms from the sacred tower.

THE CITY

O, DEAR is the song of the pine
   When the wind of the night-time blows,
And dear is the murmuring river
   That afar through my childhood flows;
And soft is the raindrop's beat
   And the fountain's lyric play,
But to me no music is half so sweet
   As the thunder of Broadway!

Stream of the living world
   Where dash the billows of strife!—
One plunge in the mighty torrent
   Is a year of tamer life!
City of glorious days,
   Of hope, and labor, and mirth,
With room, and to spare, on thy splendid bays
   For the ships of all the earth!

A RHYME OF TYRINGHAM

Down in the meadow and up on the hight
The breezes are blowing the willows white.
In the elms and maples the robins call,
And the great black crow sails over all
      In Tyringham, Tyringham Valley.

The river winds through the trees and the brake
And the meadow-grass like a shining snake;
And low in the summer and loud in the spring
The rapids and reaches murmur and sing
      In Tyringham, Tyringham Valley.

In the shadowy pools the trout are shy,
So creep to the bank and cast the fly!
What thrills and tremors the tense cords stir
When the trout it strikes with a tug and a whir
      In Tyringham, Tyringham Valley!

At dark of the day the mist spreads white,
Like a magic lake in the glimmering light;
Or the winds from the meadow the white mists blow,
And the fireflies glitter,— a sky below,—
      In Tyringham, Tyringham Valley.

And O, in the windy days of the fall
The maples and elms are scarlet all,
And the world that was green is gold and red,
And with huskings and cider they 're late to bed
      In Tyringham, Tyringham Valley.

Now squirrel and partridge and hawk and hare
And wildcat and woodchuck and fox beware!

The three days' hunt is waxing warm
For the Count Up Dinner at Riverside Farm
  In Tyringham, Tyringham Valley.

The meadow-ice will be freezing soon,
And then for a skate by the light of the moon.
So pile the wood on the hearth, my boy!
Winter is coming! I wish you joy
By the light of the hearth and the moon, my boy,
  In Tyringham, Tyringham Valley.

ELSIE

"Do you love me?" Elsie asked,
And her rose-leaf dimples masked
'Neath a pleading look, the while
On her pouting lips a smile
Hovered, yet was out of sight
Like a star that's hid at night
By a filmy, flying cloud.
"Do you love me?" scarce aloud
Lovely Cousin Elsie said.
"Why no answer, Cousin Ed?
Do you hate me, then, or why
From Your Highness no reply?"
So the chiding witch ran on:
"In a moment I'll be gone;
Then too late, Sir No Gallant!
Quick! I'll tell my precious aunt
That you love me not," she cries,
"That you hate me and despise."
Flash the great, gray, long-lashed eyes;
Half in earnest now the girl;
Down the pretty corners curl

Of the tiny mouth, and lo!
From those eyes two tearlets flow; —
Just two kisses, and they go!
Like a sunburst after showers,
Like white light upon the flowers,
Now again the dimples show.

But she could not understand
Why so long the answer waited
For the loved and not the hated,
While he held that little hand,
And like a bird she sang and said, —
Half in earnest, half in fun, —
"Do you love me, Solemn One?
Do you love me, Cousin Ed?
Do you love me? Do you love me?
Love me, love me, Cousin Ed?"

INDIRECTION

I SAW not the leaf
 But its shadow trembling, trembling down.
I faced to northward, to my grief,
 When from the southern sky a crimson meteor lit the
  star-dark town.
I saw not naked Love
Lean from his porphyry throne above
And touch her heart to flame,
Yet on her brow I saw the swift, sweet, virgin shame.

"AH, BE NOT FALSE"

Ah, be not false, sweet Splendor!
 Be true, be good;
Be wise as thou art tender;
 Be all that Beauty should.

Not lightly be thy citadel subdued;
   Not ignobly, not untimely.
Take praise in solemn mood;
   Take love sublimely.

THE ANSWER

THROUGH starry space two angels dreamed their flight,
'Mid worlds and thoughts of worlds, through day and
   night.

Then one spake forth whose voice was like the flower
That blossoms in the fragrant midnight hour.
This white-browed angel of the other asked:
  "Of all the essences that ever basked
In the eternal presence; of all things,
All thoughts, all joys, all dreads, all sorrowings
Amid the unimaginable vast —
Being, or shall be, or forever past —
Profound with dark, or hid in endless light —
Which of all these most deep and infinite?"
  Then did the elder speak, the while he turned
On him who asked clear eyes that slowly burned
The spirit through, like to a living coal:
"No depth there is so deep as woman's soul."

HOW DEATH MAY MAKE A MAN

DEATH is a sorry plight,
   It bringeth unto man
End of all delight.
Yet many a woeful wight
   Only dying can
   Quit him like a man.

Dawdling, drawling, silly,
    Maundering, scarce a man;
Driven will y-nilly;
When he's dying will he
    Run as once he ran,
    Or quit him like a man?

Vile from out the wrack
    Crawls he less than man;
Cowering in his track
Beaten, broken, black;
    Curse him if you can —
    Death may make him man.

In life the wretch did naught
    Worthy of a man;
Now by Death he's caught,
What a change is wrought!
    Whom the world did ban
    Quits life like a man.

Braced stiff against the wall,
    Behold, at last, a man.
Lost — life and honor, all!
At Death's quick touch and call
    See, the craven can
    Quit him like a man.

"CAME TO A MASTER OF SONG"

CAME to a master of song
    And the human heart
One who had followed him long
    And worshiped his art;

One whom the poet's singing
    Had lured from death,
Joy to the crusht soul bringing
    And heaven's breath;

Came to him once in an hour
    Of terror and stress,
And cried, "Thou alone hast power
    To save me and bless;
Thou alone, pure heart and free,
    Canst pluck from disaster,
If to a wretch like me
    Thou wilt stoop, O master!"

Answered the bard with shame,
    And sorrow and trembling:
"Was I false, was my song to blame?
    Was my art dissembling?
I of all mortals the saddest,
    The quickest to fall,
And song of mine highest and gladdest
    Repentance all!"

BARDS

Some from books resound their rhymes —
    Set them ringing with a faint,
    Sorrowful, and sweet, and quaint
Memory of the olden times,
Like the sound of evening chimes.

Some go wandering on their way
    Through the forest, past the herds,
    Laughing maidens, singing birds;
On their sylvan lutes they play —
Danceth by the lyric Day!

Bards there be the deep sky under
  Who in high, authentic verse
  Mysteries and moods rehearse
With a voice like Sinai's thunder,
Chanting to a world of wonder.

And those have sung whose melody,
  Drawn from out the living heart
  With a quick, unfaltering art,
Hath power to make the listener cry:
"God in heaven! It is I."

MERIDIAN

Henceforth before these feet
Sinks the downward way;
A little while to greet
The light and life of day,
Then night's slow fall
Ends all.

Now forward, heart elate,
Tho' steep the pathway slope.
Time yet for love and hate,
Joy, and joy's comrade, hope,
Ere night's slow fall
Ends all.

Still the warm sky is blue,
No fleck the sunlight mars;
'Twixt hills the sea gleams through;
With twilight come the stars;
And night's slow fall
Ends all.

In the cool-breathing night
The starry sky is deep.
Still on through glimmering light
Till we lie down to sleep;
Then let night's fall
End all.

EVENING IN TYRINGHAM VALLEY

What domes and pinnacles of mist and fire
  Are builded in yon spacious realms of light
All silently, as did the walls aspire
  Templing the ark of God by day and night!
Noiseless and swift, from darkening ridge to ridge,
  Through purple air that deepens down the day,
Over the valley springs a shadowy bridge.
  The evening star's keen, solitary ray
Makes more intense the silence, and the glad,
  Unmelancholy, restful, twilight gloom —
So full of tenderness, that even the sad
  Remembrances that haunt the soul take bloom
Like that on yonder mountain.
                                Now the bars
  Of sunset all burn black; the day doth fail,
And the skies whiten with the eternal stars.
  O, let thy spirit stay with me, sweet vale!

PART III

A WEEK'S CALENDAR

I — NEW YEAR

Each New Year is a leaf of our love's rose;
It falls, but quick another rose-leaf grows.
So is the flower from year to year the same,
But richer, for the dead leaves feed its flame.

II — A NEW SOUL

To see the rose of morning slow unfold
Each wondrous petal to that heart of gold;
To see from out the dark, unknowing night
A new soul dawn with such undreamed-of light,
And slowly all its loveliness and splendor
Pour forth as stately music pours, magnificently tender!

III — "KEEP PURE THY SOUL"

KEEP pure thy soul!
Then shalt thou take the whole
Of delight;
Then, without a pang,
Thine shall be all of beauty whereof the poet sang —
The perfume, and the pageant, the melody, the mirth
Of the golden day, and the starry night;
Of heaven, and of earth.
O, keep pure thy soul!

IV — "THY MIND IS LIKE A CRYSTAL BROOK"

THY mind is like a crystal brook
Wherein clean creatures live at ease,
In sun-bright waves or shady nook.
Birds sing above it,
The warm-breathed cattle love it,
It doth sweet childhood please.

Accurst be he by whom it were undone,
Or thing or thought whose presence
The birds and beasts would loathly shun,
Would make its crystal waters foully run,
And drive sweet childhood from its pleasance.

V — "ONE DEED MAY MAR A LIFE"

ONE deed may mar a life,
 And one can make it;
Hold firm thy will for strife,
 Lest a quick blow break it!
Even now from far on viewless wing
Hither speeds the nameless thing
 Shall put thy spirit to the test.
Haply or e'er yon sinking sun
 Shall drop behind the purple West
All will be lost — or won!

VI — THE UNKNOWN

How strange to look upon the life beyond
Our human cognizance with so deep awe
And haunting dread; a sense as of remorse,
A looking-for of judgment, a great weight
Of things unknown to happen! We who live
Blindly from hour to hour in very midst
Of mysteries; of shapeless, changing glooms;
Of nameless terrors; issues vast and black;
Of airy whims, slight fantasies, and flights
That lead to unimaginable woe:
The unweighed word cloying the life of love;
One clod of earth outblotting all the stars;
Some secret, dark inheritance of will,
And the scared soul plunges to conscious doom!
Thou who hast wisdom, fear not Death, but Life!

VII — IRREVOCABLE

WOULD the gods might give
Another field for human strife;
Man must live one life

Ere he learns to live.
— Ah, friend, in thy deep grave,
What now can change, what now can save?

PART IV

SONGS

"BECAUSE THE ROSE MUST FADE"

BECAUSE the rose must fade,
    Shall I not love the rose?
Because the summer shade
    Passes when winter blows,
Shall I not rest me there
In the cool air?

Because the sunset sky
    Makes music in my soul,
Only to fail and die,
    Shall I not take the whole
Of beauty that it gives
While yet it lives?

Because the sweet of youth
    Doth vanish all too soon,
Shall I forget, forsooth,
    To learn its lingering tune;
My joy to memorize
In those young eyes?

If, like the summer flower
    That blooms — a fragrant death,
Keen music hath no power
    To live beyond its breath,

Then of this flood of song
Let me drink long!

Ah, yes, because the rose
　　Fades like the sunset skies;
Because rude winter blows
　　All bare, and music dies —
Therefore, now is to me
Eternity!

"FADES THE ROSE"

FADES the rose; the year grows old;
The tale is told;
Youth doth depart —
Only stays the heart.

Ah, no! if stays the heart,
Youth can ne'er depart,
Nor the sweet tale be told —
Never the rose fade, nor the year grow old.

THE WINTRY HEART

ON the sad winter trees
　　The dead, red leaves remain,
Tho' to and fro the bleak winds blow,
　　And falls the freezing rain.

So to the wintry heart
　　Clings color of the past,
While through dead leaves shudders and grieves
　　The melancholy blast.

HAST THOU HEARD THE NIGHTINGALE?

Yes, I have heard the nightingale.
  As in dark woods I wandered,
  And dreamed and pondered,
  A voice past by all fire
  And passion and desire;
  I rather felt than heard
  The song of that lone bird;
Yes, I have heard the nightingale.

Yes, I have heard the nightingale.
  I heard it, and I followed;
  The warm night swallowed
  This soul and body of mine,
  As burning thirst takes wine,
  While on and on I prest
  Close to that singing breast;
Yes, I have heard the nightingale.

Yes, I have heard the nightingale.
  Well doth each throbbing ember
  The flame remember;
  And I, how quick that sound
  Turned drops from a deep wound!
  How this heart was the thorn
  Which pierced that breast forlorn!
Yes, I have heard the nightingale.

"IN THAT DREAD, DREAMED-OF HOUR"

In that dread, dreamed-of hour
  When in her heart love's rose flames into flower,
'T is never, never *yes*,
  But *no, no, no*, whate'er the startled eyes confess.

Her frail denial at last
    Swept clean away like burnt leaves in the blast,
No longer *no, no, no!*
    But *yes*, forever *yes*, while love's red rose doth blow.

"ROSE-DARK THE SOLEMN SUNSET"

ROSE-DARK the solemn sunset
    That holds my thought of thee;
With one star in the heavens
    And one star in the sea.

On high no lamp is lighted,
    Nor where the long waves flow,
Save the one star of evening
    And the shadow star below.

Light of my Life! the darkness
    Comes with the twilight dream;
Thou art the bright star shining,
    I but the shadowy gleam.

"WINDS TO THE SILENT MORN"

WINDS to the silent morn;
    Waves to the ocean;
Voice to the song unsung;
    Song to emotion;
Light to the golden flower;
    Bird to the tree;
Love to the heart of love,
    And I to thee!

Dawn to the darkened world;
    Hope to the morrow;

Music to passion; and
 Weeping to sorrow;
Love to the heart that longs;
 Moon to the sea;
Heaven to the earthborn soul,
 And thou to me.

THE UNRETURNING

I

SILENT, silent are the unreturning!
What tho' word may reach to them, and yearning,
Never through the stillness of the night,
Never in the daytime or the dark
Comes the long-lost voice, or smile of light;
Lifts no hand from sea or sunken bark.
Silent, silent are the unreturning!

II

Silent, silent are the unreturning!
Silent they? — or are we undiscerning?
Child, my child! is this thy answering voice
Murmuring far down the mountain lone?
Evening's smile, that whispers: "Heart, rejoice!"
Mother mine! is this thy very own?
Nay! nay! Silent are the unreturning;
Silent, silent are the unreturning!

TWO YEARS

O, THAT was the year the last of those before thee;
 All my world till then but dark before the dawn.
If then I had died, O, never had I known thee,
Never had beheld thee; I who won, who own thee;
Who chose thee, who sing thee, crown thee, and adore
   thee;
 O, death it were indeed to die before that dawn!

This was the year when first I did behold thee,
    Thou who on my darkness dawned with lyric light.
This the golden hour when first thy lover found thee,
Followed and beguiled thee, and with his singing bound
            thee;
When all the world with music rang to drown thee and
            enfold thee—
    Thou who turned the darkness to song, and love, and
            light!

IN PALESTINE

AND OTHER POEMS

IN PALESTINE

AND OTHER POEMS

PART I

IN PALESTINE

Aʜ, no! that sacred land
Where fell the wearied feet of the lone Christ
Robs not the soul of faith. I shall set down
The thought was in my heart. If that hath lost
Aught of its child-belief, 't was long ago,
Not there in Palestine; and if 't were lost,
He were a coward who should fear to lose
A blind, hereditary, thoughtless faith —
Comfort of fearful minds, a straw to catch at
On the deep-gulfed and tempest-driven sea.

Full well I know how shallow spirits lack
The essence, flinging from them but the form.
I have seen souls lead barren lives and curst, —
Bereft of light, and all the grace of life, —
Because for them the inner truth was lost
In the frail symbol — hated, shattered, spurned.

But faith that lives forever is not bound
To any outward semblance, any scheme
Fine-wrought of human wonder, or self-love,
Or the base fear of never-ending pain.
True faith doth face the blackness of despair,

Blank faithlessness itself; bravely it holds
To duty unrewarded and unshared;
It loves where all is loveless; it endures
In the long passion of the soul for God.

'T was thus I thought: —
At last the very land whose breath he breathed,
The very hills his bruisèd feet did climb!
This is his Olivet; on this Mount he stood,
As I do now, and with this same surprise
Straight down into the startling blue he gazed
Of the fair, turquoise mid-sea of the plain.
That long, straight, misty, dream-like, violet wall
Of Moab — lo, how close it looms! The same
Quick human wonder struck his holy vision.
About these feet the flowers he knew so well.
Back where the city's shadow slowly climbs
There is a wood of olives gaunt and gray,
And centuries old; it holds the name it bore
That night of agony and bloody sweat.

I tell you when I looked upon these fields
And stony valleys, — through the purple veil
Of twilight, or what time the Orient sun
Made shining jewels of the barren rocks, —
Something within me trembled; for I said:
This picture once was mirrored in his eyes;
This sky, that lake, those hills, this loveliness,
To him familiar were; this is the way
To Bethany; the red anemones
Along yon wandering path mark the steep road
To green-embowered Jordan. All is his:
These leprous outcasts pleading piteously;
This troubled country, — troubled then as now,

And wild and bloody,—this is his own land.
On such a day, girdled by these same hills,
Prest by this dark-browed, sullen, Orient crowd,
On yonder mount, spotted with crimson blooms,
He closed his eyes, in that dark tragedy
Which mortal spirit never dared to sound.
O God! I saw those eyes in every throng.

Was he divine, and maker of all worlds,—
The Godhead veiled in suffering, for our sins,—
An unimagined splendor poured on earth
In sacrifice supreme,—this was a scene
Fit for the tears of angels and all men.
If he was man—a passionate human heart,
Like unto ours, but with intenser fire,
And whiter from the deep and central glow;
Who loved all men as never man before,
Who felt as never mortal all the weight
Of this world's sorrow, and whose sinless hands
Upstretched in prayer did seem, indeed, to clutch
The hand divine; if he was man, yet dreamed
That the Ineffable through him had power,—
Even through his touch,—to scatter human pain
(Setting the eternal seal on his high hope
And promised kingdom); was he only man,
Thus, thus to aspire, and thus at last to fall!
Such anguish! such betrayal! Who could paint
That tragedy! one human, piteous cry—
"Forsaken!"—and black death! If he was God,
'T was for an instant only, his despair;
Or was he man, and there is life beyond,
And, soon or late, the good rewarded are,
Then, too, is recompense.

                     But was he man,
And death ends all; then was that tortured death
On Calvary a thing to make the pulse
Of memory quail and stop.

                     The blackest thought
The human brain may harbor comes that way.
Face that,—face all,—yet lose not hope nor heart!
One perfect moment in the life of love,
One deed wherein the soul unselfed gleams forth,
These can outmatch all ill, all doubt, all fear,
And through the encompassing burden of the world
Burn swift the spirit's pathway to its God.

THE ANGER OF CHRIST

On the day that Christ ascended
        To Jerusalem,
Singing multitudes attended,
And the very heavens were rended
        With the shout of them.

Chanted they a sacred ditty,
        Every heart elate;
But he wept in brooding pity,
Then went in the holy city
        By the Golden Gate.

In the temple, lo! what lightning
        Makes unseemly rout!
He in anger, sudden, frightening,
Drives with scorn and scourge the whitening
        Money-changers out.

By the way that Christ descended
    From Mount Olivet,
I, a lonely pilgrim, wended,
On the day his entry splendid
    Is remembered yet.

And I thought: If he, returning
    On this high festival,
Here should haste with love and yearning,
Where would now his fearful, burning
    Anger flash and fall?

In the very house they builded
    To his saving name,
'Mid their altars, gemmed and gilded,
Would his scourge and scorn be wielded,
    His fierce lightning flame.

Once again, O Man of Wonder,
    Let thy voice be heard!
Speak as with a sound of thunder;
Drive the false thy roof from under;
    Teach thy priests thy word.

THE BIRDS OF BETHLEHEM

I HEARD the bells of Bethlehem ring —
    Their voice was sweeter than the priests';
I heard the birds of Bethlehem sing
    Unbidden in the churchly feasts.

They clung and sung on the swinging chain
    High in the dim and incensed air;
The priests, with repetitions vain,
    Chanted a never-ending prayer.

So bell and bird and priest I heard,
  But voice of bird was most to me;
It had no ritual, no word,
  And yet it sounded true and free.

I thought Child Jesus, were he there,
  Would like the singing birds the best,
And clutch his little hands in air
  And smile upon his mother's breast.

NOËL

STAR-DUST and vaporous light, —
  The mist of worlds unborn, —
A shuddering in the awful night
  Of winds that bring the morn.

Now comes the dawn: the circling earth;
  Creatures that fly and crawl;
And Man, that last, ĭmperial birth;
  And Christ, the flower of all.

"THE SUPPER AT EMMAUS"

WISE Rembrandt! thou couldst paint, and thou alone,
Eyes that had seen what never human eyes
Before had looked on; him that late had past
Onward and back through gates of Death and Life.

O human face where the celestial gleam
Lingers! O, still to thee the eyes of men
Turn with deep, questioning worship; seeing there,
As in a mirror, the Eternal Light
Caught from the shining of the central Soul
Whence came all worlds, and whither shall return.

THE DOUBTER

THOU Christ, my soul is hurt and bruised!
  With words the scholars wear me out;
My brain o'erwearied and confused,
  Thee, and myself, and all I doubt.

And must I back to darkness go
  Because I cannot say their creed?
I know not what I think; I know
  Only that thou art what I need.

THE PARTHENON BY MOONLIGHT

I

THIS is an island of the golden Past
  Uplifted in the tranquil sea of night.
In the white splendor how the heart beats fast,
  When climbs the pilgrim to this gleaming hight;
As might a soul, new-born, its wondering way
  Take through the gates of pearl and up the stair
Into the precincts of celestial day,
  So to this shrine my worshiping feet did fare.

II

But look! what tragic waste! Is Time so lavish
  Of dear perfection thus to see it spilled?
'T was worth an empire; — now behold the ravish
  That laid it low. The soaring plain is filled
With the wide-scattered letters of one word
  Of loveliness that nevermore was spoken;
Nor ever shall its like again be heard:
  Not dead is art — but that high charm is broken.

III

Now moonlight builds with swift and mystic art
   And makes the ruin whole — and yet not whole;
But exquisite, tho' crusht and torn apart.
   Back to the temple steals its living soul
In the star-silent night; it comes all pale —
   A spirit breathing beauty and delight,
And yet how stricken! Hark! I hear it wail
   Self-sorrowful, while every wound bleeds white.

IV

And tho' more sad than is the nightingale
   That mourns in Lykabettos' fragrant pine,
That soul to mine brings solace; nor shall fail
   To heal the heart of man while still doth shine
Yon planet, doubly bright in this deep blue;
   Yon moon that brims with fire these violet hills:
For beauty is of God; and God is true,
   And with His strength the soul of mortal fills.

THE OTTOMAN EMPIRE

Let fall the ruin propt by Europe's hands!
   Its tottering walls are but a nest of crime;
Slayers and ravishers in licensed bands
   Swarm darkly forth to shame the face of Time.

False, imbecile, and cruel; kept in place
   Not by its natural force, but by the fears
Of foes, scared each of each; even by the grace
   Of rivals — not blood-guiltless all these years!

Ay, let the ruin fall, and from its stones
   Rebuild a civic temple pure and fair;
Where freedom is not alien; where the groans
   Of dying and ravished burden not the air!

1896.

KARNAK

I

OF all earth's shrines this is the mightiest,
  And none is elder. Pylon, obelisk,
Column enormous — seek or east or west,
  No temple like to Karnak 'neath the disk
Of the far-searching sun. Since the first stone
  Here lifted to the heavens its dumb appeal,
Empires and races to the dread unknown
    Have past — gods great and small 'neath Time's
      slow wheel
Have fallen and been crusht; — the earth hath shaken
Ruin on ruin — desolate, dead, forsaken.

II

Since first these stones were laid, the solid world,
  Ay, this whole, visible, infinite universe,
Hath shifted on its base; suns have been hurled
  From heaven; the ever-circling spheres rehearse
A music new to men. Yet still doth run
  This river, throbbing life through all its lands;
Those desert mountains lifted to the sun
  Live as of old; and these devouring sands;
And, under the changing heavens, amazed, apart —
Still, still the same the insatiate human heart.

III

And Thou, Eternal, Thou art still the same;
  Thou unto whom the first, sad, questioning face
Yearned, for a refuge from the insentient frame
  Of matter that doth grind us; seeking grace
From powers imagined 'gainst the powers we know; —
  Some charm to avert the whirlwind, bring the tide

And harvest; turn the blind and awful flow
   Of nature! Thou Eternal dost abide
Silent forever, like the unanswering skies
That send but empty echoes to men's cries!

IV

But not in temples now man's only hope,
   Nor secret ministries of king and priest
Chanting beyond dark gates that never ope
   Unto the people; now no hornèd beast
Looms 'twixt the worshiper and the adored,
   Nor any creature's likeness; He remains
Unknown as erst; yet Him whom we call Lord
   Is worshiped in the fields as in the fanes.
We have but faith; we know not; yet He seems
More near, more human, in our passionate dreams.

V

We know not, yet the centuries in their course
   Have built an image in the mind of man;
We have but faith, yet that mysterious Force
   Less darkly threatens, looms a friendlier plan.
Far off the singing of the morning stars,
   Yet age by age such words of light are spoken
(Like whispered messages through prison bars),
   Sometimes men deem the dreadful silence broken,
And hearts that late were famished and afeared
Leap to the Voice and onward fare well cheered.

VI

Cheered for a little season, but the morrow
   Brings the old heartbreak; gone is all the gain;
Tho' the bowed soul be schooled to its own sorrow,
   Ah, heaven! to feel earth's heritage of pain, —

The unescapable anguish of mankind,
 That blots out natural joy! — O human soul,
Learn Courage, tho' the lightning strike thee blind;
 Let Duty be thy worship; Love, thy goal:
Love, Duty, Courage — these make thou thy own,
Till from the unknown we pass into the unknown.

"ANGELO, THOU ART THE MASTER"

I

ANGELO, thou art the master; for thou in thy art
Compassed the body, the soul; the form and the heart.
Knew where the roots of the spirit are buried and twined,
The springs and the rocks that shall suckle — and tor-
  ture and bind.
Large was thy soul like the soul of a god that creates —
Converse it held with the stars and the imminent Fates.
Knewest thou — Art is but Beauty perceived and exprest,
And the pang of that Beauty had entered and melted thy
  breast.
Here by thy Slave, again, after long years do I bow —
Angelo, thou art the master, yea, thou, and but thou.

Here is the crown of all beauty that lives in the world;
Spirit and flesh breathing forth from these lips that are
  curled
With sweetness and sorrow as never, O, never before,
And from eyes that are heavy with light, and shall weep
  nevermore;
And lo, at the base of the statue, that monster of shape —
Thorn of the blossom of life, mocking face of the ape.
So cometh morn from the shadow and murk of the night;
From pain springeth joy, and from flame the keen beauty
  of light.

II

Beauty! — O, well for the hearts that bow down and
adore her:
Heart of mine, hold thou in all the world nothing before
her.
All the fair universe now to her feet that is clinging
Out of the womb of her leapt with the dawn, and the
singing
Of stars. O thou Beautiful! — thee do I worship and
praise
In the dark where thy lamps are; again in thy glory of
days,
Whose end and beginning thou blessest with piercing
delight
Of splendors outspread on the edge of the robe of the
night.

Ah, that sweetness is sent not to him whose dull spirit
would rest
In the bliss of it; no, not the goal, but the passion and
quest;
Not the vale, but the desert. O, never soft airs shall
awake
Thy Soul to the soul of all Beauty, all heaven, and all
wonder;
The summons that comes to thee, mortal, thy spirit to
shake,
Shall be the loud clarion's call and the voices of thunder.

A WINTER TWILIGHT IN PROVENCE

A STRANGER in a far and ancient land,
At evening-light I wander. Shade on shade
The mountain valleys darken, and the plain

Grows dim beneath a chill and iron sky.
The trees of peace take the last gray of day —
Day that shone soft on olives, misty-green,
And aisles of wind-forbidding cypresses,
And long, white roads, whitely with plane-trees lined,
And farms content, and happy villages —
A land that lies close in the very heart
Of history, and brave, and free, and gay;
In all its song lingering one tone of pain.

But now the wintry twilight silent falls,
And ghosts of other days stalk the lone fields;
While through yon sunk and immemorial road,
Rock-furrowed, rough, and like a torrent's bed,
Far-stretching into night 'twixt twilight farms,
I see in dream the unhistoried armies pass,
With barbarous banners trailing 'gainst the gloom;
Then, in a thought's flash (centuries consumed),
In this deep path a fierce and refluent wave
Brims the confined and onward-pressing march
With standards slantwise borne; so, to the mind,
The all-conquering eagle northward takes its flight,
And one stern empire widens o'er the world.

There looms the arch of war where once, long gone,
In these still fields, against those thymy slopes,
An alien city reared imperial towers:
See sculptured conqueror, and slave in chains
Mournful a myriad years; and near the arch
The heaven-climbing, templed monument
Embossed with horse and furious warrior!
Millenniums have sped since those grim wars
Here grimly carved, the wonder of the churl, —
The very language dead those warriors cried.
Deepens the dusk, and on the neighboring hight
A rock-hewn palace cuts the edge of day

In giant ruin stark against the sky:
Ah, misery! I know its piteous tale
Of armed injustice; monstrous, treacherous force.
Deepens the dusk, and the enormous towers,
Still lording o'er a living city near,
Are lost to sight; but not to thought are lost
A hundred stories of the old-time curse —
War and its ravagings. Deepens the dusk
On westward mountains black with olden crime
And steeped in blood spilled in the blessèd name
Of him the Roman soldiers crucified —
The Prince of Peace. Deepens the dusk, and all
The nearer landscape glimmers into dark,
And naught shows clear save yonder wayside cross
Against the lurid west whose dying gleam
Of ghastly sunlight frights the brooding soul.

Dear country mine! far in that viewless west,
And ocean-warded, strife thou too hast known;
But may thy sun hereafter bloodless shine,
And may thy way be onward without wrath,
And upward on no carcass of the slain;
And if thou smitest, let it be for peace
And justice — not in hate, or pride, or lust
Of empire. May'st thou ever be, O land!
Noble and pure as thou art free and strong:
So shalt thou lift a light for all the world
And for all time, and bring the Age of Peace.

St.-Remy de Provence, January, 1896.

PART II

"THE POET'S DAY"

THE poet's day is different from another,
Tho' he doth count each man his own heart's brother.
So crystal-clear the air that he looks through,
It gives each color an intenser hue;
Each bush doth burn, and every flower flame;
The stars are sighing; silence breathes a name.
The world wherein he wanders, dreams, and sings
Thrills with the beating of invisible wings;
And all day long he hears from hidden birds
The low, melodious pour of musicked words.

"HOW TO THE SINGER COMES THE SONG?"

I

How to the singer comes the song?
At times a joy, alone;
A wordless tone
Caught from the crystal gleam of ice-bound trees;
Or from the violet-perfumed breeze;
Or the sharp smell of seas
In sunlight glittering many an emerald mile;
Or the keen memory of a love-lit smile.

II

Thus to the singer comes the song:
Gazing at crimson skies
Where burns and dies
On day's wide hearth the calm celestial fire,
The poet with a wild desire

Strikes the impassioned lyre,
Takes into tunèd sound the flaming sight
And ushers with new song the ancient night.

III

How to the singer comes the song?
Bowed down by ill and sorrow
On every morrow —
The unworded pain breaks forth in heavenly singing;
Not all too late dear solace bringing
To broken spirits winging
Through mortal anguish to the unknown rest —
A lyric balm for every wounded breast.

IV

How to the singer comes the song?
How to the summer fields
Come flowers? How yields
Darkness to happy dawn? How doth the night
Bring stars? O, how do love and light
Leap at the sound and sight
Of her who makes this dark world seem less wrong —
Life of his life, and soul of all his song!

"LIKE THE BRIGHT PICTURE"

LIKE the bright picture ere the lamp is lit,
Or silent page whereon keen notes are writ;
So was my love, all vacant, all unsaid,
Ere she the lamp did light, ere she the music read.

REMEMBRANCE OF BEAUTY

LOVE'S look finds loveliness in all the world:
Ah, who shall say — This, this is loveliest!

Forgetting that pure beauty is impearled
A thousand perfect ways, and none is best.
Sometimes I deem that dawn upon the ocean
Thrills deeper than all else; but, sudden, there,
With serpent gleam and hue, and fixèd motion,
Niagara curves its scimitar in air.
So when I dream of sunset, oft I gaze
Again from Bellosguardo's misty hight,
Or memory ends once more one day of days —
Carrara's mountains purpling into night.
There is no loveliest, dear Love, but thee —
Through whom all loveliness I breathe and see.

MUSIC IN SOLITUDE

I

In this valley far and lonely
Birds sang only,
And the brook,
And the rain upon the leaves;
And all night long beneath the eaves
(While with soft breathings slept the housèd cattle)
The hivèd bees
Made music like the murmuring seas;
From lichened wall, from many a leafy nook,
The chipmunk sounded shrill his tiny rattle;
Through the warm day boomed low the droning flies,
And the huge mountain shook
With the organ of the skies.

II

Dear these songs unto my heart;
But the spirit longs for art,
Longs for music that is born

Of the human soul forlorn,
Or the beating heart of pleasure.
Thou, sweet girl, didst bring this boon
Without stint or measure!
Many a tune
From the masters of all time
In my waiting heart made rhyme.

III

As the rain on parchèd meadows,
As cool shadows
Falling from the sultry sky,
As loved memories die,
But live again when a well-tunèd voice
Makes with old joy the grievèd heart rejoice,
So came once more with thy clear touch
The melodies I love —
Ah, not too much,
But all earth's natural songs far, far above!
For they are nature felt, and living,
And human, and impassioned;
And they full well are fashioned
To bring to sound and sense the eternal striving,
The inner soul of the inexpressive world,
The meaning furled
Deep at the heart of all —
The thought that mortals name divine,
Whereof all beauty is the sign,
That comes,—ah! surely comes,—at music's solemn call.

"A POWER THERE IS"

A POWER there is that trembles through the earth;
It lives in nature's mirth,

Making that fearful as the touch of pain;
It strikes the sunlit plain,
And harvests flash, or bend with rushing rain;
It is not far when tempests make their moan,
And lightnings leap, and bursts the thunder-stone.
It comes in morning's beam of living light,
And the imperial night
Knows it, and all its company of stars,
And the auroral bars.
Through nature all, the subtile current thrills;
It built in flood and fire the crystal hills;
It molds the flowers,
And all the branchèd forests that abide
Forever on the teeming mountain-side.
It lives where music times the soft, processional hours;
And where on that lone hill of art
Proud Phidias carved in stone his lyric heart;
And where wild battle is, and where
Glad lovers breathe in starry night the quivering air.

THE SONG'S ANSWER

Me mystic? Have your way!
But sing me, if ye may; —
    Then shall ye know the power
    Of the seed's thought of the flower,
Of the dawn's thought of the day.

THE 'CELLO

When late I heard the trembling 'cello play,
  In every face I read sad memories
  That from dark, secret chambers where they lay
Rose, and looked forth from melancholy eyes.

So every mournful thought found there a tone
  To match despondence; sorrow knew its mate;
  Ill fortune sighed, and mute despair made moan;
  And one deep chord gave answer, "Late,—too late."
Then ceased the quivering strain, and swift returned
  Into its depths the secret of each heart;
  Each face took on its mask, where lately burned
A spirit charmed to sight by music's art;
  But unto one who caught that inner flame
  No face of all can ever seem the same.

THE VALLEY ROAD

By this road have past
  Hope and Joy adance;
And one at dark fled fast,
  Quick breath, and look askance;
And in this dust have dropt
Tears that never stopt.

Childhood, caught by flowers,
  Cannot choose but dally;
Slowly through the hours
  Age creeps down the valley;
Only Youth goes swift —
Eager, and head alift.

Summer, and the night,
  Calm and cloudless moon,
And lo! a path of light!
  Heaven would come too soon
To lovers wandering slowly
Through the starlight holy.

And by this road was borne, —
  Betwixt sweet banks of fern,
And willow rows, and corn, —
  He, who will return
Not, tho' others may,
The old, familiar way.

Two streams within these walls
  For ever and ever flow;
Back and forth the current falls,
  The long processions go;
A hundred years have flown,
The human tides pour on —

And shall, when you and I
  Pass no more again.
Beneath the bending sky
  Shall be no lack of men;
Never the road run bare,
Tho' other feet may fare.

HAWTHORNE IN BERKSHIRE

Mountains and valleys! dear ye are to me:
  Your streams wild-wandering, ever-tranquil lakes,
  And forests that make murmur like the sea;
  And this keen air that from the hurt soul takes
Its pain and languor. — Doubly dear ye are
  For many a lofty memory that throws
  A splendor on these hights. — 'Neath yon low star,
  That like a dewdrop melts in heaven's rose,
Dwelt once a starry spirit; there he smote
  Life from the living hills; a little while
  He rested from the raging of the world.

This Brook of Shadows, whose dark waters purled
  Solace to his deep mind, it felt his smile —
Haunted, and melancholy, and remote.

LATE SUMMER

Tho' summer days are all too fleet,
  Not yet the year is touched with cold;
Through the long billows of the wheat
  The green is lingering in the gold.

The birds that thrilled the April copse,
  Ah! some have flown on silent wings;
Yet one sweet music never stops:
  The constant vireo sings and sings.

AN HOUR IN A STUDIO

Each picture was a painted memory
Of the far plains he loved, and of their life, —
Weird, mystical, dark, inarticulate, —
And cities hidden high against the blue,
Whose sky-hung steps one Indian could guard.
The enchanted Mesa there its fated wall
Lifted, and all its story lived again —
How, in the happy planting time, the strong
Went down to push the seeds into the sand,
Leaving the old and sick. Then reeled the world
And toppled to the plain the perilous path.
Death climbed another way to them who stayed.
He showed us pictured thirst, a dreadful sight;
And many tales he told that might have come,
Brought by some planet-wanderer — fresh from Mars,
Or from the silver deserts of the moon.

But I remember better than all else
One night he told of in that land of fright —
The love-songs swarthy men sang to their herds
On the high plains to keep the beasts in heart;
Piercing the silence one keen tenor voice
Singing "Ai nostri monti" clear and high:
Instead of stakes and fences round about
They circled them with music in the night.

ILLUSION

WHAT strange, fond trick is this mine eyes are playing!
   I know 'tis but the visioning mind perplexes,—
   The inward sight the outer sense betraying,—
   Yet the sweet lie the spirit wounds and vexes:
As at still midnight pondering here, and reading,
   Right on the book's white page, and 'twixt the lines,
   And wreathing through the words, and quick receding,
   Only to come again (as 'mid the vines
The dryads flash and hide), white arms are gleaming,
   A light hand hovers, curvèd lips are red,
   Locks in a warm and soundless wind are streaming
Across the image of one glorious head;
   No more, — no more, — shut now the volume lies
   On that swift, piercing look, those haunting eyes.

A SONG OF THE ROAD

SPEED, speed, speed
Through the day, through the night!
Cities are beads on the thread of our flight;
Peaks melt in peaks and are lost in the air.
   Speed, speed, speed —
      But, O, the dearth of it,
      Thou not there!

Every journey is good if love be the goal of it.
What's all the world if love's not the soul of it;
  What were the worth of it —
  Thou not there!

"NOT HERE"

I

Not here, but somewhere, so men say,
More bright the day,
And the blue sky
More nigh;
Somewhere, afar, the bird of dawn sings sweeter;
Somewhere completer
The round of hopes and heart-beats that make life
More than a bootless strife.

II

But, ah! there be that know
Where joy alone doth grow.
Led by one true star,
The journey is not far.
'T is in a garden in no distant land,
High-walled on every hand;
And the key thereof
Is love.

"'NO, NO,' SHE SAID"

"No, no," she said;
"I may not wed;
  If say I must — *nay* must I say;
  I cannot stay;
  Nay, nay, I needs must flout thee!"

He turned about;
His life went out;
"If go I must, so must I go!"
Cried she — "No, no;
Ah, what were life without thee!"

A SOUL LOST, AND FOUND

I

Lo! here another
Soul has gone down.
Hope led each morrow;
Honor was all;
Faith had no fall;
Fortune no frown.
Brother by brother
Bowed to each sorrow.
None had lost heart;
Life was love, life was art.

II

We could but follow!
Quenchless his fire;
The mightier the burden
The stronger his soul,
The higher the goal.
Now see the mire
Soil him and swallow!
Heaven! what guerdon
Worth such a cost!
Love, art, life — lost, all lost.

III

Down to the pallid
Figure of death

Love's face is pressing;
Listens and waits,
Beseeching the Fates
For heart-beat and breath —
Sign clear and valid,
Life still confessing.
Dead! He is dead!
All is lost! — He has fled.

IV

Behold now, a moving,
A flutter of life!
Forth from the starkness,
Horror, and slime,
See, he doth climb.
With himself is the strife;
Back to the loving
From mire and the darkness,
Back to the sun!
He has fought — he has won.

"THIS HOUR MY HEART WENT FORTH, AS IN OLD DAYS"

This hour my heart went forth, as in old days,
To one I loved, forgetting she was dead —
So fluttered back the message, like the dove
That found no rest in all the weltering world.
Is it then so — all blankness and black void,
No welcome, no response, no voice, no sign?
Ah, Heaven! let us be foolish — give us faith
In what is not; cheat us a little longer;
Comfort us mortals with envisioned forms;
Let us, tho' but in dreams, see spirits near,

And touch the draperies of imagined shapes
That hold the souls we love — that have gone forth
Into the land of shadows, but still live
In memory, O, most dear! Beguile our lives
With dim, half-fashioned phantoms of dead hours,
Lest the long way grow hateful; give us faith
Unreasoned, vague, unsubstanced, but still faith;
For faith is hope, and hope alone is life.

"EVEN WHEN JOY IS NEAR"

Even when joy is near
These ghosts of banished thoughts do haunt the mind:
The awful void of space wherein our earth,
An atom in the unending whirl of stars,
Circles, all helpless, to a nameless doom;
The swift, indifferent marshaling of fate
Whereby the world moves on, rewarding vice
And punishing angelic innocence
As 't were the crime of crimes; the brute, dull, slow
Persistence in the stifled mind of man
Of forces that drive all his being back
Into the slime; the silent cruelty
Of nature, that doth crush the unseen soul
Hidden within its sensitive shell of flesh;
The anguish and the sorrow of all time, —
These are forever with me, — but grow dim
When I remember my sweet mother's face.
Somewhere, at heart of all, the right must reign
If in the garden of the infinite
Such loveliness be brought to perfect bloom.

RESURRECTION

BACK to my body came I in the gray of the dawning,
Back to my bed in the mold, 'neath the sod and the
blossoms;
Not strange seemed my natural couch, not new, not
afflicting;
But strange now, and new, and afflicting my natural body,
Alien long while my soul took the wings of the morning.
I lifted my hands to the light — then swiftly I followed,
With fingers that carefully prest, the curve of the
muscles;
All was familiar; this was the frame I had nurtured,
I had loved as a man loves the body so long his com-
panion;
Again was I 'ware of the brow where the dew of sweet
kisses
Fell, ere forth went the stripling to life and the shudder
Of battle; — again from the mirror of waters the features
Not unloved of dear comrades looked forth. I beheld in
amazement
The bodily presence so long laid aside and forgotten;
Overwhelmed was my soul with its shackles; I grieved,
I lamented
As a prisoner dragged back to his cell, as an eagle re-
captured.

"AS SOARS THE EAGLE"

As soars the eagle, intimate of light,
Fear not the face of the sun;
Nor all the blasts of earth.
Child of Him, the untrembling One,
O, prove thee worthy of thy birth!

Let no ill betray thee!
Let no death dismay thee!

The eagle seeks the sky,
Nor fears the infinite light;
Thus, soul of mine, escape the night
And 'gainst the morning fly!

PART III

ROBERT GOULD SHAW

(THE MONUMENT BY AUGUSTUS SAINT-GAUDENS)

I

FIXT in one desire,
Thrilled by one fierce fire,
Marching men and horse,
And he the youthful rider — one soul, one aim, one force.

II

Onward he doth press;
Moving, tho' motionless;
Resolute, intent,
As on some mighty errand the willing youth were bent.

III

Onward, tho' he hears
Father's, sisters' tears;
Onward, tho' before him
— Grief more near, more dear — the breaking heart that
    bore him.

IV

Onward, tho' he leaves
One who lonely grieves;

O, keep him, Fate! from harm,
For on his dewy lips the bridal kiss is warm.

V

What doth he behold
Making the boy so bold?
Speak with whispering breath!
O Fate, O Fame, O radiant soul in love with glorious
      Death!

VI

Eyes that forward peer —
Why have they no fear?
Because, through blood and blight,
They see the golden morning burst and bring the living
      light;

VII

See War the fetters strike
From white and black alike;
See, past the pain and scorn,
A nation saved, a race redeemed, and freedom newly
      born;

VIII

See, in days to come, —
When silent War's loud drum,
Ere civic wrong shall cease, —
Heroes as pure and brave arise on battlefields of peace.

"THE NORTH STAR DRAWS THE HERO"

(TO H. N. G.)

THE North Star draws the hero; he abides
      Stedfast tho' death defends the unending quest.
But, ah, more faithful still the love that hides
      In woman's empty arms and aching breast!

GLAVE

THIS day I read in the sad scholar's page
    That the old earth is withered and undone;
    That faith and great emprize beneath the sun
    Are vain and empty in our doting age;
'T were best to calm the spirit's noble rage,
    To live in dreams, and all high passion shun,
    While round and round the aimless seasons run —
    Pleasured alone with dead art's heritage.
Then, as I read, outshone thy face of youth,
    Hero and martyr of humanity,
    Dead yesterday on Afric's shore of doom!
Ah, no; Faith, Courage fail not, while lives Truth,
    While Pity lives, while man for man can die,
    And deeds of glory light the dark world's gloom.

OF HENRY GEORGE

WHO DIED FIGHTING AGAINST POLITICAL TYRANNY AND CORRUPTION

Now is the city great! That deep-voiced bell
    Tolls for a martyred hero. Such is he
Who loved her, strove for her, and nobly fell.
    His fire be ours — the passion to be free.

NEW YORK, 1897.

SCORN

WHO are the men that good men most despise?
    Not they who, ill begot and spawned in shame,
    Riot and rob, or rot before men's eyes, —
    Who basely live, and dying leave no name.
These are the piteous refuse of mankind,
    Fatal the ascendant star when they were born,

Distort in body, starved in soul and mind;
Ah, not for them the good man's bitter scorn!
He, only, is the despicable one
Who lightly sells his honor as a shield
For fawning knaves, to hide them from the sun;
Too nice for crime, yet, coward, he doth yield
For crime a shelter. Swift to Paradise
The contrite thief, not Judas with his price!

THE HEROIC AGE

He speaks not well who doth his time deplore,
Naming it new and little and obscure,
Ignoble and unfit for lofty deeds.
All times were modern in the time of them,
And this no more than others. Do thy part
Here in the living day, as did the great
Who made old days immortal! So shall men,
Gazing long back to this far-looming hour,
Say: "Then the time when men were truly men:
Tho' wars grew less, their spirits met the test
Of new conditions; conquering civic wrong;
Saving the state anew by virtuous lives;
Guarding the country's honor as their own,
And their own as their country's and their sons':
Proclaiming service the one test of worth;
Defying leaguèd fraud with single truth;
Knights of the spirit; warriors in the cause
Of justice absolute 'twixt man and man;
Not fearing loss; and daring to be pure.
When error through the land raged like a pest
They calmed the madness caught from mind to mind
By wisdom drawn from eld, and counsel sane;
And as the martyrs of the ancient world

Gave Death for man, so nobly gave they Life:
Those the great days, and that the heroic age."
ATHENS, 1896.

THE SWORD OF THE SPIRIT

(IN MEMORY OF JOE EVANS)

TOO much of praise for the quick, pitiless blow!
Justice doth lean on strength, full well we know;
But the sharp, glittering sword that strikes for right
Takes fame too easily. Thank Heaven for might,
Which is Heaven's servant, oft! Yet he's not man
Who, when the heart's afire, no brave deed can.
Praise thou the clencht fist that, when blood is hot,
On itself tightens, but descendeth not.
Ay, praise the sword undrawn, the bolt unsped,
The rage supprest till the true word is said.
Might of the spirit, this shalt thou extol,
And holy weakness of the conquering soul.

And on this day, when one well loved has past
From suffering to the unknown peace, at last,
Would I might praise, as nobly as I ought,
The hero-soldier who no battle fought —
Or, rather, one who, facing fate's worst frown,
The spirit's sword but with his life laid down.
The soul that from that body, bent and frail,
Peered out, did at no earthly terror quail.
To face an army he was brave enough;
Martyrs and conquerors are of that stuff.
And in the civic conflict that was waged
Year after year, his knightly spirit raged;
He could not bear his country should have blame,
So this slight warrior did the mighty shame.

Yet Beauty was his passion, and the art
To paint it — that it might not all depart.
He loved the gentlest things; there was a grace
In his sad look surpassing many a face
More beautiful. Ah, back, ye bitter tears!
He, lover of light and gladness, all these years
Fighting twin demons of keen pain and doom;
He, of such humor that the very tomb
Might snatch a brightness from his presence there!
But no; not bright the tomb. We, in despair,
Seek through the world again a charm like this —
That which our friend has taken we shall forever miss.

April, 1898.

"THROUGH ALL THE CUNNING AGES"

THROUGH all the cunning ages
  Mankind hath made for man
From out his loves and rages
  A god to bless and ban.

When he his foe despises
  This god he calls to curse;
And would he win earth's prizes
  His praise doth man rehearse.

So, when he craves the guerdon
  Of others' land and pelf,
He flings the blame and burden
  On this shadow of himself.

If, spite of all their ranting,
  There reigns a God indeed,
How well He hates the canting
  That framed their sordid creed!

"Lay not to me your hollow
  And broken words of faith —
To sin that good may follow
  No law of mine," He saith.

"If, 'twixt your tribes and nations,
  There lives no law but might,
Not myriad incantations
  Can make your evil right.

"Ye call me 'God of battle';
  I weary while ye slay.
Are ye my hornèd cattle
  To find no better way?"

ONE COUNTRY — ONE SACRIFICE

(ENSIGN WORTH BAGLEY, MAY 11, 1898)

IN one rich drop of blood, ah, what a sea
  Of healing! Thou, sweet boy, wert first to fall
In our new war; and thou wert Southron all!
There is no North, no South, remembering thee.

"WHEN WITH THEIR COUNTRY'S ANGER"

WHEN with their country's anger
  They flame into the fight, —
On sea, in treacherous forest,
  To strike with main and might, —

He shows the gentlest mercy
  Who rains the deadliest blows;
Then quick war's hell is ended,
  And home the hero goes.

What stays the noblest memory
  For all his years to keep?
Not of the foemen slaughtered,
  But rescued from the deep!

Rescued with peerless daring!
  O, none shall forget that sight,
When the unaimed cannon thundered
  In the ghastly after-fight.

And, now, in the breast of the hero
  There blooms a strange, new flower,
A blood-red, fragrant blossom
  Sown in the battle-hour.

'T is not the Love of Comrades, —
  That flower forever blows, —
But the brave man's Love of Courage,
  The Love of Comrade-Foes.

For since the beginning of battles
  On the land and on the wave,
Heroes have answered to heroes,
  The brave have honored the brave.

1898.

A VISION

ALL round the glimmering circuit of the isle
Audibly pulsed the ocean. In the dark
Of the thick wood a voice not of its own
Might come to sharpened ears; a sound supprest,
The rustling of an armèd multitude
Who toss in sleep, or, wakening, watch for death.
Beneath the tropic stars that in strange skies
Drew close and glittered large, I saw in dream
A Soul pass hoveringly.

Then came I near
And questioned of that Ghost, who answer made
Like a deep, murmuring wind that slowly draws
Through dim memorial aisles of ancient time: —

"I am the mother of men, and from my womb
Came all the dead and living. I am curst
With memory, with knowledge of what is,
And what shall be; yet, verily, am I blest
With these three knowledges, — my children I
Have seen these myriad years grow, age by age,
More wise, more just, more joyous, yet have I
Seen mutual slaughter sow the earth with tears.
In this New World here had I hoped my children
Would learn to unlearn the path mankind has climbed
Over its slain to happiness and power;
For soon or late I know that boon shall come,
And in the wars of peace the race shall wax
Manlier, purer, gentler, and more wise.

"But now again the sacred truce is broken,
And bleeds this breast at every wound and sigh,
And aches my mother-heart with the new pain
Of mortal mothers comfortless forever."

Then past the Spirit from my dream at dawn;
I woke into another day of war
With news of splendid deeds, and victory —
Yet still I heard that brooding shade lament.

1898.

THE WORD OF THE WHITE CZAR

THIS day, a strange and beautiful word was spoken, —
Not with the voice of a child, nor the voice of a woman,
Nor yet with the voice of a poet, the melody sounded, —

Forth from the lips of a warrior, girt for the battle,
Breathed this word of words o'er a world astonished.

Prisoners returning from war, and conquering armies,
Navies flusht with new and amazing victory,
Heard the message, so strange, so high, so entrancing,
And soldiers dying of wounds or the wasting of fever.
In tropic islands it sounded, through wrecks of cities;
O'er burning plains where warlike death was in wait-
    ing;
Armies and navies confronting, in watchful silence,
Heard it and wondered; statesmen stopt their debates,
And turning their eyes toward the voice, with its mean-
    ing unlooked for,
Listened and smiled with the smile and the sneer of the
    cynic.
But the mothers of youths who had died of their wounds
    and of fever,
And the poor crusht down by the price of the glory of
    battle
And the weight of the wars that have been, and that yet
    are preparing,
They from their burdens looked up and uttered their
    blessing:
For Peace,— the Peace of God,— was the warrior's
    prayer!

And I, who heard, I saw in a waking vision
An image familiar long to the hearts of mortals,
A face of trouble, a brow celestial, yet human —
In a dream of the day, I saw that suffering spirit,
Him accustomed to labor, to anguish not alien,
Still mourning for men alone in the valley of shadows; —
I dreamed that he lifted that face of infinite sorrow,

And harkened — when lo! a light in those eyes of sad-
    ness
Came sudden as day that breaks from the mountains of
    Moab.

PART IV

A SONG FOR DOROTHEA, ACROSS THE
SEA

A SONG for you, my darling,
    For your own, dear, only sake.
You bid me sing — so does the spring
    Bid the birds awake,
    And quick with molten music the dewy branches quake.

A song for you, my darling,
    To follow you all the day;
And in sweet sleep the song shall keep
    Singing along the way,
    Through dreamland's silver meadows with golden
        lilies gay.

A song for you, my darling,
    For those deep and darkling eyes,
That stedfast shine as the stars divine
    Bright in the midnight skies,
    When the winds blow the clouds from heaven, and we
        gaze with a glad surprise.

A song for you, my darling,
    A song for that faithful heart
That as true abides as the throbbing tides,
    Tho' half a world apart —
    So far away is the girl I sing, with only a lover's art.

A BLIND POET

CALL him not blind
Whose keen, anointed sight,
Pierced every secret of the heart, the mind,
The day, the night.

ON A WOMAN SEEN UPON THE STAGE

("TESS," AS PLAYED BY MRS. FISKE)

ALAS, poor, fated, passionate, shivering thing!
So through brief life some dagger-haunted king
Wears a bright sorrow. Thus her life rehearse:
She was a woman; this her crown, her curse.

OF ONE WHO NEITHER SEES NOR HEARS

(HELEN KELLER)

SHE lives in light, not shadow;
   Not silence, but the sound
Which thrills the stars of heaven
   And trembles from the ground.

She breathes a finer ether,
   Beholds a keener sun;
In her supernal being
   Music and light are one.

Unknown the subtile senses
   That lead her through the day;
Love, light, and song and color
   Come by another way.

Sight brings she to the seeing,
   New song to those that hear;
Her braver spirit sounding
   Where mortals fail and fear.

She at the heart of being
   Serene and glad doth dwell;
Spirit with scarce a veil of flesh;
   A soul made visible.

Or is it only a lovely girl
   With flowers at her maiden breast?
— Helen, here is a book of song
   From the poet who loves you best.

FOR THE ESPOUSALS OF JEANNE ROUMANILLE, OF AVIGNON

WHILE joy-bells are ringing
   And the high Fates meet thee,
Child of the South, and of singing,
   Singing I greet thee.

In thy chaplet one flower
   From a far world! Wilt wear it?
Rich tho' thy land, and this hour,
   Thou may'st not forbear it;

Thou wilt welcome and win it;
   It will breathe on, caress thee;
For the fame of thy father is in it;
   His lover doth bless thee!

His lover — the lover of thee, O Provence;
   Thy blue skies, thy gray mountains;
The heart-beat of Freedom and France
   Shakes thy rivers and fountains,

And makes thee a dream and a passion
  In the souls of all poets forever,
While from thy fire thou dost fashion
  Beauty and music and art that shall perish, O, never!

TO MARIE JOSEPHINE GIRARD, QUEEN OF THE FÉLIBRES

ON HER WEDDING-DAY

QUEENS have there been of many a fair domain
  Of arts, of hearts, of lands.
  Thy sovereignty a threefold realm commands
Who o'er Provence, and Poetry, and Love dost reign.

INSCRIPTION FOR A TOWER IN FLORENCE

(WRITTEN FOR THE CHATELAINE)

I

FOUR-WALLED is my tower:
The first wall is for the dawn that comes from Vallom-
    brosa,
The second wall is for the day that fills with soft fire the
    green vase of Tuscany,
The third is for the evening twilight that darkens from
    the Valley of the Arno,
The fourth is for the night and the stars of night.

II

Four-walled is my tower:
One wall is for the South and the sun,
One is for the West and for memory,

One is for the North and the star that never sets,
And one is for the East and a faith that fares beyond
    the stars.

III

Four-walled is my tower:
One wall is for the Spring and for Hope,
One is for Summer and for Love,
One is for Autumn and the Harvest,
One is for Winter and for Waiting.

IV

Four-walled is my tower:
One is for Childhood and the Innocence of Life,
The second is for Youth and the Joy of Life,
The third is for Manhood and the Fullness of Life,
The fourth is for Old Age and the Wisdom of Life.

V

Four-walled is my tower:
A Rock for Strength,
A Hight for Seeing,
A Beacon for the Stranger,
And a Hearth for Friendship.
Four-walled is my tower
On the Hill of Bellosguardo.

WITH A VOLUME OF DANTE

O THOU whom Virgil and thy Beatrice
Through life and death, Hell, Purgatory, Heaven,
Led upward into unimagined light —
Lead thou this soul the way thou, too, didst go
Unto the Light that lights the eternal stars!

POEMS AND INSCRIPTIONS

POEMS

AUTUMN AT FOUR-BROOKS FARM

No song-bird, singing, soaring,
But the brooks are up and roaring!
Along the lane one lonely tree
Starts a sound like a storm at sea.
The round, black clouds pursue
Across the gulfs of blue;
So fast they fly the mountain crest
Reels backward to the blowing west.
Shadow and sun rush on together
Across the hills in the gusty weather,
And leaves like flocks of golden birds
Take flight above the huddling herds.
Hark, hark that bell-like baying! —
The wily fox with the hound is playing;
All is motion, and air, and strife;
Down the valley the floods are pouring;
This is Autumn, O, this is life;
No song-bird sings, but the hawks are soaring,
And the brooks are up and roaring!

INDOORS IN EARLY SPRING

I

In the old farm-house living-room
Four shrunken doors shut out the gloom;
Two curtained windows hide night's pall;

These openings six in the ancient wall
Let in the breeze in seams.
The air in spark-lit, pouring streams
From hearth to heaven leaps.
Against the black of the chimney-soot
The forkèd flames upshoot,
And the blaze a-roaring keeps.

II

Every log is a separate flute;
And every chink a singing wire
Of some unseen Æolian lyre
Tuned to the music of the fire.
The little tinkling sounds; the low,
Sweet whistlings of the bubbling wood;
The thundering bass of winds that blow
In leafless maples by the road —
All make a music in the mind;
While, book in hand, in musing mood, —
My body here, my soul in flight, —
Through the true poet's world I wind,
And there a spirit-music find
That mixes with the sounding night.

THE NIGHT PASTURE

I

In a starry night of June, before the moon had come
over into our valley from the high valley beyond,

Up the winding mountain-lane I wandered, and, stop-
ping, leaned on the bars, and listened;

And I heard the little brook sliding from stone to
stone; and I heard the sound of the bells as the cows
moved — heavily, slowly,

In various keys, deep, or like sleigh-bells tinkling, sounded the chiming cow-bells —

Starting and stilling, irregular; near or far away in the dusk —

And the nearer cows I heard chewing the cud, and breathing warm on the cool air of the mountain slope

In the night pasture.

II

Terrace on terrace rises the farm, from meadow and winding river to forest of chestnut and pine;

There by the high-road, among the embowering maples, nestles the ancient homestead;

From each new point of vantage lovelier seems the valley, and the hill-framed sunset ever more and more moving and glorious;

But when in the thunderous city I think of the mountain farm, nothing so sweet of remembrance,— holding me as in a dream,—

As the silver note of the unseen brook, and the clanging of the cow-bells fitfully in the dark, and the deep breathing of the cows

In the night pasture.

III

Then I think, not of myself — but an image comes to me of one who has past,

Of an old man bent with labor;

He, like his father before him, for many and many a year,

When the cows down the mountains have trudged in the summer evening, and after the evening milking,

Night after night, and year after year, back up the lane he has driven them, while the shepherd-dog leaped and barked —

Back up the lane, and past the orchard, and through the bars
Into the night pasture.

IV

There in the twilight I see him stand:
He listens to the sounds of the field and the forest,
On his brow strikes the cool mountain air;
Hard is the old man's life and full indeed of sorrow —
But now, for a moment, respite from labor, in the pause 'twixt day and night!
Perhaps to his heart comes a sense of the beauty that fills all this exquisite valley —
A sense of peace and of rest; a thought of the long and toilless night that comes to all,
As he leans on the bars and listens, and hears the deep-breathed cows, and the scattered sound of the bells
In the night pasture.

A LETTER FROM THE FARM

TELL you the news
From Four-Brooks Farm?
Well,
But there *is* news to tell,
As long as my arm!
"What! a new she-calf born
To this world forlorn?"
Few things are finer
Than a fine heifer-calf,
And most things are minor;
But 't is better by half
The news that I 've got now!
Such a wonderful lot now

Of heifers,—why, what now
Such farm news as this!
You were here, when, what bliss!
Alpha dropt on our planet,
And we all ran to scan it:
How the soft thing, with silk down,
Had learned to bring milk down
Without any teaching,
Example, or preaching!

Not this is the news
From Four-Brooks Farm —
Nor the ice-pond built
Where Hermit Brook spilt;
Nor the great pine we found
Thunder-burst in the middle
And spread on the ground
Like the strings of a fiddle;
Not of this, not of that, —
Such news now were flat, —
But something far racier!
Muir, of Alaska,
Path-finder, cliff-basker,
Known of bird, known of deer
(Grizzlies know him, won't harm),
John Muir has been here,
And has hitched to the farm
A great blanket glacier!
Don't flout it! don't doubt it!
'T is as sure and as clear
As if on the rock,
With chisel and knock,
A giant of eld
His message had spelled,

And ten thousand years after
We read it, — with laughter
And loyal acclaim, —
His ancestry, name,
The work he was doing,
The place whence he came,
And the journey pursuing.
"This giant of eld!
  See his path," said John Muir,
"Here it held
Northwest to southeast;
Slow and sure,
Like a king at a feast
Eating down through the list;
Inch by inch, crunch by crunch;
Yonder hollow his lunch,
Of this valley — one gobble,
Then he supped light on Cobble!
This big boulder, he bore it;
Through eons uncounted
That range there he mounted,
He tore it.
Rock-grinding; strata rending;
Always pausing; never ending;
O what a grand rumpus!
Now, down on your knees,"
Said Muir, "an you please,
And out with your compass!"
(By the way — 't was Thoreau's
As Muir well knows)
And then, in a trice,
Where the quartz glistens white,
Smooth as ice,
In the clear, slanting light

The fine striæ show, —
Like arrows they go
Northwest to southeast,
Just as John Muir pleased!

And as he spoke I saw the huge creature glide,
With speed that scarcely lessened or increased,
From the far pole to ocean's melting tide.
Through countless boreal hours
It moved on its torn pathway deep and wide;
Its shining bulk I saw
Crunching the mountain tops with monstrous maw; —
To make our Four-Brooks Farm with all its flocks and
flowers.

SUMMER BEGINS

THE bright sun has been hid so long,
Such endless rains, such clouds and glooms!
But now, as with a burst of song,
The happy Summer morning blooms.

The brooks are full, it is their youth;
No hint of shrunken age have they;
They shout like children, and in truth,
No human child so careless-gay.

How fresh the woods, each separate leaf
Is shining in the joyful sun.
Strange! I have half forgotten grief;
I think that life has just begun.

"STROLLING TOWARD SHOTTERY"

STROLLING toward Shottery on one showery day,
We saw upon the turf beside the path

A clown who, stooping by the pleasant way,
   Rough-cobbled his torn shoes and spoke in feignèd
      wrath.

At first we thought him brain-touched and askew,
   But, as we listened to his shrilling talk,
We found him prating of some things he knew,
   Tho' others he but guessed; — we halted in our walk.

His was the wisdom shrewd of roadside men,
   Gathered in wanderings through the country wide;
He had a cynic wit, and to his ken
   The world wagged wickedly — saved by its humorous
      side.

Racy his speech and, tho' it bit, good-hearted;
   There was an honest freshness in the tramp;
We felt his debtor, therefore when we parted
   Some pennies wealthier the philosophic scamp!

Laughing we followed on to sweet Anne's cot:
   — Perhaps like us her lover left the town;
Like us he crossed the pretty pasture lot,
   And met, — and made immortal, — one more Shake-
      speare clown.

STRATFORD BELLS

ONE Sabbath eve, betwixt green Avon's banks,
   In a dream-world we hour by hour did float;
   The ruffling swans moved by in stately ranks;
   With soft, sad eyes the cattle watched our boat.
We, passionate pilgrims from a far-off land,
   Beyond the vexed Bermoothes: O, how dear

That strange, sweet picture — by the Enchanter's
    wand
Familiar to our spirits made, and near!
But suddenly a rich and resonant sound
    Thrilled from the skies and waters; lo, the chimes
    Of Stratford rang and rang; the very ground
Murmured, as with a deep-voiced poet's rhymes;
    Then swift melodious tone on tone was hurled:
    'T was Shakespeare's music brimmed the trembling
      world.

IN WORDSWORTH'S ORCHARD

DOVE COTTAGE

IN Wordsworth's orchard, one sweet summer day,
    Breathless we listened to his thrushes sing;
    We heard the trickling of the little spring
    Beneath the terrace; saw the tender play
Of breezes 'midst the leaves; scarce could we say
    The well-loved verses whose rich blossoming
    Was on this narrow hillside; strange they ring
    For tears that choke the numbers on their way.
Then home by winding Rothay did we turn
    While bird, and bloom, and mountain seemed his voice
    Deep sounding to the spiritual ear —
And this its message: Let love in thee burn,
    Here learn in holy beauty to rejoice,
    Here learn true living, and the song sincere.

SIR WALTER SCOTT

I

RHYMERS and writers of our day,
Too much of melancholy!
Give us the old heroic lay;

A whiff of wholesome folly;
The escapade, the dance;
A touch of wild romance:
Wake from this self-conscious fit;
Give us again Sir Walter's wit;
His love of earth, of sky, of life;
His ringing page with humor rife;
His never-weary pen;
His love of men!

II

Builder of landscape, who could make
Turret and tower their stations take
Brave in the face of the sun;
Of many a mimic world creator,
Alive with fight and strenuous fun;
Of nothing human he the hater.
Nobly could he plan:
Master of nature, master of man.

III

Sometimes I think that He who made us,
And on this pretty planet laid us,
Made us to work and play
Like children in the light of day —
Not like plodders in the dark,
Searching with lanterns for some mark
To find the way.
After the stroke of pain,
Up and to work again!

IV

Such was his life, without reproach or fear:
A lonely fight before the last eclipse —

A broken heart, a smile upon the lips;
And, at the end,
When Heaven bent down and whispered in his ear
The word God's saints waited and longed to hear,
I ween he was as quick as they to comprehend;
And, when he past beyond the goal,
Entered the gates of pearl no sweeter soul.

A DAY IN TUSCANY

I

I KNEW the Rucellai had choice of villas:
This day has proved it, this thrice happy day
Stolen from care, and many a saddened thought.
Have we not seen, we wanderers from afar,
Fountained Caneto, standing watch and ward
Over Bisenzio's lovely, curving vale! —
Caneto, olive-cinctured, cypress-crowned,
And wreathed in vine; Caneto, whose high hall
Bears record of a proud and noble race,
Friendly to art and letters (Cimabue
Be witness paramount; and the brave front
Of Santa Maria Novella; the Academe
That in the Garden of the Rucellai
Relit the Athenian fire!). Yes, Edith dear,
I love Caneto well, but well I love
This "Villa of the Little Fields," that hides
Embowered among its farms; in rose and lilac
Radiant and scented like an April bride;
'Mid busy sounds secluded and remote.
But most I love this tower you call my own,
This musing tower that wins the soul to song,
From whose four windows, see! the Apennines
Make a walled paradise of Tuscany.

II

Beyond the ilex-dome, against the west,
The sunset sky was crimson: "Then," you say,
"Fair is to-morrow, if the sky was red."
"Fair is to-morrow"? O, to-morrow fair
That wakes me from this dream? — Here from my
    tower
One planet marks where Prato lies below,
And yonder, through the tender gray and green
Of the high-branching plane-tree, shines a light
Betwixt the earth and heaven — a lure that means
Florence, and all its wonder; now, ah, now
The hour draws nigh when Italy once more
To me is of the past, a thought, a passion,
But all ungrasped of sense.
And what is that our Cosimo has said?
"To-day the nightingales have come." — Have come?
And I, tho' listening long, and with my soul,
I have not heard one tone.

In the Tower at CAMPI BISENZIO.

A SACRED COMEDY IN FLORENCE

IN WHICH TAKES PART A CERTAIN STATUE ON THE FAÇADE OF THE DUOMO

LONELY Pope upon his throne,
Cold in marble, high in air,
On the Duomo's checkered front —
Benediction, as is wont,
Falling from his saintly face
Down upon the clattering square:
Falls, to-day, a special grace,
For, in fact, he 's not alone —
Solemn Pope upon his throne,

White in marble, cold in air! —
To those priestly fingers there,
Lifted o'er the peopled square,
A purple pigeon sudden flits,
Lightly 'lights and lingering sits.
By the Baptistery gates,
Where I stand, I can but smile,
Thinking that the potentate's
Lips are curving, too, the while;
And I wonder what the bird
Said that Papa, smiling, heard.

MICHAEL ANGELO'S AURORA

THE MEDICI CHAPEL, FLORENCE

O MAJESTY and loveliness in one!
Why art thou sorrowful, now night is done?
This is the dawn; why doth thy spirit quake?
O thou who wakenest! is it pain to wake?

THE OLD MASTER

OF his dear Lord he painted all the life,
But not that ancient land, nor the old days;
Not curious he to seek, through learnèd strife,
The look of those far times and unknown ways.
But in his solemn and long-living art
Well did he paint that which can never die:
The life and passion of the human heart,
Unchanged while sorrowing age on age goes by.
Beneath his brush his own loved people grew,
Their rivers and their mountains, saints and lords;
The dark Italian mothers whom he knew,

The sad-eyed nuns, the warriors with drawn swords;
And the young Savior, throned at Mary's breast,
Was but some little child whom he loved best.

AT LUTHER'S GRAVE

WITTENBERG

HERE rests the heart whose throbbing shook the earth!
High soul of courage, we do owe thee much;
Thee and thy warrior comrades, who the worth
Of freedom proved and put it to the touch!
Because, O Luther, thou the truth didst love,
And spake the truth out,— faced the sceptered lie,—
E'en we, thy unforgetting heirs, may move
Fearless, erect, unshackled, 'neath the sky.
Yet at this shrine who doth forever linger
Shall know not that true freedom Luther won;
"Onward," his spirit points, with lifted finger,
"Onward lies truth! My work were never done
If souls by me awakened climbed not higher —
Ever to seek, and fear not, the celestial fire."

BEETHOVEN

VIENNA

I CAME to a great city. Palaces
Rose glittering, mile on mile. Here dwells the King,
The Emperor and King; here lived, here ruled
How many mountainous far-looming fames;
Here is the crown of shadowy Charlemagne.
What housing of what glorious dignities!
Yet in a narrow street, unfrequented,
No palace near — one name upon a wall,
And all these majesties seem small and shrunk:
For here unto the bitter end abode

He who from pain wrought noble joy for men;
He who from silence gave the world to song;
For in his mind an awful music rose
As when, in darkness of the under-seas,
Currents tremendous over currents pour.
He heard the soundless tone, its voice he was,
And he of vast humanity the voice,
And his the empire of the human soul.

THE DESERT

Souls live for whom the illimitable sands
Not lonely are; they see white, phantom hands
Beckoning in spectral twilights, and they hear
Voices that come not to another ear.
The mystic desert calls them, as doth call
The sea to those who once have known its thrall —
The desert that (like to the eternal sea)
Creates a visible infinity;
There, where the day its quivering fire outpours,
A silent ocean breaks on silent shores.
Who would be wise —
Let him consort with Time 'neath desert skies.

EGYPT

I thought, in Egypt, Death was more than Life,
It seemed so long; its monuments so great;
The emptiness of tombs was such high state,—
No living thought, or power, or potentate
So glorious seemed, wrapt in such splendid gloom.
For I perceived that in each ancient tomb,
Long ages since, dead kings for Death made room.
Not here the Dead, but Death — alone, supreme:
In Egypt Death was real — Life a wingèd Dream.

SYRIA

I THOUGHT in Syria, Life was more than Death.
A tomb there was forsaken of its dead,
But Death filled not the place; here with bowed head
Worships the world forever at the tread
Of one who lived, who liveth, and shall live —
Whose grave is but a footstep on the sod;
Men kiss the ground where living feet have trod.
Here not to Death but Life, they worship give.
August is Death, but this one tomb is rife
With a more mighty presence; it is Life.

THE DEAD POET

A. H.

His was the love of art and song,
  And well he loved the flowery way;
Yet great his wrath at prospered wrong;
  When evil triumphed day by day
  Then plunged he in the fray.

And when brave innocence went down
  Then did the vanquished find a friend.
With him went justice through the town;
  No foeman ever saw him bend;
  He scorn for scorn could send.

Men said his heritage was lost;
  For, born to gentler use, his youth
Was wasted in rude strife; the cost
  Too great, they deemed, altho', in sooth,
  Through him men learned of Truth.

So were his songs but brief and few;
  Yet of some lives they were a part,
And on some souls they fell like dew;
  Dead — now men say: he gave to art
  The epic of the heart.

WAR

I

Two men on thrones, or crouched behind,
With cunning words the world would blind.
With faces grave, averse from spoils,
They weave their thieving, cynic toils.
One thing they mean, another speak;
Bland phrases utter, tongue in cheek.
Stale truths turn lies on velvet lips;
The candid heavens are in eclipse;
From crooked minds, and hearts all black,
Comes WAR upon its flaming track,
And reeking fiends in happy hell
Shout, "All is well!"

II

Then lives surprise!
While not a devil dares to shirk,
But all his hellish malice plies —
The angels, too, begin their work.
Now every virtue issues forth
And busy is from south to north:
Self-sacrifice, and love, and pity
Tramp all the rounds in field and city;
Mercy beyond a price, sweet ruth,
Courage and comradeship and truth,

And gentlest deed and noblest thought,
Into the common day are brought.
Man lives at heaven's gate, and dies
For fellow-man with joyful cries.

III

And all the while hell's imps are free
To work their will with fearful glee.
The beast in man anew is born;
Revenge, and lust, and pride, and scorn,
And glory false, and hateful hate,
All join to desecrate the state.

THE BLAMELESS KNIGHT

WHERE led the bright and blameless plume
  We charged the shameless foe;
Whether to win or lose our doom
  We never cared to know.

His voice was as a scimitar,
  Superb and sure his stroke;
And where he came their men-of-war
  In panic fury broke.

Once more we gathered for the fight
  Against the ranks of shame;
Again we called the blameless knight
  And cheered him as he came.

But, God of grace! not with us now
  Our valiant knight doth go:
A plume of black above his brow —
  He leads the shameless foe!

They are the same, that shameful horde,
  The same their shameless song;
Beneath his shield they draw the sword
  For rapine and for wrong.

Fight on! fight on! brave comrades all,
  Nor weep the blameless knight;
They cannot fail, what tho' they fall,
  Who battle for the right.

One Captain less in our good war,
  But see! a thousand spring
Intent as never men before
  To strike the Accursèd Thing.

THE DEMAGOGUE

ALL mouth, no mind; a mindless mouth in sooth;
He does not bend his strength to seek the truth,
But, shrewdly guessing what may take the crowd,
With tragic grimace, this he shouts aloud.
No true opinion, no fixed faith has he,
But gravely simulates sincerity.
His many causes swift resolve to one:
You find him his own cause when all is done.

THE TOOL

THE man of brains, of fair repute, and birth,
Who loves high place above all else of earth;
Who loves it so, he 'll go without the power
If he may hold the semblance but an hour;
Willing to be some sordid creature's tool
So he but seem a little while to rule;
On him even moral pigmies would look down;
Were prizes given for shame, he 'd wear the crown.

THE NEW POLITICIAN

WHILE others hedged, or silent lay,
He to the people spoke all day;
Ay, and he said precisely what
He thought; each time he touched the spot.
"In heaven's name, what does he mean!
Was ever such blind folly seen!"
The wag-beard politicians cried:
"Can no one stop the man?" they sighed.
"This 'talking frankly' may be fun,
But when have such mad tactics won?
He may be happy, but the cost
Is ours! The whole election's lost!"

And still the people at his feet
Followed and cheered from street to street.
Truly this ne'er was known before:
No soldier, sailor, orator,
No hero home from battle he
Whom welcoming thousands rush to see;
But just a man who dared to take
His stand on justice, make or break;
'T was all because the people found
A man by no conventions bound;
Who sought to heal their black disgrace
By treating rich and poor the same,
Giving to crime its ugly name,
Damning the guilty to their face.

And when the votes, at last, were read
Our candidate ran clear ahead!
This be his glory and renown:
He told the truth — and took the town.

A LADY TO A KNIGHT

Sir Knight, thou lovest not,
    If thou wouldst be too dear;
And I less worshipful, I wot,
    If thou couldst kneel so near!

So must thy shield of flawless fame
    Shine clear in honor's light;
Lest I should know a queenly shame
    To find thee less a knight.

"IS HOPE A PHANTOM?"

Is Hope a phantom? Holds the crystal cup
Sweet madness only — an we drink it up?
A respite ere the poor, doomed soul is killed?
— Then spake one who had loved: "*Hope is no lie,*
But real as answered Love, or unfulfilled;
Yet were Hope phantom-false, still would I cry,
'*Hail, Thou Bright Poisoner! let me drink, and die!*'"

SONG

If, lest thy heart betray thee,
Thou to one lover wouldst not constant be,
And yet thou couldst love me —
This boon I pray thee:
Divide the dark from light,
Love me by night.

If thy sweet thought would find me,
Not through the garish day, O, give it wing:
In shadows clasp and cling,

And bless and blind me!
When stars are still and bright —
Love me by night.

In longing dreams I'll name thee;
In secret hours, when breathes the midnight rose,
Thy heart in mine shall close,
Great love shall claim thee:
O mine in dark and light,
In day and night!

MEMORY

INTO this musing, Memory! thou hast brought
Me, thy true vassal; into this delight
That is more poignant for the haunting grief;
And as thou leadest on I follow, follow,
Down the deep, woody pathway of my dream,
Feeling the breath of flowers colorless
And airs that change their seasons as I wander,
Falling or cool or warm upon the brow.
The river shimmers 'twixt the shadowy boles;
Scarce seen the stars for the high, monstrous leaves
That make a lovers' screen; while the large moon,
Late risen, sends three beams athwart the path.
It is not night, nor day, it is the time
Of the clear spirit's life; the soul's high noon;
The hour most fit for passion's holy birth.
O mellow eve, unstartled by a bird!
O night whose light is deepening up the sky!
    'T was such a night when one low-murmured word, —
A word all miracle, — made of my soul
Naught but a singing rapture.

"O GLORIOUS SABBATH SUN"

I

O GLORIOUS Sabbath sun, thou art
A balm and blessing to my heart;
Dark sorrow flies, and in thy shine
Bursts o'er the world a flood divine.

II

So may the light beyond the skies
Illume and bless my inward eyes,
That each new day may bring to me
The splendor of eternity.

MOTTO FOR A TREE–PLANTING

STAY as the tree — go as the wind;
Whate'er thy place, serve God and kind!

The tree holds commerce with the skies
Tho' from its place it never flies.

They serve their God; they do not roam,
The stormy winds that have no home.

JANET

I REMEMBER
That November
When the new November child
On this old world woke and smiled.

Here 's a woman,
Sweet and human,
And they call her Janet, now —
I can't make it out, I vow.

It only seems
One night of dreams;
Years they say; how *do* they plan it?
What's become of Little Janet?

Never mind;
She's good; she's kind;
Age can never bend or win her;
There's a heart of youth within her.

ON BEING ASKED FOR A SONG

CONCERNING THE DEDICATION OF A MOUNTAIN IN SAMOA
TO THE MEMORY OF STEVENSON

A Letter to I. O. S.

BUT, friend of mine,— and his,— I am afraid!
How can I make a song
When the true song is made!
For this you say:
Because that Tusitala loved the birds,
They who named Tusitala (weaver of charmèd words —
Teller of Tales)
Have given his mountain to the birds forever!
There all day long
Bright-plumaged island-birds make gay the dales,
From off the sea the swift white bosun over the mountain
        sails,
From many a large-leaved tree
The gray dove cooes its low, insistent song.
From those green hights and vales
They shall be absent never —
To show what love can be from man to man.
Lovers of Birds and Poets — this is glory!
It *is* a poem,— that which these Chiefs have done, —

In memory of him, the only one.
And yet our Tusitala could have sung again the pretty
    story —
Alas, none other can!

TO AUSTIN DOBSON

LAUREATE of the Gentle Heart!
Only art like your own art,
Limpid, gracious, happy-phrased,
Could praise you as you should be praised.
Many a lyric you have writ,
Grave with pathos, gay with wit,
Or conceived in larger mood,
Shall outlast the clattering brood
That usurp our noisy day;
Shall, with all that's noble, stay
In our well-loved English tongue
Till the ending song is sung;
For no purer tone was heard
Since men sought Beauty and the Word.

TO L. R. S.

LISA Romana! no mean city gave
    Thee to the world, sired by as true a knight
    As e'er the flying paynim's helmet clave,
    Leading a hope forlorn in glorious fight!
And thou, dear, stately maid, no knight of old,
    That eastward battles down the pleasant page
    Of chivalry, ever in heart did hold
    A queenlier image — face more brightly grave.
Be kind to her, ye seas, ye winds that blow,
    On the long journey homeward, and one day,
    Ocean and wild sea-winds! swift make return

Of her ye take from us; — ay, let her yearn
　　Back, back to us once more; before this gray
　　Whitens, and hearts that love her are laid low.

A NAME

MANY the names, the souls, the faces dear
That I have longed to frame in verse sincere;
But one high name, sweet soul, and face of love
Seemed ever my poor art, O, far above.
Like Mary's, stricken with sorrow was that face;
Like hers it wore a most majestic grace.
That soul was tender as the sunset sky,
And full of lofty dream her days went by;
That name — than God's alone there is no other
Holy as thine to me, O sacred Mother!

JOHN GEORGE NICOLAY

WASHINGTON, D. C., SEPTEMBER, 1901

THIS man loved Lincoln, him did Lincoln love;
　　Through the long storm, right there, by Lincoln's side,
　　He stood, his shield and servitor; when died
The great, sweet, sorrowful soul — still high above
All other passions, love for the spirit fled!
　　To this one task his pure life was assigned:
　　He strove to make the world know Lincoln's mind:
He served him living, and he served him dead.
　　So shall the light from that immortal fame
　　Keep bright forever this most faithful name.

THE COMFORT OF THE TREES

McKINLEY: SEPTEMBER, 1901

GENTLE and generous, brave-hearted, kind,
　　And full of love and trust was he, our chief;

He never harmed a soul! O, dull and blind
And cruel, the hand that smote, beyond belief!
Strike him? It could not be! Soon should we find
'T was but a torturing dream — our sudden grief!
Then sobs and wailings down the northern wind
Like the wild voice of shipwreck from a reef!
By false hope lulled (his courage gave us hope!)
By day, by night we watched — until unfurled
At last the word of fate! Our memories
Cherish one tender thought in their sad scope:
He, looking from the window on this world,
Found comfort in the moving green of trees.

THE CITY OF LIGHT

THE PAN-AMERICAN EXPOSITION

WHAT shall we name it
As is our bounden duty —
This new, swift-builded fairy city of Beauty;
What name that shall not shame it;
Shall make it live beyond its too short living
With praises and thanksgiving!

Its name — how shall we doubt it,
We who have seen, when the blue darkness falls,
Leap into lines of light its domes, and spires, and walls,
Pylons, and colonnades, and towers,
All garlanded with starry flowers!
Its name — what heart that did not shout it
When, from afar, flamed sudden against the night
The City of Light!

AMHERST HOUSE, BUFFALO, May, 1901.

INSCRIPTIONS

FOR THE

PAN-AMERICAN EXPOSITION

BUFFALO, 1901

INSCRIPTIONS

FOR THE PROPYLÆA

PANEL I

HERE, BY THE GREAT WATERS
OF THE NORTH, ARE BROUGHT
TOGETHER THE PEOPLES OF THE
TWO AMERICAS, IN EXPOSITION
OF THEIR RESOURCES, INDUS-
TRIES, PRODUCTS, INVENTIONS,
ARTS, AND IDEAS

PANEL II

THAT THE CENTURY NOW BEGUN
MAY UNITE IN THE BONDS OF
PEACE, KNOWLEDGE, GOOD-WILL,
FRIENDSHIP, AND NOBLE EMULA-
TION ALL THE DWELLERS ON
THE CONTINENTS AND ISLANDS
OF THE NEW WORLD

FOR THE STADIUM

PANEL I

NOT IGNOBLE ARE THE DAYS OF
PEACE, NOT WITHOUT COURAGE
AND LAURELED VICTORIES

PANEL II

HE WHO FAILS BRAVELY HAS
NOT TRULY FAILED, BUT IS HIM-
SELF ALSO A CONQUEROR

PANEL III

WHO SHUNS THE DUST AND
SWEAT OF THE CONTEST, ON
HIS BROW FALLS NOT THE COOL
SHADE OF THE OLIVE

FOR THE GREAT PYLONS
OF THE TRIUMPHAL
CAUSEWAY

ON THE PYLONS WERE STATUES
OF COURAGE, LIBERTY, TOLER-
ANCE, TRUTH, BENEVOLENCE,
PATRIOTISM, HOSPITALITY, AND
JUSTICE

PANEL I

THE SPIRIT OF ADVENTURE IS
THE MAKER OF COMMON-
WEALTHS

PANEL II

FREEDOM IS BUT THE FIRST
LESSON IN SELF-GOVERNMENT

PANEL III

RELIGIOUS TOLERANCE A SAFE-
GUARD OF CIVIL LIBERTY

PANEL IV

A FREE STATE EXISTS ONLY IN
THE VIRTUE OF THE CITIZEN

PANEL V

WHO GIVES WISELY BUILDS MAN-
HOOD AND THE STATE — WHO
GIVES HIMSELF GIVES BEST

PANEL VI

TO LOVE ONE'S COUNTRY ABOVE
ALL OTHERS IS NOT TO DESPISE
ALL OTHERS

PANEL VII

THE BROTHERHOOD OF MAN,
THE FEDERATION OF NATIONS,
THE PEACE OF THE WORLD

PANEL VIII

BETWEEN NATION AND NATION,
AS BETWEEN MAN AND MAN,
LIVES THE ONE LAW OF RIGHT

DEDICATORY INSCRIPTIONS

PANEL I

TO THE ANCIENT RACES OF
AMERICA, FOR WHOM THE NEW
WORLD WAS THE OLD, THAT
THEIR LOVE OF FREEDOM AND
OF NATURE, THEIR HARDY COUR-
AGE, THEIR MONUMENTS, ARTS,
LEGENDS, AND STRANGE SONGS
MAY NOT PERISH AND BE
FORGOTTEN

PANEL II

TO THE EXPLORERS AND PIO-
NEERS WHO BLAZED THE WEST-
WARD PATH OF CIVILIZATION,
TO THE SOLDIERS AND SAILORS
WHO FOUGHT FOR FREEDOM
AND FOR PEACE, AND TO THE
CIVIC HEROES WHO SAVE A
PRICELESS HERITAGE

PANEL III

TO THE GREAT INVENTORS AND
FARSEEING PROJECTORS, TO THE
ENGINEERS, MANUFACTURERS,
AGRICULTURISTS, AND MER-
CHANTS WHO HAVE DEVELOPED
THE RESOURCES OF THE NEW
WORLD, AND MULTIPLIED THE
HOMES OF FREEMEN

PANEL IV

TO THOSE WHO IN THE DEADLY
MINE, ON STORMY SEAS, IN THE
FIERCE BREATH OF THE FUR-
NACE, AND IN ALL PERILOUS
PLACES WORKING CEASELESSLY
BRING TO THEIR FELLOW MEN
COMFORT, SUSTENANCE, AND
THE GRACE OF LIFE

PANEL V

TO THE SCHOLARS AND LABORI-
OUS INVESTIGATORS WHO, IN
THE OLD WORLD AND THE NEW,
GUARD THE LAMP OF KNOW-
LEDGE AND, CENTURY BY CEN-
TURY, INCREASE THE SAFETY OF
LIFE, ENLIGHTEN THE MIND AND
ENLARGE THE SPIRIT OF MAN

PANEL VI

TO THOSE PAINTERS, SCULPTORS,
AND ARCHITECTS, TELLERS OF
TALES, POETS, AND CREATORS OF
MUSIC, TO THOSE ACTORS AND
MUSICIANS WHO IN THE NEW
WORLD HAVE CHERISHED AND
INCREASED THE LOVE OF
BEAUTY

PANEL VII

TO THE PROPHETS AND HEROES,
TO THE MIGHTY POETS AND DI-
VINE ARTISTS, AND TO ALL THE
LIGHTBEARERS OF THE ANCIENT
WORLD WHO INSPIRED OUR
FOREFATHERS AND SHALL LEAD
AND ENLIGHTEN OUR CHIL-
DREN'S CHILDREN

PANEL VIII

TO THE STATESMEN, PHILOSO-
PHERS, TEACHERS, AND PREACH-
ERS, AND TO ALL THOSE WHO, IN
THE NEW WORLD, HAVE UPHELD
THE IDEALS OF LIBERTY AND
JUSTICE, AND HAVE BEEN FAITH-
FUL TO THE THINGS THAT ARE
ETERNAL

"IN THE HIGHTS"

"IN THE HIGHTS"

"IN THE HIGHTS"

ONE who this valley passionately loved
  No more these slopes shall climb, nor hear these
    streams
That, like the murmured melody of dreams,
His happy spirit moved.

He knew the sudden and mysterious thrill
  That takes the heart of man on mountain hights,
These autumn days that flame from hill to hill,
  These deep and starry nights.

O vanished spirit! tell us, if so may be,
  Are our wild longings, stirred by scenes like this —
Our deep-breathed, shadowless felicity —
  A mocking, empty bliss?

No answering word, save from the inmost soul
  That cries: all things are real — beauty, youth;
All the heart feels; of sorrow and joy the whole;
  That which but seems is truth.

This mortal frame, that harbors the immortal,
  Mechanic tho' it be, in our life's fires
Turns spiritual; it becomes the portal
  Wherethrough the soul aspires.

The soul's existence in its human sheath
  Is life no more than is the spirit's life

In this wide nature whose keen air we breathe;
   Whose strife arms us to strife.

And they are wise who seek not to destroy
   The unreasoned happiness of the outpoured year.
To him, the lost, this vale brought no false joy,
   And therefore is most dear.

Wherever in the majesty of space,
   Near or afar, but not from God afar,
Where'er his spirit soars, whatever grace
   Is his, whatever star —

The aspirations and imaginings
   That in these glorious paths his soul sublimed,
They are a part of him; they are the wings
   Whereby he strove and climbed.

Nature to man not alien doth endure;
   Her spirit in his spirit is transfused;
On this high mystery dream the humble-pure,
   The mightiest poets mused.

The white clouds billow down the blowing sky,
   Then, O my heart, be lifted up, rejoice!
   The trumpet of the winds, to that wild voice
Let all my soul reply!

HOME ACRES

A sense of pureness in the air,
   Of wholesome life in growing things;
   Waving of blossom, blade, and wings;
Perfume and beauty everywhere;
Sky, trees, the grass, the very loam —
I love them all; this is our home.

God! make me worthy of Thy land
　Which mine I call a little while;
　　This meadow where the sunset's smile
Falls like a blessing from Thy hand,
And where the river singing runs
'Neath wintry skies and summer suns!

Million on million years have sped
　To frame green fields and bowering hills:
　　The mortal for a moment tills
His span of earth, then is he dead:
This knows he well, yet doth he hold
His paradise like miser's gold.

I would be nobler than to clutch
　My little world with gloating grasp;
　　Now, while I live, my hands unclasp,
Or let me hold it not so much
For my own joy as for the good
Of all the gentle brotherhood.

And as the seasons move in mirth
　Of bloom and bird, of snow and leaf,
　　May my calm spirit rise from grief,
In solace of the lovely earth;
And tho' the land be dark or lit,
O, let me gather songs from it.

A CALL TO THE MOUNTAINS

I CALLED you once to the sea,
　Come now to the mountains;
Climb the earth's ramparts with me,
　Drink her deep fountains!

On the food that you love make merry;
　Forget grind and grief

In the red and the tang of the berry,
　The bronze of the leaf.

Chestnuts are ripe on the bough,
　And the burrs all are bursting;
For a tramp with you, John, I vow!
　I am hungering and thirsting.

Come, John, or you 'll be to blame;
　The birds wait your biding.
One of them, hearing your name,
　Flashed forth from its hiding; —

See, it is searching for you —
　Its pretty head cocking;
Pecking, and looking askew,
　On the bare bough rocking.

And yonder a stray wing flitters;
　A great hawk soars;
The lakelet gleams and glitters;
　The high wind roars.

Nearer, from field and thicket,
　Come musical calls;
The tinkling, clear note of the cricket,
　Chime of ripples and falls.

From the meadow far up to the hight
　The leaves all are turning;
By the time you have come to the sight
　The world will be blazing and burning.

John of Birds, tarry not till
　The first wild snow-flurry;
Voices of forest and hill
　Cry hurry, O hurry!

SPRING SURPRISE

Lo, now it comes once more; lo, my heart leaps again;
Comes swift the dear surprise, not at the spring, alone,
But, as a soul that knew, many a year agone,
All the full bloom of love, since the gray ashes —
    Feels all the glad surprise when the o'er-wearied heart
Still knows the joy of life, as in the olden days;
That love can thrill again; — so the spring calls once
      more
With the old tenderness; till my heart trembles.

AUTUMN TREES

But yesterday a world of haze,
    To-day, a glory of color and light!
Like golden voices shouting praise
    The bright trees flame along the hight.

Who would have thought, the summer through,
    Each separate tree of all the choir,
Lifting its green against the blue,
    Held at its heart such flame and fire?

"THE LIGHT LIES ON THE FARTHER HILLS"

The clouds upon the mountains rest;
    A gloom is on the autumn day;
But down the valley, in the west,
    The hidden sunlight breaks its way —
    A light lies on the farther hills.

Forget thy sorrow, heart of mine!
    Tho' shadows fall and fades the leaf,

Somewhere is joy, tho' 't is not thine;
    The power that sent can heal thy grief;
    And light lies on the farther hills.

Thou wouldst not with the world be one
    If ne'er thou knewest hurt and wrong;
Take comfort, tho' the darkened sun
    Never again bring gleam or song,
    The light lies on the farther hills.

"AH, NEAR, DEAR FRIEND"

AH, near, dear friend of many and many years!
I have known thy lovelinesses — known thy tears,
Thy smiles, like sunlight crossing shade,
Thy spirit unafraid.

All these have been like music to my soul;
These, having fashioned me, should I extol,
It were, in sooth, myself to praise —
O Light of all my days!

Thy smiles, thy tears, thy exquisite sad words —
Mystic as, in the moonlight, songs of birds;
But, O, more wonderful than these,
Thy lonely silences.

MUSIC IN DARKNESS

I

AT the dim end of day
I heard the great musician play:
Saw her white hands now slow, now swiftly pass;
Where gleamed the polished wood, as in a glass,

The shadow hands repeating every motion.
Then did I voyage forth on music's ocean,
Visiting many a sad or joyful shore,
Where storming breakers roar,
Or singing birds made music so intense,—
So intimate of happiness or sorrow,—
I scarce could courage borrow
To hear those strains: well-nigh I hurried thence
To escape the intolerable weight
That on my spirit fell when sobbed the music: late, too
     late, too late!
While slow withdrew the light
And, on the lyric tide, came in the night.

II

So grew the dark, enshrouding all the room
In a melodious gloom,
Her face growing viewless; line by line
That swaying form did momently decline
And was in darkness lost.
Then white hands ghostly turned, tho' still they tost
From tone to tone; pauseless and sure as if in perfect
     light;
With blind, instinctive, most miraculous sight,
On, on they sounded in that world of night.

III

Ah, dearest one; was this thy thought, as mine,
As still the music stayed?
"So shall the loved ones fade,—
Feature by feature, line on lovely line;
For all our love, alas,
From twilight into darkness shall they pass!
We in that dark shall see them nevermore,

But from our spirits they shall not be banished;
For on and on shall the sweet music pour
That was the soul of them, the loved, the vanished;
And we, who listen, shall not lose them quite
In that mysterious night."

THE ANGER OF BEETHOVEN

THIS night the enchanting musicians rendered a trio of
        Beethoven —
Light and lovely, or solemn, as in a Tuscan tower
The walls with gracious tapestries gleam, and the deep-
        cut windows
Give on landscapes gigantic, framing the four-square
        world —
When sudden the music turned to anger, as nature's
        murmur
Sometimes to anger turns, speaking, in voice infuriate,
Cruel, quick, implacable; inhuman, savage, resistless —
And I thought of that sensitive spirit flinging back in
        scorn tempestuous
And in art supreme, immortal, the infamous arrows of
        fortune.

MOTHER AND CHILD

MOTHER and Child! There is no holier sight
In all the realms of morning and of night;
And all the meaning of that word, DIVINE,
Shines in the tender glory of this sign. .
The world learns Worship here; it kneels in awe,
Seeing a mystery, knowing a mighty law.
Sin cannot live in presence of this grace,
No least unworthiness perplex the place.

Here Good doth dwell, but never baneful Doubt,
For Love and Loveliness would cast it out.
Were prophet voices still, the heavens brass,
Here would a new Evangel come to pass;
Out from the dark a rose-leaf hand would leap,
Close to the Eternal Throne the ancient world to keep.

ALICE FREEMAN PALMER

When fell, to-day, the word that she had gone,
Not this my thought: Here a bright journey ends,
Here rests a soul unresting; here, at last,
Here ends that earnest strength, that generous life —
For all her life was giving. Rather this
I said (after the first swift, sorrowing pang):
Radiant with love, and love's unending power,
Hence, on a new quest, starts an eager spirit —
No dread, no doubt, unhesitating forth
With asking eyes; pure as the bodiless souls
Whom poets vision near the central throne
Angelically ministrant to man;
So fares she forth with smiling, Godward face;
Nor should we grieve, but give eternal thanks —
Save that we mortal are, and needs must mourn.

"MOTHER OF HEROES"

SARAH BLAKE SHAW

Mother of heroes, she — of them who gave
Their lives to lift the lowly, free the slave.
Her, through long years, two master passions bound:
Love of our free land; and of all sweet sound.
'T was praising her to praise this land of grace;
And when I think on music — lo, her face!

THE GREAT CITIZEN

ABRAM STEVENS HEWITT

MOURN for his death, but for his life rejoice,
Who was the city's heart, the city's voice.

Dauntless in youth, impetuous in age,
Weighty in speech, in civic counsel sage;

Talents and wealth to him were but a trust
To lift his hapless brother from the dust; —

This his chief aim: to wake, in every man,
The soul to do what only courage can.

He saw the evil, as the wise must see,
But firm his faith in what the world shall be.

Following the truth, he led his fellow-men —
Through years and virtues the great citizen!

By being great, he made the city great;
Serving the city, he upheld the state.

So shall the city win a purer fame
Led by the living splendor of his name.

ON READING OF A POET'S DEATH

I READ that, in his sleep, the poet died
    Ere the day broke;
In a new dawn, as rose earth's crimson tide,
    His spirit woke.

Yet still with us his golden spirit stayed:
  On the same page
That told his end, his living verse I read—
  His lyric rage.

Behold! I thought, they call him cold in death,
  But hither turn—
See where his soul, a glorious, flaming breath,
  Doth pulse and burn!

This is the poet's triumph, his high doom! .
  After life's stress,
For him the silent, dark, o'er-shadowing tomb
  Is shadowless.

And this the miracle, the mystery:
  In that he gives
His soul away, magnificently free —
  By this he lives.

JOHN HENRY BONER

In life's hard fight this poet did his part;
He was a hero of the mind and heart.
Now rests his body 'neath his own loved skies,
And from his tomb Courage! his spirit cries.

"A WONDROUS SONG"

A wondrous song,
Rank with sea smells and the keen lust of life;
Echoing with battle trumpets, and the moan
Of dying men in reeking hospitals;
Thrilling all through with human pity and love
And crying courage in the face of doom; —
With all its love of life still praising death

Enchantingly, as death was never praised;
And with high anger and a god-like scorn
Passionately proclaiming life in death
And the unquenched, immortal soul of man —
A wondrous song,
Trembling with unshed tears and life's full joy,
Burst the tense meshes of the critic's web
And sang itself into eternal day.

A NEW POET

I

FRIENDS, beware!
Stop babbling! Hark, a sound is in the air!
Above the pretty songs of schools
(Not of music made, but rules),
Above the panic rush for gold
And emptinesses manifold,
And selling of the soul for phantom fame,
And reek of praises where there should be blame;

Over the dust and muck,
The buzz and roar of wheels,
Another music steals;
A right, true note is struck.

II

Friends, beware!
A sound of singing in the air!
The love-song of a man who loves his fellow-men;
Mother-love and country-love, and the love of sea and fen;
Lovely thoughts and mighty thoughts and thoughts that
        linger long;
There has come to the old world's singing the thrill of a
        brave new song.

III

They said there were no more singers,
But listen! — a master voice!
A voice of the true joy-bringers!
Now will ye heed and rejoice,
Or pass on the other side,
And wait till the singer has died,
Then weep o'er his voiceless clay?
Friends, beware!
A keen, new sound is in the air; —
Know ye a poet's coming is the old world's judgment day!

THE SINGER OF JOY

HE sang the rose, he praised its fragrant breath;
(Alas, he saw the gnawing worm beneath.)
He sang of summer and the flowing grass;
(He knew that all the beauty quick would pass.)
He said the world was good and skies were fair;
(He saw far, gathering clouds, and days of care.)
Immortally he sang pure friendship's flame;
(Yet had he seen it shrivel to a name.)
And, ah, he praised true love, with golden speech;
(What tho' it was a star he could not reach.)
His songs in cowering souls the hero woke ;
(He in the shadows waited the last stroke.)
He was the singer of the joyous art;
(Down to the grave he bore a broken heart.)

BREAD UPON THE WATERS

A MELANCHOLY, life o'er-wearied man
Sat in his lonely room, and, with slow breath,
Counted his losses: thrice-wreckt plan on plan,

Failure of friend, and hope, and heart, and faith —
This last the deadliest, and holding all.
Help was there none through weeping, for the years
Had stolen all his treasury of tears.
Then on a page where his eyes chanced to fall
There sprang such words of courage that they seemed
Cries on a battlefield, or as one dreamed
Of trumpets sounding charges. On he read
With fixèd gaze, and sad, down-drooping head,
And curious, half-remembering, musing mind.
The ringing of that voice had something stirred
In his deep heart, like music long since heard.
"Brave words," he sighed; and looked where they were
        signed;
There, reading his own name, tears made him blind.

LOST

An old, blind poet, sitting sad and lone,
Thinking his scribe was near, chimed slowly forth
Into the empty and unheeding air
A song, of all his songs the loveliest.
That night he died, and the sweet song was lost.

A million roses and uncounted worlds
Unknown, save to their Maker, strew the flood
Of heedless and immeasurable time.

"WHAT MAN HATH DONE"

Thus did he speak, thus was he comforted:
"I yet shall learn to live ere I am dead;
  I shall be firm of will, know false from true:
  Each error will but show me how to do,

When next the occasion calls. I shall pursue
The path that grim experience has taught."
This was his solace, this his saving thought.
 Then came a sudden knocking at the door.
He rose — and did what he had done before:
He looked into the dark, he flinched, he quailed;
The occasion came, and once again he failed.

Thus wrote a man who had seen much of men:
"What man hath done, that will he do again."

Yet are there souls who, having clinched with fate,
Have learned to live, ere it was all too late.
Be it thy hope, tho' seven times a fool,
To get some lessons in life's fearful school.

"HE PONDERED WELL"

HE pondered well, looked in his heart,
And bravely did his part.
Then spake the Ironic Powers
That rule the prostrate hours:
"Look now on this your deed; —
Despite your heroic creed,
Your pondering and your prayers,
Behold how ill the pretty project fares!
Not hotly were you driven;
For thought and thought the days were seven;
All was wisdom, all was cool —
And now one name you to yourself have given:
'T is fool, fool, fool, and only fool!"

Hast thou kept honor, and sweet courtesy kept,
Then is no loss that may be wailed or wept.

"THOU THINKEST THOU HAST LIVED"

THOU thinkest thou hast lived
If fortune fair hath touched thee with its wand,
If thou hast known, but once, the top of life
In giving royally, in truly loving,
In braving some great deed in sight of men,
Or issuing victorious from strife.
Not so; nor hast of life the flower and hight
In suffering that others may go free.
For thee the sequent years still proudly hold
A keener sense of the rich depths of being,
When thou, brave novice, shalt endure the lore
Of fate's immeasurable ironies.
Thou may'st behold the scorn of thee and thine
Sit on the laureled brow of him thy hand
Helped to that heaven; yes, thou yet may'st see
Success, in them thou gavest strength to rise,
Used for thine own disfigurement and loss;
May'st know betrayal and forgetfulness,
And knowing shalt thy spirit hold in calm;
Pitying the arrogant, the meanly vain,
Unbitterly, and with no cloying hate,
Disdain, nor envy; comforted and blest
With the high thought of knowledge, worthily gained,
And the humility which makes men wise,
And the uncensured pride of purity.

THE GOOD MAN

WHAT do you know of me, my gentlest one!
You who have watched my life from day to day
Through half a lifetime! Who have seen, indeed,
My comings and my goings; my dull years
In sunshine and in shade; in getting bread;

Gathering a little gold, a little fame,
A thousand nothings. What, I say, know you
Of my deep, inward, real, wonderful life?
My wild emprizes, foolishnesses, fears,
Failures, and shames, and all but acted crimes;
My half-mad waking dreams, O, yes, stark mad;
My spiritual comedies, my glooms —
Unutterable, intense, and without hope;
My secret, true, and unpraised heroisms;
My tragedies — played on the bare soul's stage,
With no eye witnessing but mine, alone —
Great God! not thine, I pray, not thine, not thine!

"SO FIERCE THE BUFFETS"

So fierce the buffets of untimely fate
He bowed his youthful head in mortal pain,
And cried: "Alas, my happy life is slain!"
Then came true sorrow, and he knew, too late,
His early woe was but a feather's weight.

TWO HEROES

Two heroes do the world's insistent work:
One rushes in the battle's blood and murk,
          And, knowing the foeman flies,
          In one rich moment dies.

The other, on a path he long has feared,
By bugle blast and drum-beat all uncheered,
          At duty's chill behest
          Gives life to want and waste.

For him, the battle hero, high we pile
The sculptured stone; his ringing name, the while,
          In praises and in songs
          Its lyric life prolongs.

For the other, we fashion a heaven of late reward;
His life, all dark, and desolate, and hard,
      Down to oblivion goes —
      Unless some great God knows!

THE WORLD'S END

ONCE wandering far in Asia, lo, we came
    Unto a valley falling toward the east;
    Naked its sides as if a spreading flame
    Had swept all bare; devouring, in mad feast,
Forest and herb, all beasts and singing choirs.
    With ardent colors were the vast hills strewn,
    Glowing like unquenched embers of great fires;
    Then sank the red sun, rose immense the moon.
So builded were those walls, so leaned the earth, —
    With slow, unnatural, and awful trend, —
    It seemed, at last, in this strange land of dearth,
Even just beyond, the solid world had end —
    And, moving on, our vision might take flight
    Into that pit whence issue day and night.

SHELLEY'S "OZYMANDIAS"

THIS timeless river — oldest of all time,
These desolate mountains, deserts stretching vast;
These pyramids and temples; this domain
Of tombs; and empty shadows of the dead,
And mockery of old fame ; — here day and night
I wander, not alone, nor with sad heart:
One line of Shelley singing in my soul.

LA SALLE

EXPLORER OF THE MISSISSIPPI

BATTLING, through trackless lands, 'gainst savage foes;
Striving, enduring, knowing the bitterness
Of foul betrayal, still in front he goes;
Onward through swamp and forest see him press,
Proud, silent, suffering, misunderstood;
The weight he bore, it seemed that no man could;
Then at the last, when the infernal stroke
Fell, 't was as if the silent leader spoke:
"This river I first traced to the far sea —
If monument I need, this let it be;
Then shall I live with the chief sons of time.
This is the path of empire: onward to empire climb!"

INAUGURATION DAY

ON this great day a child of time and fate
On a new path of power doth stand and wait.

Tho' heavy-burdened shall his heart rejoice,
Dowered with a nation's faith, an empire's choice.

Who hath no strength, but that the people give,
And in their wills, alone, his will doth live.

On this one day, this, this, is their one man,
The well-beloved, the chief American!

Whose people are his brothers, fathers, sons:
In this his strength, and not a million guns.

Whose power is mightier than the mightiest crown,
Because that soon he lays that power down.

Whose wish, linked to the people's, shall exceed
The force of civic wrong and banded greed.

Whose voice, in friendship or in warning heard,
Brings to the nations a free people's word;

And, where the opprest out from the darkness grope,
'T is as the voice of freedom and of hope.

O pray that he may rightly rule the state,
And grow, in truly serving, truly great.

THE WASHINGTON MONUMENT

AT WASHINGTON, D. C.

STRAIGHT soars to heaven the white magnificence —
  Free as man's thought, high as one lonely name; —
True image of his soul, serene, immense,
  Mightiest of monuments and mightiest fame.

BUILDERS OF THE STATE

WHO builds the state? Not he whose power
  Rooted in wrong, in gold intrenched,
Makes him the regent of the hour;
  The eternal light cannot be quenched:

This shall outlive his little span;
  Shine fierce upon each tainted scheme;
Shall show where shame blots all the plan;
  The treachery in the dazzling dream.

He builds the state who builds on truth, —
  Not he who, crushing toward his aim,
Strikes conscience from the throne, and ruth,
  To win a dark, unpiteous fame.

Not he, tho' master among men,
  Empire and ages all his thought —
Tho' like an eagle be his ken:
  Down to the ground shall all be brought.

For this I hold, and shall for aye,
  Till Heaven sends death, that they who sow
Hate, and the blood of brothers, they
  Shall harvest hate and want and woe —

The curse of Earth's dread agonies
  Whereto they added, in their hour,
And all the unheeded tears and cries
  They caused in lust of lawless power.

He builds the state who to that task
  Brings strong, clean hands, and purpose pure;
Who wears not virtue as a mask;
  He builds the state that shall endure —

The state wherein each loyal son
  Holds as a birthright from true sires
Treasures of honor, nobly won,
  And freedom's never-dying fires.

IMPROMPTUS

TO WILLIAM WATSON

ON HIS CORONATION ODE

(These lines were first published on the day the King was to have been crowned.)

IN this high ode with its great shadow-kings,
    More real than real things;
In this proud pageant of imperial verse
    That nobly doth rehearse
England's true glories, for the world to read,
    The King is crowned indeed!

"LIFE IS THE HAMMER"

(SIDNEY LANIER)

LIFE is the hammer that strikes
From the bell of the poet's heart
Art.

And whether he lives or dies
The music in widening rings
Sings.

"THE CRITIC SCANNED THE POET'S BOOK"

THE critic scanned the poet's book
And ranged it calmly in its place · —
A soul that felt its music shook
As if a bolt struck down through space;
And in that soul, like flower from seed,
The music turned to lofty deed
That sanctified a race.

"HER DELICATE FORM"

HER delicate form, her night of hair,
    Took me, unaware.
They called her *poet*, and the word
    Strangely I heard;
For that I thought: Can she
A poem write, and be?

FRANCESCA MIA

No verses I can bring her,
No song that I can sing her,
Can be so sweet, by half,
As the music of her laugh,
As the murmur of her voice,
As the sound of her violin.
These make my heart rejoice,
These me to heaven can win.
But something in her face,
Sad, wild, and full of grace —
A look in those dark eyes
That dream, and flash, and dance,
And with soft shadows fill —
These bring one long-loved glance,
Tender, and deep, and wise;
Then doth my heart stand still.

AGE, AND THE SCORNER

As I hobble, old and halt,
Daily, nightly,
By you, hectoring on the corner,
I know you for a graybeard scorner,
Tho' you raise your hat politely:

I know you hold it for a fault
That I bend with burdening years,
Dull of eye, and dull of ears;
That this poll
Whitens like a flax-wigged doll.
'T is a fault, you think; but wait!
Something marches, men call Fate;
If you, boy! succeed in keeping
Safe from sweep of Old Time's reaping,
You'll be the bent-back one that hobbles
Over the cobbles —
Wondering why, all young at heart,
With the old you're pushed apart.

TO JACOB A. RIIS

ON HIS SILVER WEDDING

WERE true hearts bells, all breezes would be bringing,
Straight to your heart to-day, a silver ringing
From those you've blest, the heavy hearts and sore; —
Hark the sweet sound from here to Elsinore!

MUSIC AND FRIENDSHIP

THRICE is sweet music sweet when every word
And lovely tone by kindred hearts are heard;
So when I hear true music, Heaven send,
To share that heavenly joy, one dear, dear friend!

FRIENDSHIP

TO ——

FROM the happy first time
  That we met — and wondered,
I from thee and thou from me
  Ne'er in soul were sundered.

No regret, no blaming;
  Absence has not shaken:
Far apart, still close in heart;
  Undoubting, unforsaken.

As the circle narrows
  We draw near and nearer;
So, old friend! as comes the end
  Thou art dearer, dearer.

TO E. C. S.

ON HIS SEVENTIETH BIRTHDAY

HIS life was generous as his life was long —
Filled to the brim with friendship and with song.

"TELL ME GOOD-BY"

DARK Southern girl! the dream-like day is past,
  The harbor light burns red against the sky;
In the high blue, star follows star full fast;
  The ship that takes me northward loometh nigh;
"Tell me good-by!"

Good-by to the red rose that is your mouth,
  The tender violets that are your sigh;
The sweetness that you are — that is my South;
  Ah, not too soon, Enchantress, do I fly!
"Tell me good-by."

"Tell me good-by," — but not too sweetly tell
  Lest all too hard the going, lest I cry
"Never, no never!" tho' the parting bell
  Ring madly in the night; not then could I
Tell you good-by.

FAREWELL TO CHARLESTON

ENCHANTED city, O farewell, farewell!
If farewell it can be
When here, 'twixt the dark pines and sunrise sea,
Our hearts remain,
While fare our bodies to the North again!
Here stay our hearts amid these mansions stately,
These oaks, forever green, that guard sedately
The living and the dead —
Thrilled through with song that hath interpreted
The beauty and the gladness of the day.
O, yes, our hearts remain; they must forever stay
'Midst happy gardens, unforgettable,
And where St. Michael's chimes
The fragrant hours exquisitely tell,
Making the world one loveliness, like a true poet's rhymes.

"THE PINES"

THESE are the sounds that I heard at the home in "The
    Pines":
The frightened cry of the yellowthroat hid in the trees;
The chipmunk's rustling tread on the autumn leaves
That fringe with brown the green of the wave and the
    wood;
The purr of the quick canoe where it curves the wave
And the liquid push of the oar; the voice of the wind
Now far, now near, as it sighs through the swaying
    boughs —
Through the boughs that sway with a slow and wave-
    like motion
Like growths of the sea that swing in the moving waters;
The voice of the wind I heard, now near, now far;
Voice of the grieving world that murmurs and calls
And wakes in the spirit of man an answering cry.

"NOT WREATHS ALONE"

Not wreaths alone, for him who wins the fight
  'Twixt public Wrong and Right; —
The heavy burden of the people's cares
  The civic conqueror bears.
So to the chief, on this victorious night,
Pledge hands and hearts and heaven-climbing prayers.

FOR THE CITY CLUB

In Love of City here we take our stand: —
  Love of the City is no narrow love;
Who loves it not he cannot love his land
  With love that shall protect, exalt, endure.
Here are our homes, our hearts; great God above!
The City *shall* be noble, *shall* be pure.

TO C. H. RUSSELL

WHOSE FATHER WAS ONE OF LINCOLN'S HELPERS

I give this token to the son of him
That was a type of those brave, prescient souls
Who when dire trouble fell upon the land
From the beginning saw the fateful end,
Bending strong backs to the tremendous strain.
  Higher than knighthood's honor lives your line
For that the mighty Lincoln hurriedly called
To your true sire, in a perilous hour,
And got true answer — succor swift, complete.
  On such as he the patient President,
The tender elder brother of us all,
The sad, wise leader leaned, and not in vain.
Therefore the nation lives — therefore shall live,
Inheriting the spirit of great days.

"GIVE THY DAY TO DUTY"

GIVE thy day to Duty!
To that high thought be given
Thine every hour.
So shall the bending heaven,
As from the root the flower,
Bring to thy glad soul Beauty.

TWO OPTIMISTS

(A LETTER TO JOSEPH JEFFERSON, ACKNOWLEDGING A COPY OF
HELEN KELLER'S ESSAY ON "OPTIMISM")

To send fit thanks, I would I had the art,
For this small book that holds a mighty heart,
Enshrining, as it does, brave Helen's creed.
  In thought and word; in many a lovely deed;
In facing what would crush a lesser soul,
Making of barriers helps to reach the goal;
In sympathy with all; in human kindness
To the blind of heart (dear girl! not this *her* blindness!),
As well as to her brethren of the dark
And silent world, who through her see and hark;
In bringing out of darkness a great light,
Which burns and beacons high in all men's sight,
That exquisite spirit is true optimist!
  Yet there are other names in the bright list:
If faith in man and woman that still lasts,
Tho' chilled by seventy winters' bitter blasts;
If seeing, as you see, the good in evil,
And even something Christian in the devil;
If power to take misfortune as a friend
And to be cheerful to the darkening end;
Not to be spoiled by praise, nor deeply stung
By the detractor's sharp and envious tongue;

If living in fairy-land as really now
As when heaven's dew was fresh on childhood's brow;
If seeing, in fine, this world as through a prism
Of lovely colors be true optimism,
Then Jefferson is true optimist no less,
And Heaven sent both this troubled world to bless.

THE PASSING OF JOSEPH JEFFERSON

SOME element from nature seems withdrawn,
The world we lived in being of his spirit wrought —
His brightness, sweetness, tender gayety,
His childlike, wistful, and half-humorous faith
That turned this harsh earth into fairy-land.
He made our world, and now our world is changed.

The sunniest nature his that ever breathed;
Most lovable of all the sons of men;
Who built his joy on making others happy;
Like Jesus, lover of the hills and shores,
And like him to the beasts and flowers kin,
And with a brother's love for all mankind,
But chiefly for the loving — tho' the lost.
In his own art,— ineffable, serene,
And mystical (not less to nature true
And to the heart of man),— his was the power
To shed a light of love on human waifs
And folk of simple soul. Where'er he went,
Sweet childhood followed and all childlike hearts.
His very presence made a holiday —
Affectionate laughter and quick, unsad tears.

Now, he being gone, the sun shines not so bright
And every shadow darkens.

                     Kind Heaven forbid
Our lives should lack forever what he gave;
Prove mirage-haunted, every good unreal!
Let the brave cheer of life we had through him
Return, reflected from his joyous soul
That cannot all be lost, where'er it hides,—
Hides, but is quenched not,— haply smiling still
Near where his well-loved Shakespeare smiling sits,
Whose birthday for his own new birth he took
Into the unseen world, to him not far
But radiant with the same mysterious light
That filled his noontime with the twilight dream.
And it was Easter, too — the golden day
Of resurrection, and man's dauntless hope.

   Into the unseen he past, willing and glad,
And humbly proud of a great nation's love;
In honored age, with heart untouched by years
Save to grow sweeter, and more dear, more dear —
Into that world whereon, so oft, he mused;
Where he forgets not this, nor shall we him —
That magic smile, that most pathetic voice,
That starry glance, that rare and faithful soul.

   From dream to dream he past on Shakespeare's
      day —
So dedicate his mind to pleasant thought,
So deep his fealty to that supreme shade;
He being, like him of Avon, a fairy child,
High-born of miracle and mystery,
Of wonder, and of wisdom, and of mirth.

"SHALL WE NOT PRAISE THE LIVING?"

I

UNGENEROUS!

Shall we not praise the living as the dead?
And I, who lately sang a beautiful spirit fled,
Shall I not praise a living spirit we know,
Dear heart! we know full well,
And long have known, in utmost joy and woe;
In our own sorrows, and delights;
Her days of brightness and lone-weeping nights!
  If she should die, alas the day! how swift this verse
      would tell
Our anguish, our large loss, irreparable,
In a wild passion of praise
For her dear virtues, her sweet friendship's ways,
That many know; but only a sacred few
Know, as to the evening hour is known the dew,
As the still dawn knows the great, melting stars,
As night is intimate to those who love,
As sorrow's voice is known to the mourning dove,
As memoried twilight holds the sunset's crimson bars.

II

Shall we not praise the loveliness
God gave her, and the true heart that cannot help but
      bless?
For she is not of those
Who virtues wear like graceful draperies,
But breathes them as her life. Where'er she goes
Go pleasure and pure thoughts, and baseness dies.
A holy ministry her life is, even without intent;
For, tho' she worships duty,

Such elements in her are exquisitely blent
She cannot but be kind;
A spiritual radiance in her beauty
Makes itself inly felt, even by the blind.
    Ah, thou and I, dear soul! we know
How the rich courtesy that touched full many a heart
Is no mere learnt and gracious art;
For when, to those she loved, keen trouble came,
How leaped her spirit, like a flame;
How quick, sure, self-forgetting, beyond thought,
The angelic succor that brave spirit brought!

III

How may I fitly name them all —
The graces, gentlenesses, benedicities,
That in a white processional
Move before these musing eyes;
Nor would I shame
That proud humility which is the crown and chief
Of all the virtues that make up her golden sheaf;
Tho' should I name
Each separate goodness, clearly, that is her very own,
To her calm eyes, alone,
The authentic picture would be never known —
The portrait of another it would seem;
And should one say, "This, this indeed is you!"
"No," she would cry, "'t is but a poet's dream,
And, save as a dream, it cannot all be true!"

IV

This, then, the dream: Large, innocent eyes,
Lit with life's romance and surprise,
And with a child's strange wisdom wise.

A child in nature, eager, gay,
And, yet, in all a woman's way
Wifely and motherly her day.

  Curious, but constant; slow to wrath,
Yet nobly scornful; pride she hath
That sheds a splendor on her path.

  She breathes a heaven-born sympathy;
For her there is no low nor high;
Goodness is honor in her eye:

  So, in the throng, each separate one
Deems her glad welcome his alone,
As if some special grace were shown.

  The great world, seeing her afar,
Claims her, and names her for a star;
But, among nearer watchers, are

  Some who a sacred tale could tell
How those bright beams, ineffable,
On one great hero-spirit fell.

v

Shall we not praise the living?
Too soon the living pass
Like images on the unremembering glass,
Scarce even a breath's length! shall we not thanksgiv-
    ing
Upraise, or e'er the everlasting sleep
Hath dulled the ear? that slumber deep
Whereof we know so little, however we may hope —
Mortals who see a closing door, and never see it
    ope.

HYMN

WRITTEN FOR THE SERVICE IN MEMORY OF DR. J. L. M.
CURRY, HELD BY THE SOUTHERN EDUCATION CONFER-
ENCE, RICHMOND, VIRGINIA, APRIL 26, 1903

GOD of the strong, God of the weak,
  Lord of all lands, and our own land;
Light of all souls, from Thee we seek
  Light from Thy light, strength from Thy hand.

In suffering Thou hast made us one,
  In mighty burdens one are we;
Teach us that lowliest duty done
  Is highest service unto Thee.

Teach us, Great Teacher of mankind,
  The sacrifice that brings Thy balm;
The love, the work that bless and bind;
  Teach us Thy majesty, Thy calm.

Teach Thou, and we shall know, indeed,
  The truth divine that maketh free;
And knowing, we may sow the seed
  That blossoms through eternity; —

May sow in every living heart
  That to the waiting day doth ope.
Not ours, O God! the craven part,
  To shut one human soul from hope.

Now, in the memory of Thy Saint,
  To whom Thy little ones were dear,
Help us to toil and not to faint,
  Till earth grows dark and heaven comes near.

JOHN WESLEY

WRITTEN FOR THE CELEBRATION OF THE TWO-HUN-
DREDTH ANNIVERSARY OF THE BIRTH OF JOHN
WESLEY, AT WESLEYAN UNIVERSITY, MIDDLETOWN,
CONNECTICUT, JUNE, 1903

I

In those clear, piercing, piteous eyes behold
The very soul that over England flamed!
Deep, pure, intense; consuming shame and ill;
Convicting men of sin; making faith live;
And,— this the mightiest miracle of all,—
Creating God again in human hearts.

What courage of the flesh and of the spirit!
How grim of wit, when wit alone might serve!
What wisdom his to know the boundless might
Of banded effort in a world like ours!
How meek, how self-forgetful, courteous, calm!
A silent figure when men idly raged
In murderous anger; calm, too, in the storm,—
Storm of the spirit, strangely imminent,—
When spiritual lightnings struck men down
And brought, by violence, the sense of sin,
And violently oped the gates of peace.

O hear that voice, which rang from dawn to night,
In church and abbey whose most ancient walls
Not for a thousand years such accents knew!
On windy hilltops; by the roaring sea;
'Mid tombs, in market-places, prisons, fields;
'Mid clamor, vile attack, or deep-awed hush,
Wherein celestial visitants drew near
And secret ministered to troubled souls!

Hear ye, O hear! that ceaseless-pleading voice,
Which storm, nor suffering, nor age could still —
Chief prophet-voice through nigh a century's span!
Now silvery as Zion's dove that mourns,
Now quelling as the Archangel's judgment-trump,
And ever with a sound like that of old
Which, in the desert, shook the wandering tribes,
Or, round about storied Jerusalem,
Or by Gennesaret, or Jordan, spake
The words of life.

        Let not that image fade
Ever, O God! from out the minds of men,
Of him Thy messenger and stainless priest,
In a brute, sodden, and unfaithful time,
Early and late, o'er land and sea, on-driven;
In youth, in eager manhood, age extreme —
Driven on forever, back and forth the world,
By that divine, omnipotent desire,
The hunger and the passion for men's souls!

Ah, how he loved Christ's poor! No narrow thought
Dishumaned any soul from his emprize;
But his the prayer sincere that Heaven might send
Him chiefly to the humble; he would be,
Even as the Galilean, dedicate
Unto the ministry of lowliness:
That boon did Heaven mercifully grant;
And gladly was he heard; and rich the fruit;
While still the harvest ripens round the earth;
And many own the name once given in scorn;
And all revere the holy life he led,
Praise what he did for England, and the world,
And call that greatness which was once reproach.
Would we were worthy for his praise.

Dear God!
Thy servant never knew one selfish hour!
How are we shamed, who look upon a world
Ages afar from that true kingdom preached
Millenniums ago in Palestine!

Send us, again, O Spirit of all Truth!
High messengers of dauntless faith and power
Like him whose memory this day we praise,
We cherish and we praise with burning hearts.
Let kindle, as before, from his bright torch,
Myriads of messengers aflame with Thee
To darkest places bearing light divine!

II

As did one soul, whom here I fain would sing,
For here in youth his gentle spirit took
New fire from Wesley's glow.

How oft have I,
A little child, harkened my father's voice
Preaching the Word in country homes remote,
Or wayside schools, where only two or three
Were gathered. Lo, again that voice I hear,
Like Wesley's, raised in those sweet, fervent hymns
Made sacred by how many saints of God
Who breathed their souls out on the well-loved tones.
Again I see those circling, eager faces;
I hear once more the solemn-urging words
That tell the things of God in simple phrase;
Again the deep-voiced, reverent prayer ascends,
Bringing to the still summer afternoon
A sense of the eternal. As he preached
He lived; unselfish, famelessly heroic.
For even in mid-career, with life still full,
His was the glorious privilege and choice

Deliberately to give that life away
For country and for comrades; for he knew
No rule but duty, no reward but Christ.

III

Increase thy prophets, Lord! give strength to smite
Shame to the heart of luxury and sloth!
Give them the yearning after human souls
That burned in Wesley's breast! Through them, great
    God!
Teach poverty it may be rich in Thee;
Teach riches the true wealth of Thine own spirit.
To our loved land, Celestial Purity!
Bring back the meaning of those ancient words,—
Not lost but soiled, and darkly disesteemed,—
The ever sacred names of husband, wife,
And the great name of Love, whereon is built
The temple of human happiness and hope!
Baptize with holy wrath thy prophets, Lord!
By them purge from us this corruption foul
That seizes on our civic governments,
Crowns the corrupter in the sight of men,
And makes him maker of laws, and honor's source!

Help us, in memory of the sainted dead,
Help us, O Heaven! to frame a nobler state,
In nobler lives rededicate to Thee:
Symbol and part of the large brotherhood
Of man and nations; one in one great love,
True love of God, which is the love of man,
In sacrifice and mutual service shown.

Let kindle, as before, O Heavenly Light!
New messengers of righteousness, and hope,
And courage, for our day! So shall the world
That ever, surely, climbs to Thy desire
Grow swifter toward Thy purpose and intent.

A TEMPLE OF ART

WRITTEN FOR THE OPENING OF THE ALBRIGHT ART
GALLERY, BUFFALO, MAY 31, 1905

I

SLOWLY to the day the rose,
The moon-flower suddenly to the night,
Their mysteries of light
In innocence unclose.

II

In this garden of delight,
This pillared temple, pure and white,
We plant the seed of art,
With mystic power
To bring, or sudden or slow, the perfect flower,
That cheers and comforts the sad human heart;
That brings to man high thought
From starry regions caught,
And sweet, unconscious nobleness of deed;
So he may never lose his childhood's joyful creed,
While years and sorrows to sorrows and years succeed.

III

Tho' thick the cloud that hides the unseen life
Before we were and after we shall be,
Here in this fragment of eternity;
And heavy is the burden and the strife —
The universe, we know, in beauty had its birth;
The day in beauty dawns, in beauty dies,
With intense color of the sea and skies;
And life, for all its rapine, with beauty floods the earth.
Lovely the birds, and their true song,
Amid the murmurous leaves, the summer long.

Whate'er the baffling power
Sent anger and earthquake and a thousand ills,
It made the violet flower,
And the wide world with breathless beauty thrills.

IV

Who built the world made man
With power to build and plan,
A soul all loveliness to love,
Blossom below and lucent blue above,
And new unending beauty to contrive.
He, the creature, may not make
Beautiful beings all alive —
Irised moth nor mottled snake,
The lily's splendor,
The light of glances infinitely tender,
Nor the day's dying glow nor flush of morn,
And yet his handiwork the angels shall not scorn,
When he hath wrought in truth and by Heaven's law,
In lowliness and awe.
Bravely shall he labor, while from his pure hands
Spring fresh wonders, spread new lands;
Son of God, no longer child of fate,
Like God he shall create.

V

When, weary ages hence, this wrong world is set right;
When brotherhood is real
And all that justice can for man is done;
When the fair, fleeing, anguished-for ideal
Turns actual at last; and 'neath the sun
Man hath no human foe;
And even the brazen sky, and storms that blow,
And all the elements have friendlier proved,

By human wit to human uses moved —
Ah, still shall art endure,
And beauty's light and lure,
To keep man noble, and make life delight,
Tho' shadows backward fall from the engulfing night.

VI

In a world of little aims,
Sordid hopes and futile fames,
Spirit of Beauty! high thy place
In the fashioning of the race.
In this temple, built to thee,
We thy worshipers would be,
Lifting up, all undefiled,
Hearts as lowly as a child;
Humble to be taught and led
And on celestial manna fed;
So to take into our lives
Something that from Heaven derives.

THE FIRE DIVINE

THE FIRE DIVINE

THE FIRE DIVINE

HE who hath the sacred fire
Hidden in his heart of hearts,
It shall burn him clean and pure,
Make him conquer, make endure.
He to all things may aspire,
King of days, and souls, and arts.
Failure, fright, and dumb dismay
Are but wings upon his way.
Imagination and desire
Are his slaves and implements.
Faiths and foul calamities,
And the eternal ironies,
Are but voices in his choir.
Musician of decreed events —
Hungers, happinesses, hates,
Friendships lost, all adverse fates,
All passions and all elements,
Are but golden instruments
In his glorious symphonies.
Subject to his firm decrees
Are the heavens, are the seas;
But in utter humbleness
Reigns he, not to ban, but bless —
Cleansed, and conquering, and benign
Bearer of the fire divine.

THE INVISIBLE

(AT A LECTURE)

SUCH pictures of the heavens were never seen.
We stood at the steep edge of the abyss
And looked out on the making of the suns.
The skies were powdered with the white of stars
And the pale ghosts of systems yet to be;
While here and there a nebulous spiral told,
Against the dark, the story of the orbs —
From the impalpable condensing slow
Through ages infinite.

     Each mighty shape
Seemed as the shape of speed — a whirling wheel
Stupendously revolving,
And yet no eye of man may see it stir.
(That moveless motion brings to the human brain
A hint of the large measurements of time —
Eternity made present.)

      Such new sense
Of magnitudes that make our world an atom
Might crush the soul, did not this saving thought
Leap to the mind and lift it to clear hights: —
"'T is but the unseen that grows not old nor dies,
Suffers not change, nor waning, nor decay.
This that we see — this casual glimpse within
The seething pit of space; these million stars
And worlds in making, these are naught but matter;
These all are but the dust upon our feet,
And we who gaze forth fearless on the sight
Find not one equal, facing from the vast
Our sentient selves. Not one, sole, lonely star
In all the infinite glitter and deep light
Can make one conscious movement; all are slaves

To law material, immutable —
That Power immense, mysterious, intense,
Unseen as our own souls, but which must be
Like them the home of thought, with will and might
To stamp on mindless matter the soul's will.
Yea, in these souls of ours triumphant dwells
Some segment of the large creative Power —
A thing beyond the things of sight and sense;
A strength to think, a force to conquer force.
One are we with the ever-living One."

DESTINY

(AFTER READING A WORK ON ASTRONOMY)

I SEE it all; my soul the dregs hath drunk
  Of man's last, helpless, hopeless destiny;
  Born of the primal ooze, where slow light sunk,
  And climbing to the secrets of the sky;
Through countless million years the spiral mounts
  Till nature, a companionable slave,
  Bows to man's bidding; lo, then, the deep founts
  Run gradual dry, earth turns its own chill grave:
The insatiate desert marches on the sown,
  The sea exhales, the very air is gone,
  And, gasping in the silent void, the race
Dies with the planet. — But not this the doom
  Of man's outlooking soul; that hath no tomb,
  Being quenchless as the law and lord of space.

THE OLD FAITH

ON that old faith I will take hold once more —
Now that the long waves bear me to the shore
And life's brief voyage is o'er;

Near is the looked-for land —
One wild leap on the strand
And the dear souls I loved of old
I shall again behold,
And arms that held me once shall hold again.
In blinding ways of men
Long did I mourning doubt,
Saying: "Into the universe have they gone out
And shall be lost
In the wide waves of unseen, infinite force;
For nature heeds not all the bitter cost,
But rushes on its course
Unto the far, determined goal,
Without self-conscious knowledge, or remorse."
But now the time is come, the test draws near,
And sudden my soul is innocent of fear.
O ye beloved! I come! I cry
With the old passion ye shall not deny!
I know you, as I knew
When life was in its dew;
Ah, naught of me has suffered inward change,
Nor can be change essential even in you,
However far the freer spirit's range.
Soul shall find soul; there is no distance
That bars love's brave insistence,
And nothing truly dies
In all the infinite realm of woe and weal;
Throughout creation's bound thrill answers thrill
And love to love replies.

THE DOUBTER'S SOLILOQUY

A WHITE lie, even as the black, I learned to hate;
Being taught clear truth by honest parentage,

And, haply, somewhat morbid in this matter.
'T would come, I fear, not easy to deceive
Even death-beds, for their good, that men, indeed,
Might, as they say, "die happy." (Not that I
Have never eased, by little lies that helped,—
Being gray with years,— to smooth a neighbor's path,
Or even mine own.) And when I've read brave tales
Wherein the hero like a hero lied,
And saved the other hero from some shame,
Or loss, or ill that seemed itself a lie,
Such tragi-comedies, I've thought, mayhap
Argued a sophist mind in them who wrote.
　　Once reading such a pretty history
The thought came on me with a sickening stroke:
'But what of all the martyrs who died singing,
Smiling and singing in the face of pain,
Of tortured, useless death; seeing just beyond
The flame, the scorch, the shudder — sudden joy;
Joy so intense it threw a splendor back
Into the midst of unfelt agonies!
And what of those, the unknown martyrdoms,
The myriads of faithful, humble souls
Who horribly suffered through long, faithful lives,
Seeing the peace of God beyond the strife!
What of all these if there be no awakening?
If He permitted the Colossal Lie
As opiate for the agony of life —
Who were the sophist then?"
　　　　　　　　　　　　But a voice spake
And said: "Your argument requires a God
All powerful, all present, and all wise,
Who could prevent false notions of Himself
And His designs to fasten on men's minds.
If such a God exists, this is most sure —

He wills not to make plain His character
And mode of government; witness through time
A thousand gods, religions without end,
Each in some souls,— all reverent and sincere,—
Supreme, unquestioned; gods that grimly held
Races and ages round about their thrones.

"Your very doubt creates a mighty Power,
Invisible, yet having human traits,
And Him you judge with your sole, finite mind —
You doubt, you dread, you trouble your sad soul.
Were it not best to follow those twin stars
Which light each mortal path: the double stars
Of Love and Duty? If by these you walk
(This has been proved), a solace shall arrive —
A noble solace, a majestic joy.
Whatever of life is worthy of the soul
Then shall be yours. Disdain, disdain all else!"

LAW

TRUE love to liberty is never foe,
  And he who truly loves is truly free:
    Thus thought I when I heard the pulsing flow
    Of mighty music rushing gloriously
Along the channels of unchanging law;
    Thus thought I when I gazed upon the skies
    And there the circling universe I saw
    Moving obedient in glad harmonies
About a central, inescapable power:
    No sun, nor planet, nor wild comet's course
    But owns that sway in every separate hour
Of all its centuries; to that one force
    Freely it yields, — as hearts that never rove,
    But pour their being in a single love.

IDENTITY

AND can it be?
The heart that in the earth's far dawn knew God;
The thought that seized the circling of the stars;
The soul of fire that on that hill of Athens
Builded immortal beauty; the brain enorm
That peopled for all men and for all time
A world Shakespearian; and can it be? —
The mind imperial named Beethoven,
Majestically chanting harmonies
That hold the motions of the rhythmic worlds,
And to far doomsday stir all living hearts;
And he the framer of earth's mightiest dome,
Painter sublime and poet marvelous,
Who carved the likeness of his soul in stone,
And in cold marble the hot heart of man
Imprisoned eternally; and can it be? —
These, these and all the potencies of time
Which throbbed in human form; and can it be
That the intensive fire which made them men,
Not trees, nor creeping beasts, nor stones, nor stars,
And gave identity to every soul
Making it individual and alone
Among the myriads; and can it be
That, when the mortal framework failed, this fire,—
Which flamed in separate and lonely life,—
These souls, slipt out of being and were lost,
Eternally extinguished and cast out:
Only to some obscure electric wave
Giving new force, to some stray flower new grace,
Unto some lover's vow more ardency;
Making some island sunset more intense,
Passing from fiery thought to chemic heat —

But all the universe empty of that one high
And exquisite accomplishment and power,
Forever and forever — can it be?

"SPARE ME MY DREAMS"

I

RELENTLESS Time, that gives both harsh and kind,
　　　Brave let me be
To take thy various gifts with equal mind,
　　　And proud humility;
But, even by day, while the full sunlight streams,
Give me my dreams!

II

Whatever, Time, thou takest from my heart,
　　　What from my life,
From what dear thing thou yet may'st make me part —
　　　Plunge not too deep the knife;
As dies the day, and the long twilight gleams,
Spare me my dreams!

HYMN

(THANKSGIVING FOR SAINTS AND PROPHETS)

To Thee, Eternal Soul, be praise!
Who, from of old to our own days
Through souls of saints and prophets, Lord,
Hast sent Thy light, Thy love, Thy word.

We thank Thee for each mighty one
Through whom Thy living light hath shone;
And for each humble soul and sweet
That lights to heaven our wandering feet.

We thank Thee for the love divine
Made real in every saint of Thine;
That boundless love itself that gives
In service to each soul that lives.

We thank Thee for the word of might
The Spirit spake in darkest night;
Spake through the trumpet voices loud
Of prophets at Thy throne who bowed.

Eternal Soul, our souls keep pure,
That like Thy saints we may endure;
Forever through Thy servants, Lord,
Send Thou Thy light, Thy love, Thy word.

THE VALLEY OF LIFE

WHEN I was a child joyfully I ran, hand claspt in hand, now with my mother, now with my father, or with younger, blithe companions, now in sunlight, now in shadow and dread, through the strange new Valley of Life.

Sometimes on the high-road, then over the fields and meadows, or through the solemn forests; sometimes along the happy brook-side, listening to its music or the clamor of the falls, as the pleasant waters hurried or grew still, in the winding way down the Valley of Life.

And as we moved along, hand claspt in hand, sometimes the hand-clasp was broken, and I, a happy child, ran swiftly aside from the path to gather flower or fruit or get sight of a singing bird; or to lean down and pluck a pearly stone from under the lapping waves; or climbed a tree and swayed, shouting, on its waving boughs — then returning to the clasp of loving hands, and so passing on and on down the opening Valley of Life.

In the bright morning I walked wondering; wondering
I walked through the still twilight and many-colored
sunset; watching the great stars gather, and lost in the
mystery of worlds beyond number, and spaces beyond
thought, till, side by side, we lay down to sleep under the
stars in the Valley of Life and of Dreams.

Then there came a time when the hands that held me,
— the loving hands that guided my steps and drew me
gently on,— turned cold, and slipt from my grasp; I
waited, but they came not back, and slowly and alone
I plodded on down the Valley of Life and of Death.

"Where went they?" I asked my heart and the
whispering waters and the sighing trees. "Where went
my loving and well-belovèd guides? Did they climb the
hills and tarry; did they, tired, lie down to sleep and forget me forever; leaving me to journey on without their
dear care down the long Valley of Life?"

I could not know, for I heard no answer except my own
heart's beating. But other comrades came,— one dearer
than all,— and as time went on I felt the little hands of
my own children clasping mine while, once more happy
and elate, with them I traveled down the miraculous Valley of Life.

But, as on we wander, hearing their bright voices, and
seeing their joy upon the way,— their happy chasings
here and there, their eager run to hold again our hands,
— how soon, I think, shall I feel the slipping away of the
clasping fingers while I fall asleep by the wayside, or
climb the cloud-enveloped hills, and leave those I love
to journey on down the lonely Valley of Life?

And I say: "Surely the day and the hour hasten; grief
will be theirs for a season; then will they, as did I, with
brave hearts journey on the appointed way." But where
then shall my spirit rest? Will it sink unconscious into

endless night? or shall I, in some new dawn, and by some unimagined miracle not less than that which brought me here, wander, with those that led me once, and those I led, hand claspt in hand, as of old, by the murmuring waters and under the singing trees of the ever-wonderful, the never-ending Valley of Life?

TO ONE IMPATIENT OF FORM IN ART

I

CHIDE not the poet that he strives for beauty,
If still forthright he chants the thing he would —

If still he knows, nor can escape, the dire
Necessity and burden of straight speech;

Not his the fault should music haunt the stroke,
When to the marrow cleaves the lyric knife.

Who poured the violent ocean, and who called
Earthquake and tempest and the crash of doom,

He spread the sea all beautiful at dawn,
And curved the bright bow 'gainst the black, spent storm;

He framed these late and lovely violets
That under autumn leaves surprise the heart.

Blame not the seeker of beauty if his soul
Seeks it, in reverent and determined quest,

And in the sacred love of loveliness
Which God, the all-giver, gave — and satisfies;

Fearing lest he match not life's poignant breath
And the keen beauty of the blossoming day.

II

No poet he who knows not the great joy
That pulses in the flow and rush of rhythm,—

Rhythm which is the seed and life of life,
And of all art the root, and branch, and bloom,—

Knows not the strength that comes when vibrant thought
Beats 'gainst the bounds of fixèd time and space;

For law unto the master is pure freedom,
The prison-house a garden of delight.

So doth the blown breath from the bugle's walls
Issue in most triumphant melody;

So doth the impassioned poet's perfect verse,
Confined in law eternal, mate the stars.

TO THE POET

Let not thy listening spirit be abashed
By the majestic ranks of ancient bards
Or all the clarion singers of thy day:
For in thy true and individual song
Thou art a voice of nature; as the wind,
And cries of moving waters, and all shows
And speaking symbols of the universe
Are but the glorious sound and utterance
Of the mysterious power that spake the Word —
The immense first word that filled with splendid light
And vibrant potency the house of life;
Whose candles are a million, million stars,
Whose windows look on gulfs unthinkable
That bound our world. Think not on thine own self,

But on the enormous currents silently
That flood the unseen channels of still force,
Or with the sound of earthquake and the shout
Of circling storms complete an unknown doom.
   Thine is the fate and function mystical,
In forms of lyric and eternal art,
Clearly to utter and re-syllable
The primal Word: — So is thy verse of kin
To the sea-shell, the lily, and the leaf.
It hath a natural right and majesty,
Being of the infinite, all-evolving power
True jet and symbol; kin to the morning star
That in the sky of dawn sings with its mates.

COMPENSATION

THE Angel of Life stood forth on the threshold of Birth
And converse held with a spirit about to be born;
And the Angel announced to the Soul awaiting its world:
Choose thou! for now thou must choose, and never here-
      after.
And if thou to beauty shalt bow, to Beauty and Art,
And if to thy spirit all exquisite things be revealed,
If the fate of the poet be thine, if a god thou wouldst be,
If thou in thy soul wouldst joyfully seize and encompass
The glories and grandeurs of earth, the sweetness supreme,
The vision angelic, forbidden to eyes unanointed,
The melodies silent to all save the holy of spirit,
The signs and the secrets, the splendors, the exaltations,
If these thou shalt choose, if these thou wouldst know
      and impart,
Even so — but forget not the price of the infinite wisdom,
For the price of the passion of joy is the passion of sorrow,
And the cost of thy heaven is the burning and anguish of
      hell.

THE POET'S SECRET

THE secret — he has learned it
    And only, only he:
Heaven in his heart hath burned it;
    To him alone 't is free,
And them from him who learned it
    In wise simplicity.
From thousand suns it flashes,
    It leaps in flower and flame;
The spring, from winter's ashes,
    Cries out its silent name —
The secret of the ages
    That, to the poet came.
Unknown to all the sages,
    However wise they be,
Through his quick veins it rages
    And soul of ecstasy;
It lightnings from his pages,
    In all his songs 't is sung:
The secret of the ages —
    To be forever young.

"THE DAY BEGAN AS OTHER DAYS BEGIN"

THE day began as other days begin,
The round of work, the implacable city's din;
The New World's Babel, louder with each hour.
    Then in a by-way,— a still, secret bower,—
A temple given to silence and to books;
And in its heart a sacred nook of nooks.
There, in the silence, from a priceless store
Of written tomes, a guardian of their lore
A manuscript uplifted to my view,
With reverent, loving hands — and then withdrew.

Opening the book my gaze fell on that line
Wherein the marvelous poet, the divine
Singer of Endymion, his deathless song
Began, and so beginning made immortal.
O dead, undying bard! now all the wrong
Fate did thee rose; through Memory's drapèd portal
Trooped, in wan figures, all thy tragic story —
But mightier still the wonder and the glory
Of that white page whereon thy soul was poured.
Then with thy spirit my spirit likewise soared;
Something immortal entered in this breast
Miraculously; and like one confessed
And throughly shriven, back to the world I turned
While a new heart within me flamed and burned.

And yet that morn, when grew the glare and din,
The day began, as other days begin.

A POET'S QUESTION

WHAT, then, shall make these songs of mine more real;
More tuneful, piercing, bright — miraculous,
As art should be? Shall some high, fortunate chant,
Some song to come, flood backward on them all, —
Over every word in all the singing flock, —
A light, a meaning; a power to seize, to thrill;
A swift beatitude and haunting beauty;
Shall make of them a trouble to the base,
Scourge to the false, sun to the darkened soul,
Help to the fainting, succor to the bruised,
A judgment to the heeding and unheeding?
Or shall a flame leap from the singer's flight,
Making them luminous in sudden dawn —
Bright in the chrism of Death.

PRELUDE FOR "A BOOK OF MUSIC"

WITHOUT intent, I find a book I've writ
And music is the pleasant theme of it;
For tho' I can no music make, I trust
Here's proof I love it.
                      Tho' no reasoning fine
Should any ask to show this art divine,
Yet have I known even poets who refuse
To name pure music as an equal muse.
If music pleased them, 't was not deeply felt,
And in its charms they deemed it shame to melt;
For that, they held, it is an art where might
Even children give its votaries delight,
And therefore lacking in the things of mind.

But 't is not argued well. There is a kind
Of music that a little child can give,
Echoing great masters; but the masters live
Not in such echo — elfish, immature;
'T is but a part of them. Ah, be ye sure
Tho' lovely, not the loveliest; that must wait
For him who noble moods can recreate
With solemn, subtile, and deep-thoughted art
That wins the mind or e'er it takes the heart.
For that a child may gracious music make
Is but a sign that music doth partake
Of something deep, primeval, that began
When God dreamed of Himself, and fashioned man.
'T is near the source of being; it repeats
The vibrancy that runs in rhythmic beats
Through all the shaken universe; and tho'
Its language shall take not the ebb and flow
Of speech articulate, it is that tone

Cleaves closer to life's core; the thing alone
Well-nigh it is, not thought about the thing;
No pictured flight across a painted sky —
The bird itself, the beating of its wing;
The pang that is a cry;
Not human language, but pure ecstasy.

In this my BOOK OF MUSIC which hath come
As does a lover's litany by some
Miraculous chance, with added song to song,
I trust I have my Lady done no wrong,
My Lady of Melody I worshipt long.

Blameless the artist praises the sweet rose
If in his art he aim not to compose
An image, all inanimate, that seeks
To copy shrewdly those inviolate cheeks
Or the rich, natural odor imitate;
But shows, as best he can, its grace and state,
The love that in him burns for this fair flower,
And all his joy therein, for one sweet hour.
Nor shall the poet subtly strive to phrase
For any heart save his what music says;
For,— as before the autumn skies and woods,—
A meaning gleams through our own human moods:
Yet is the meaning real; and many a wound
Wherewith our spirits are beaten to the ground
Heals 'neath the sanctity of noble sound.

Ah, not to match the music of the wires
Or trembling breath, the instruments and choirs,
But to tell truly how that moves the soul
In the impassionate and rhythmic word,
By poesy's proper art — which must be heard

Even as music is! Not to forget
The viol and the harp, the clarinet,
The booming organ; too, the intertwined
Voices wherewith the sounding, rich clavier,
Struck by the master's hand, enchants the ear—
If so may be to catch a fleeting strain
And in new art imprison it again!
Then let him list to music who would rhyme;
For every art, tho' separate, may learn,
From the great souls in all, how to make burn
Brighter the light of beauty through all time.
And scorn not thou to read of music's power
Over one soul that in great humbleness
His memory brings of many a happy hour,
Hoping these echoed tones some wounded heart may
    bless.

MUSIC AT TWILIGHT

I

O, GIVE me music in the twilight hour!
Then, skilled musician! thou of the magic power,
Summon the souls of masters long since gone
Who through thine art live on!

As the day dies I would once more respire
The passion of that spirit whose keen fire
Flashes and flames in yearning and unrest
And never-ending quest.

Or listen to the quick, electric tones,
Or moods of majesty, of him who owns
The secret of the thrill that shakes the earth
And moves the stars in mirth

And I would walk the shore of sound with him
Whose voice was as the voice of cherubim:
Musician most authentic and sublime
Of all the sons of time.

Bring their deep joys, the breath of solitudes,
Dear dreams and longings, and high, hero moods;
Ay, bring me their melodious despairs
To die in twilight airs.

For, given a rhythmic voice, re-uttered so,
Sorrow itself is lost in the large flow
Of nature; and of life is made such part
As doth enrich the heart;

And on the tide of music, to my soul
Shall enter beauty's solace — life be whole,
Not broken by chords discordant, but most sweet,
In sequent tones complete.

II

Great is the true interpreter, for like
No other art, two sentient souls must strike
The spark of music that in blackness lies
'Mid silent harmonies,

Till, at a cunning touch, the long-lost theme
Newly imagined, and new-born in dream,
Clothed gloriously in garment of sweet sound
Wakes from its darkened swound.

So would I ask, Musician! of thy grace
That thou wouldst bless and sanctify the place
With august harmonies, well-loved of old; —
But from thy manifold

Miraculous memory fail not of thine own
Imaginings enraptured of pure tone,
That I may nearer draw to music's shrine,
And mystery divine.

MUSIC IN MOONLIGHT

WAS ever music lovelier than to-night?
'T was Schumann's Song of Moonlight; o'er the vale
The new moon lingered near the western hills;
The hearth-fire glimmered low; but melting tones
Blotted all else from memory and thought,
And all the world was music. Wondrous hour!
Then sank anew into our trancèd hearts
One secret and deep lesson of sweet sound —
The loveliness that from unloveliness
Outsprings, flooding the soul with poignant joy,
As the harmonious chords to harsh succeed,
And the rapt spirit climbs through pain to bliss:
Eternal question, answer infinite;
As day to night replies; as light to shade;
As summer to rough winter; death to life —
Death not a closing, but an opening door;
A deepened life, a prophecy fulfilled.
    Not in the very present comes reply,
But in the flow of time. Should the song cease
Too soon; ere yet the rooted answer blooms,
Lo, what a pang of loss and dissonance!
But time with the resolving and intended tone
Heals all, and makes all beautiful and right.
Even so our mortal music-makers frame
Their messages melodious to men;
Even so the Eternal His high harmonies
Fashions, supreme, of life, and fate, and time.

THE UNKNOWN SINGER

ONE singer in the oratorio,
Her only did I see, nor can forget;
Nor knew her name, nor have I seen her more,
Nor could I in the chorus find her voice.
Her swaying, gracious form, her face alight
As with an inner flame of melody —
These seized me; seemed the white embodiment
Of all the angelic voices richly poured
In a great rushing and harmonious flood.
That human form, all beautiful and bright,
Lived the pure, conscious, glorious instrument
Wherethrough the master made his message felt —
Conscious, but with no shallow vanity,
A breathing image of a thought in sound,
A living statue, symbol of a tone.
That which she sang she was; and, unaware,
Made music visible not less than heard.

THE VOICE

RICH is the music of sweet instruments, —
The separate harp, cornet, oboe, and flute,
The deep-souled viola, the 'cello grave,
The many-mooded, singing violin,
The infinite, triumphing, ivoried clavier;
And when, with art mysterious, some god
Thrills into one the lone and various tones,
Then is no hiding passion of the heart,
No sigh of evening winds, no breath of dawn,
No hope or hate of man that is not told.
    But when a human voice leaps from that surge,
'T is as a flower that bursts from th' trembling earth;

Something more wonderful assails the soul,
As, with exultant cries, up-curving, swift,
The shrill Walküre clamor against the sky,
Or pale Brünhilde moans her bitter fate.

WAGNER

THIS is the eternal mystery of art:
He told the secretest secret of his heart —
How many mortals, with quick-flaming brow,
Whispered, "Lo, this am I — and that art thou!"

"THE PATHETIC SYMPHONY"

(TSCHAIKOWSKY)

WHEN the last movement fell, I thought: Ah, me!
Death this indeed; but still the music poured
On and still on. O, deathlier it grew,
And then, at last, my beating heart stood still—
Beyond all natural grief the music passing,
Beyond all tragedy, or last farewell.
Then, on that fatal tide, dismayed I felt
This living soul, my own, without one tear,
Slowly, irrevocably, and alone,
Enter the ultimate silence and the dark.

MACDOWELL

REJOICE! Rejoice!
The New World hath a voice;
A voice of tragedy and mirth,
Sounding clear through all the earth;
A voice of music, tender and sublime,
Kin to the master-music of all time.

Hear ye, and know,—
While the chords throb with poignant pause and flow,—
Of the New World the mystic, lyric heart,
Breathed in undaunted art:
Her pomp of days, her glittering nights;
The rich surprise
And miracle of iridescent skies;
Her lovely lowlands and imperial hights;
Her glooms and gladness;
Her oceans thundering on a thousand shores;
Her wild-wood madness;
Her streams adream with memory that deplores
The red inhabitants evanished and undone
That follow, follow to far lands beyond the setting
    sun.
And echoes one may hear of ancient lores
From the Old World's well-loved shores—
Primal loves, and quenchless hates;
Striving lives, and conquering fates;
Elves innocently antic
Or wild-eyed, frantic;
Shadow-heroes, passionate, gigantic—
Sons and daughters of the prime
That moved the mighty bards to noble rhyme.
    Rejoice! Rejoice!
The New World hath new music, and a voice.

A FANTASY OF CHOPIN

(GABRILOWITSCH)

LIGHTNINGS and tremblings and a voice of thunder;
    But when the winds are down, and spent the showers—
At the vast mountain's base, the sheer cliffs under,
    How sweet the summer flowers!

"HOW STRANGE THE MUSICIAN'S MEMORY"

How strange the musician's memory, never wrong
In symphony, sonata, fugue, or song!
Sees he the score with wide, unseeing eyes,
Or is it sound his heart doth memorize?
What is it like? Behold, from out the west,
The long light on the wild wave's flying crest.
See the swift gleam rush up the leaning strand
And die in foam upon the singing sand.

"IN A NIGHT OF MIDSUMMER"

In a night of midsummer, on the still eastern shore of
the ocean inlet,

In our hearts a sense of the inaudible pulsings of the
unseen, infinite sea,

Suddenly through the clear, cool air, arose the voice of
a wonderful tenor; soaring and sobbing in the music of
"Otello."

I knew that the singer was long dead; I knew well that
it was not his living voice;

And yet truly it was as the voice of a living man; tho'
heard as through a veil, still was it human; still was it
living; still was it tragic;

Still felt I the fire of the spirit of a man; I was moved
by the passion of his art; I perceived the flower and
essence of his person; the exquisite expression of his
mind and soul;

His soul it was that seized my soul, through his voice,
which was as the very voice of sorrow;

And then I thought: If man, by science and searching, can build a cunning instrument that takes over and
keeps, beyond the term of human existence, the essence
and flower of a man's art;

If he can recreate that most individual attribute, his
articulate and musical voice, and thus the very art and
passion which that voice conveys,

Why may not the Supreme Artificer, when the human
body is utterly dissolved and dispersed, recover and keep
forever, in some new and delicate structure, the living
soul itself?

IN THE WHITE MOUNTAINS

MOUNTAINS in whose vast shadows live great names,
On whose firm pillars rest mysterious dawns,
And sunsets that redream the apocalypse;
A world of billowing green that, veil on veil,
Turns a blue mist and melts in lucent skies;
A silent world, save for slow waves of wind,
Or sudden, hollow clamor of huge rocks
Beaten by valleyed waters manifold; —
Airs that to breathe is life and joyousness;
Days dying into music; nights whose stars
Shine near, and large, and lustrous; these, O these,
These are for memory to life's ending hour.

JOHN PAUL JONES

I

BEHOLD our first great warrior of the sea
Who, in our war to make the half world free,
His knightly sword in noble anger drew!
Born to the Old, he visioned clear the New.

II

Born to the New — and shall we lose our faith
And mourn for freedom as a fleeing wraith?
Or heroes swift as he, and valorous, find
In bloodless battles of the unfettered mind!

TO EMMA LAZARUS

(1905)

DEAR bard and prophet, that thy rest is deep
  Thanks be to God! Not now on thy heart falls
Rumor intolerable. Sleep, O sleep!
  See not the blood of Israel that crawls,
Warm yet, into the noon and night; that cries
  Even as of old, till all the world stands still
  At rapine that even to Israel's agonies
  Seems strange and monstrous, a mad dream of ill.
Thou sleepest! Yea, but as in grief we said:
  There is a spiritual life unconquerable;
  So, bard of the ancient people, tho' being dead
Thou speakest, and thy voice we love full well.
  Never thy holy memory forsakes us;
  Thy spirit is the trumpet that awakes us!

CARL SCHURZ

IN youth he braved a monarch's ire
  To set the people's poet free;
Then gave his life, his fame, his fire
  To the long praise of liberty.

His life, his fame, his all he gave
That not on earth should live one slave;
True freedom of the soul he sought
And in that battle well he fought.

He fought, and yet he loved not war,
  But looked and labored for the day
When the loud cannon silent are
  And holy peace alone hath sway.

Ah, what a life! From youth to age
Keeping the faith, in noble rage.
Ah, what a life! From knightly youth
Servant and champion of the truth.

Not once, in all his length of days,
    That falchion flashed for paltry ends;
So wise, so pure, his words and ways,
    Even those he conquered rose his friends.

For went no rancor with the blow;
The wrong and not the man, his foe.
He smote not meanly, not in wrath;
That truth might speed he cleaved a path.

The lure of place he well could scorn
    Who knew a mightier joy and fate —
The passion of the hope forlorn,
    The luxury of being great,

The deep content of souls serene
Who gain or lose with equal mien;
Defeat his spirit not subdued
Nor victory marred his noble mood.

GEORGE MACDONALD

Ah, loving, exquisite, enraptured soul,
Who wert to me a father and a friend;
Who imaged and brought near, all humanly,
The sweetness and the majesty of him
Who in Judea melted human hearts,
And won the world by loveliness and love;
Dear spirit, who to the Infinite Purity
Past, without change, and humbly unabashed —

If farewell we must say, it is that thou
So far beyond, above, we,— alien so
From grace like thine,— may hardly follow close
Thy shining feet in fields of endless light
When to the goal of souls reborn we pass.

Yet couldst thou not rest happy in that world
Thou saw'st with eyes anointed, near that Christ
Who was to thee a human brother and friend,
If we, thy brothers, with thee came not nigh.

If ever saint with the Eternal strove,
Then wouldst thou, wilt thou, strive and supplicate
That not one soul be lost or suffer ill,
If so may be, but win to the Infinite Love
That was the faith, strength, life of all thy days.

Our hearts are heavy; O, yet give we thanks,
As thou didst give when died one dear to thee,
Thanks that thou livedst — that we knew and loved,
Even in the flesh, one who was one with God.

JOSEPHINE SHAW LOWELL

IT was but yesterday she walked these streets,
Making them holier. How many years,
With all her widowed love, immeasurably
She ministered unto the abused and stricken,
And all the oppressed and suffering of mankind;
Herself forgetting, but never those in need;
Her whole, sweet soul lost in her loving work;
Pondering the endless problem of the poor.

In ceaseless labor, swift, unhurriedly,
She sped upon her tireless ministries,
Climbing the stairs of poverty and wrong,

Endeavoring the help that shall not hurt,
Seeking to build in every human heart
A temple of justice — that no brother's burden
Should heavier prove through human selfishness.

In memory I see that brooding face
That now seemed dreaming of the heroic past
When those most dear to her laid loyal lives
On the high altar of freedom; and again
That thinking, inward-lighted countenance
Drooped, saddened by the pain of humankind,
Tho' resolute to help where help might be,
And with undying faith illuminate.

She was our woman of sorrows, whose pure heart
Was pierced by many woes; and yet long since
Her soul of sympathy entered the peace
And calm eternal of the eternal mind;
Inheritor of noble lives, she held,
Even to the end, a spirit of cheerfulness,
And knowledge keen of the deep joy of being
By pain all unsubdued. Sister and saint,
Who to life's darkened passageways brought light,
Who taught the dignity of human service,
Who made the city noble by her life,
And sanctified the very stones her feet
Prest in their sacred journeys!
                              Most High God!
This city of mammon, this wide, seething pit
Of avarice and lust, hath known Thy saints,
And yet shall know. For faith than sin is mightier,
And by this faith we live — that in Thy time,
In Thine own time, the good shall crush the ill;
The brute within the human shall die down;

And love and justice reign, where hate prevents —
That love which in pure hearts reveals Thine own
And lights the world to righteousness and truth.

"ONE ROSE OF SONG"

(MARY PUTNAM JACOBI)

ONE rose of song
For one sweet deed
On her grave I fling.
But, O, how can I sing
When she takes no heed!

My rose of song
For a fragrant deed,
Tho' she takes no heed,
Still must I bring.

Tho' she needs no praise,
Tho' she hears not my song
On her journey long
In the new, strange ways —
O still must I sing,
My rose I must fling,
Just to ease my heart
Of the sorrow and smart.

In a far-off land
She stretched forth her hand
To me and to mine.
And now, for a sign,
This song I sing
And this rose I bring.

Tho' she take no heed
On her journey long,

Yet a soul shall hear,
Some soul shall take heed,
And the rose and the deed,
They shall sow their seed.

JOHN MALONE

THIS actor in great Shakespeare's shadow moved;
He thought his thoughts, he lived in Shakespeare's age.
His were the tenets of that mighty stage:
Therefore we mourn; therefore was he beloved.

"LOST LEADERS"

I

"LOST leaders" — no, they are not lost
Like shrunken leaves the wild wind tost.
Them only shall we mourn who failed;
When came the fight — who faltered, quailed.

II

Raged not through blood and battle grime
These heroes of our land and time;
The foes they fought, with dauntless deed,
Were shameless vice and maddened greed.

III

Not lost, not lost the noble dead —
By them our doubting feet are led.
Stars of our dark, sun of our day,
They guide, they light the climbing way.

IV

And if, in their celestial flight,
The mist hath hid those forms from sight,

Still, down the stormy path, we hear
Their hero-voices ringing clear.

v

Who for their fellows live and die,
They the immortals are. O sigh
Not for their loss, but rather praise
The God that gave them to our days.

ON A CERTAIN "AGNOSTIC"

AGNOSTIC! Ah, what idle name for him
Who knew — not the untruths of fables old,
Cherished in fear, or arrant ignorance;
Who knew — not the shrewd structures of keen minds
Intent on their own shrewdness; losing quite
The inner truth in outward scaffoldings,
Cunning appearances, and schemes involved;
But who knew well the central verity:
That honest thought followed, without dismay,
Unto the bitter and accepted end,
Is the one way to wisdom in this world;
Who knew not creeds, but could not help but follow
The feet of him who loved his fellow-men;
Who knew that human service is true life;
Who knew deep friendship, lived this knowledge out,
As few called "friends" have ever dared to live;
And who knew well the sacred truth of love.
Ah, call him not unknowing, for he knew
The truth of truth — the gods can know no more.

"A WEARY WASTE WITHOUT HER"

"A WEARY waste without her?" Ah, but think!
   You who were blest with the most sweet, most near

Knowledge of that high nature; who could drink
At her fresh spirit's fountain, year by year —
What were the past without her? And her dear
Image and memory — did they, too, sink
Into the abyss? — Herself was yours, and here
Still lives remembrance; a bright, golden link
'Twixt this, the visible world, and the unknown
Toward which we journey — where she now doth live,
Close to the Eternal One. Make thou no moan;
What else may pass, this twofold gift endures;
Give thanks, and mourn not, then. — But, O, forgive!
How can I chide who mix my tears with yours?

THE POET'S SLEEP

> In spite of it all I am going to sleep. Put out the lights.
> THOMAS BAILEY ALDRICH.

EVER when slept the poet his dreams were music,
And in sweet song lived the dear dream once more.
So when from sleep and dreams again he wakes,—
Out from the world of symbols passing forth
Into that spirit-world where all is real,—
What memoried music, new and exquisite,
Shall strike on ears celestial — where he walks
Reverent among the immortal melodists!

WHERE SPRING BEGAN

THE days were cold, and clouded. On a day
Before the seasonable warmth and sun
The poet died. We bore him to the tomb
And, under wreaths and flowers, we laid him down.
Then came a burst of sunshine. Bright it poured
On the banked blossoms and the leafless trees.
There, at the poet's grave, the spring began.

AVARICE

They said, "God made him," ah, the clean, great God!
  Perhaps! Even as He made the loathèd beast
  Whose use is to take offal for his feast;
  As He made viper and vermin or, at a nod,
Made hell, to do some necessary part
  In His wide-stretched, inscrutable universe.
  Yes, haply God imagined him for a curse,
  A scourge, a vengeance; with slow, patient art
Him did He fashion cunningly; saying: "This
  My sign and warning, to time's distant end,
  That all a loveless life is may be known,
And desolate horror of pure avarice;
  The world is his, — a world without a friend, —
  Without one friend an honest man would own."

PITY THE BLIND

I

"Pity the blind!" Yes, pity those
  Whom day and night inclose
  In equal dark; to whom the sun's keen flame
  And pitchy night-time are the same.

II

But pity most the blind
  Who cannot see
That to be kind
  Is life's felicity.

PROOF OF SERVICE

Thou who wouldst serve thy country and thy kind,
Winning the praise of honorable men

And love of many hearts — know the true proof
Of faithfulness lies not therein. That dwells
In the lone consciousness of duty done,
And in the scorn and contumely of souls
Self-soiled with sin: the necessary hate
Of perjured and contaminated spirits
For that whose mere existence brings reproach,
Shame, and despair for something lost forever.
When thou hast won the hatred of the vile,
Then know thou hast served well thy fellow-men.

CONQUERED

In thine anger it was said:
"Would that mine enemy were dead."
Or, if thou saidest naught,
That was thy thought.
Now thou cryest, night and day:
"Mine enemy hath conquered in our fight,
In that he fled away
Into the darkness and the night,
Ere I to justice wakened and the right.
Now this through all the anguished hours I say,
As with my soul my soul doth strive:
Would God mine enemy were alive!"

BLAME

(A MEMORY OF EISLEBEN, THE PLACE OF LUTHER'S
BIRTH AND DEATH)

In a far, lonely land at last I came
Unto a town made great by one great fame.
Born here, here died the noblest of his time,
Whose memory makes his century sublime.

But, O my God! I was not happy there,
For down below, in dark and caverned air,
Outstretched and cramped, the pallid miners lay.
Their shortened lives, their absence from the day,
Burdened my spirit with a sense of blame.
Now you, and you — I see you flush with shame.

THE WHISPERERS

(NEW YORK, 1905)

In the House of State at Albany,— in shadowy corridors and corners,— the whisperers whispered together.

In sumptuous palaces in the great city men talked intently, with mouth to ear.

Year in and year out they whispered, and talked, and no one heard save those who listened close.

Now in the Hall of the City the whisperers again are whispering, the talkers are talking.

They who once conversed so quietly, secretly, with shrugs and winks and finger laid beside nose — what has happened to their throats?

For speak they never so low, their voices are as the voices of trumpets; whisper they never so close, their words are like alarm bells rung in the night.

Every whisper is a shout, and the noise of their speech goes forth like thunders.

They cry as from the housetops — their voices resound up and down the streets; they echo from village to village and from city to city.

Over prairies and mountains and across the salt sea their whispers go hissing and shouting.

They say the thing they would not say, and quickly the shameful thing clamors back and forth over the round world;

And when they would fain cease their saying, they may not, for a clear-voiced Questioner is as the finger of fate and the crack of doom.

What they would hide they reveal, what they would cover they make plain;

What they feared to speak aloud to one another, unwilling they publish to all mankind;

And the people listen with bowed heads, wondering and in grief;

And wise men, and they who love their country, turn pale and ask: "What new shame will come upon us?"

And again they ask, "Are these they in whose keep are the substance and hope of the widow and the fatherless?"

And the poor man, plodding home with his scant earnings from his hard week's work, hears the voices, with bitterness in his soul.

And thieves, lurking in dark places and furtively seizing that which is not their own; and the petty and cowardly briber, and he who is bribed, nudge one another;

And the anarch and the thrower of bombs clap hands together, and cry out: "Behold these our allies!"

BEFORE THE GRAND JURY

A WOMAN, who has been a man's desire,
Now cast aside like ashes from a fire,
With startled breath, confessing all her shame,
Here,— looking in the faces of strange men,
Who probe remorselessly their "where" and "when," —
Falters her dreadful story, that the blame
May strike on the betrayer. In that glare
Plead piteous answers hardly might she dare
Murmur, at midnight, on a mother's breast.

Was ever secret misery confest
To such grim audience!
                    O hapless fate
For this sweet girl, and for her guiltier mate.
    Powers of the world, and O, ye Powers Unseen,
Be stern, yet be ye kind! Let be the ends
Of justice served; but hold a shield between
Souls and the smiting sword. O, make amends
In the oncoming years, or some far age.
They are but caught in Nature's deathless rage;
The fire that in their bodies burned doth hold
The sun in heaven; part is it of the force
That keeps the stars each on its mystic course,
While the all-changing universe grows never old.

"IN THE CITIES"

I

In the cities no longer the blaring of trumpets that sum-
        mon to battle,
From splendid towers the banners flash not forth in the
        breeze,
No longer the ringing of war-bells, and the clattering
        sound of horsemen,
The clangor of sword on shield, nor the cries of the feudal
        fighters
Hurrying into the streets to strike with bullet and steel;
Clamoring, battering down; assailing high walls and
        towers;
Rushing maddened, furious, to the killing of fellow-
        men.

II

Yet still a clangor of bells and a loud, shrill whistling
        and shouting,

But the sharp, quick sounds that startle proclaim not
    anger but mercy.
For now, like winds and thunders, flash by the glittering
    engines,
And the wagons, with ladders and axes, laden with well-
    trained men
Eager to quench the flame, to scale the dangerous battle-
    ments;
Eager to risk their lives in the hissing blaze and the smoke
That blinds, and that grips the throat like the throttling
    hand of murder.

III

On come the engines and wagons, and the Chief in his
    hooting chariot,
And a boy, who hears them careering, rushes out to the
    crossing of ways,
And, swinging his arms and shouting, clears a path for
    the shrieking engine,
That rushes like winds and thunders down a vale of death
    and destruction —
And every man, at his post, on the winds of the human
    tempest,
Mad for the saving of lives of men and of women and
    children —
To creep to the edge of death, to swing in dizzying chasms,
To save the children of strangers, forgetting their own
    in their madness;
And then if a comrade fall, how wild each man to the
    rescue,
Plunging into the pit, poisoned, choked, unconscious;
Revived, they struggle back 'gainst their officers' yelled
    commandings —
Mad, mad, mad, for the saving of human life.

IV

And now, in the days of peace, no squadron charging by,
But hark! down the street a sharp reiterant stroke and
    clamor,
A rhythmic beating of hoofs, a galloping louder, closer,
And again a youth leaps quick to the crossing of crowded
    ways,
And he swings his arms and shouts, and clears, through
    the human currents,
A path for the ringing ambulance, hurrying, hurrying,
    hurrying
To a place where a child has fallen, is wounded nigh
    unto death,
That the child may be tenderly lifted and skillfully nursed
    and tended —
Engine and hurrying ambulance screaming, ringing,
    impatient,
Filling the frightened streets with echoes of old-time wars,
Laden with men of might, skilled and fierce and deter-
    mined —
Not as of old to maim, to harry and scatter destruction;
Not to take life, but to save it; not to kill, but to rescue
    the perishing.

A TRAGEDY OF TO-DAY

(NEW YORK, 1905)

I

In a little theater, in the Jewry of the New World, I
sat among the sad-eyed exiles;
Narrow was the stage and meagerly appointed, and
the players gave themselves up utterly to their art;
And, before our eyes, were enacted scenes of a play
that scarcely seemed a play.

The place was a city in a wide, unhappy land;

Even in that empire which drifts to-day like a great ship toward a black and unknown coast;

While men, with blanched faces, cry out: "Unless the tempest abates quickly, behold the mightiest wreck on all the shores of time!"

And the time of the drama was our own time; and the coming and the going; and the people themselves were of our own day and generation;

The people, with strange beards, and look of the im-memorial Orient; like those men and women who, alien and melancholy, plod the New-World streets;

Like those who, in slow and pitiful procession, on a fixed day of mourning, with dirges and wailings, poured innumerous into the city's open places;

And, as the play went on, at times the very speech of the actors, in hot debate, crackled and sputtered like the fuse of a Russian bomb.

And there an old man, the preacher of a hunted race and a despised religion, all alone called to his people to follow him, and their God, the God of Israel.

Passionately he proclaimed the faith of the fathers and the saving word and protecting arm of the Almighty;

He, the voice and the prophet of the Lord High God, called aloud to them who strayed: —

"Come ye back to your God, and to His Everlasting Word.

"Ye young men who have forgotten Him, the Un-forgetting, and ye old men mumbling your prayers; ye cowards! leaving the holy shrine unprotected";

And the young men answered and called the old man the name of them who are dead and have passed away;

And the old men, unheeding, swayed to and fro, mum-bling their ancient psalms and ineffectual supplications.

Then, while the noise of the beastly rabble swelled

louder and nearer — then did the preacher turn once more to the Lord of Hosts, lifting up his voice in praise and prayer, and faith unquenchable;

Crying to God with a loud voice and saying: — "Lead me, Thou Jehovah! in the right way,

"For now hath come the great day of the Lord; now, Lord, save Thy people and bless Thy heritage,

"Thou who wert, and art, and ever shalt be! Show now Thy Almightiness, send Thy miracle as lightning from on high."

Nearer and nearer came the curses and shrieks and the wailing lamentations; and men and women fled, wounded, before the infamous and infuriate avengers;

Then the crash of guns and the terror of carnage and rapine unspeakable;

And, in the midst, the voice of an old man crying to heaven, and falling smitten and dead before the shrine of the God of Israel.

And, listening, I heard not only the sounds of the mimic drama — but, louder and more dreadful, the panting of miserable women who welcomed death, the deliverer;

And from Kishineff and Odessa I heard, once more crying to heaven, the outpoured blood of the Jew.

II

And still as I listened and dreamed, the crimson flood widened to a great and lustrous pool,

And looking therein I saw reflected the faces of many known well to my heart and to the hearts of all the world,

For there were the features of mighty warriors and makers of laws and leaders of men; of poets inspired and of painters and musicians; and of famed philosophers, and of men and women who loved, and labored for, their kind;

And the faces of preachers and prophets; of those who fervently cursed the unrighteous, and who to a world in darkness brought light everlasting;

And chief of all I saw in that crimson mirror the face of him whose spirit was bowed beneath the agonies of all mankind.

THE OLD HOUSE

I

Home of my forebears, home of my dreaming childhood,
House that I love with a love instinctive, changeless,
Ancestral, mystical, passionate, tender, sorrowful;
Old house where I was born and my mother before me —
Strangely the old house speaks to its child returning,
Speaks with a tone affectionate, intimate, sweet,
Made, mysterious, out of the voices of many —
Out of the accents of them, the loving, the loyal,
That still in memory soothe and murmur and call;
Voices that greeted my life and guided the journey,
Human voices, long hushed, and the subtler speech
That steals from the dumb, dead walls, and whispers and
        thrills,
From the shadowy chimney-places, and haunted nooks;
These centuried walls, this roof, and the buoyant branches
Of large-leaved, mottled buttonwoods, towering mightily,
And pines that my father planted, now loftily dying —
These are the vibrant notes of the one deep chord
That sings in my heart, here by the ancient hearthstone.

II

Five are the generations this place have humaned,
Leaving their impress, I think, on the breathèd air —
For full is the house of relics of lives departed:

Carvings strange that some wanderer here enharbored,
Bringing the Orient's touch to the wondering child;
And Arctic gatherings; hints of the torrid zone;
And quaint embroideries worked by hands ancestral,
Deft for the spinning of flax on these silent wheels;
Books of a day when each was a treasure, a star —
And chief of them all, to the trembling heart of a boy,
The verse of him, the singer of song sonorous,
Whose voice was the voice of trumpets and many waters,
Whose soul went forth with angels and archangels,
Nor stood dismayed before the Eternal presence.

Pictures of faces whose features I see in my own —
That I see re-imaged by laws unfathomed, fateful,
In my own children's pleading, innocent faces;
Volumes of lores outgrown, or a living art;
Bibles and books of devotion, where names are enrolled
In letters that fade like the image of souls long dead.
Not without tears may I ponder the yellowing leaves
Where record was made of secretest dreams and
        prayers —
Records of love accomplished, or unfulfilled.
Were the agèd faces I knew, the timorous maidens
Who, wistful, their innocent passions here hinted, or hid?
This wife new-married, so young, so sweet, so appealing,
Was this the angelical mother, she of great sorrows,
Loving and dreaming in age, as in palpitant girlhood?
This lock, among many a tress so lovingly treasured —
Ah, this is my own, by hands that I knew so well,
Cut from a golden head that long has been silvered.

III

The old house speaks, and low, in the glimmering twilight,
It murmurs of days that are gone, and spirits lamented;
A girlish face with a smile all radiant, loving —

Sweet cousin mine! where, in the land of shadows,
Doth that smile illume, that voice bring joy as of old?
This quaint and closeted chamber, ah, here was unfolded
The love of a child for a child, through years and
    through sorrows
Remembered and cherished by each,— the love of the old
For the old, now,— the love of the old for lost youth
And comrades long gone, and loved and remembered
    together.

And she with the heart of a queen, and the soul of a
    martyr;
In young days serene, and blithe and undaunted in age,
Who loved the old house, even as I,— her birthplace,
    her refuge,—
She in a vision comes near; and quick I remember
One night of all nights, when a messenger stood in the
    doorway —
Silent he stood, and we knew the message unspoken!
O night of nights, when a wife turned sudden a widow,
And a child, 'neath the solacing stars, passed swift into
    manhood.

IV

But of childhood the old house whispers and murmurs
    to-night,
Of the twilight hour in the arms of her the beloved
And loving sister of her who gave me my being —
Who like a second mother encompassed my childhood
With song and with story, with gleams of fairy and hero,
Chanting in twilight gray the ancient ballads,
Or crooning, as if to herself, the love-songs of girlhood;
Or, again, she fashioned the tales of her own young days:
Of the country balls, in the time when winter was winter,
And the snows were piled — high as the head of a man,
And the ringing sleighs sped over the fields and the fences

To the revels and routs in the taverns of long ago;
When the dancing would last till dawn, and the dancers
    flew
From village to village, and tavern to tavern, all night;
Turning the snow-lit dark to rollicking day.
O days and nights of a far and happy world!

V

Of childhood the old house whispers, of wintry sports
With sled and skate on the ponds long filled and forgotten;
Wild joys of meadow, and woods, and waters; of branches
Laden with black-heart cherries, where boys and birds
Alternate shared the wealth of the aery feast.
Of boyhood the old house whispers, of moonlit voyages
On the wooded stream, that wound in silent reaches,
Far through the mystic land of awakening life.

VI

And now, in the twilight hour, dear, living voices,
The voices of children I hear, they come to my call;
And I tell of the days that are gone, and they hark with
    delight—
As I, in my youth, heard the tales of the ancient days;
Then good-night, and to bed! But the teller of ancient
    tales
Stays by the dying fire and listens, again,
To the thronging voices that murmur to him alone.

"THERE'S NO PLACE LIKE THE OLD PLACE!"

I

    BACK to the old place I've come home again,
    Back at last from the big town,

After so many hard and struggling years;
Back to the old home, the old home in the mountains,
In the valley of childhood;
And I say to myself, again and again I say:
There's no place like the old place!

II

Here once more I wander, here, in the valley of brooks,
I wander a stranger — where every spring and tree and
    rock is familiar.
The little brooks tinkle down, with the old music, through
    the pine-darkened gorges;
The brooks that sometimes run dry, or hide under the
    smooth stones;
In the time of fullness leaping from ledge to ledge down
    to the big brook that never dries;
Where the trout dartle and the pools are shadowy and
    cool
And good to the hot body of a boy.
Lovely, with an intimate loveliness, is the valley,
And again and again I chant to myself:
O, there's no place like the old place!

III

There's no place like the old place!
Strangely nearer seem the walls of the valley,
Tho' far and spacious as ever the mysterious sunset.
Never before have I felt so intensely the beauty of it all —
How well-shaped the double valley;
The upper valley like a great, green bowl,
And the lower valley opening out toward the sunset like a
    trumpet;
The mountains embowered with evergreens, and maples,
    and chestnuts —

Or lying naked in the sun,
Scraped bare by the ancient glacier,
Scoured by rains and scarred by lightnings,
And with a look as if the salt sea had beaten and bitten
      there for a thousand years.

IV

Stately and gracious with elms and willows are the
      smooth and grassy meadows
Leveled for human use by the lakes of untold ages,
Then covered with forests, that the pioneers uprooted —
Rich now and full of peace; bringing back the well-loved
      images of the Bible;
Meadows where first I heard the swift song of the bobo-
      link,
Throbbing and ringing madly, back and forth in the
      meadow air,
And whence, in full summer, after a long, hot day
The boy that was I came back to the home barn
Royally charioted on the high-piled, sweet-scented hay.
Ah, there's no place like the old place!

V

There, under the hill, is the homestead;
How large the maples have grown that the old folks
      planted!
Sweet was the sap in the spring and the shade in the
      summer.
I never knew such water as from the spring at our house,
Running cold as ice in the kitchen and out in the barn.
And the little window up there was mine!
I tell you I slept well, and rose early in those days,
Tho' sometimes at night after a long rain, or when the
      ice was melting in Hayes's pond,

I could scarce sleep for the brook roaring like Niagara,
As it leapt the mill-dams and spread out over the meadows,
Scurrying great logs along, and every footbridge in the valley.
But most times it was quiet enough at the old home —
The dear old place, the old place that's the best place!

VI

O, there's no place like the old place, and no time like the old time!
The chores were rough, but the keener the zest for the play!
For chestnuting in the frosty autumn,
For the tug of the bass at Goose pond and the lake at Monterey,
And the day of fun at the county fair;
For the skim on the frozen meadow on winter nights,
Or the watch at the pickerel flags in the ice-holes on the white spread of the mountain lakes,
Or the flying plunge of the bob-sled down Papermill hill;
The chase for the woodchuck, and the far-circling fox, and the all-night tramp for the treed 'coon;
For a hay-ride with a bevy of girls and a moonlight drive with one;
For wanderings through the woods and over the hills,
When the billowing mountain-laurel from afar off
Looked like flocks of sheep on the high terraces of the old Sweet farm;
When the hiding arbutus or gossamer clematis faintly scented the clean air;
When came the child's first thrill at the boom of the startled partridge,

And when first the adventurer heard a whole, great
    blossoming linden
Humming, with honey-gathering bees, like the pluckt
    string of a violin.

VII

O, there's no place like the old place!
Mightier mountains there are, sky-piercing and snow-
    covered all the year round,
But the lion-like curve of Cobble, clear-cut against the
    southern heavens,
On still, cold nights heaves close to the thick stars;
And the white ways of the Galaxy I have seen start from
    the lion's head
And sweep over to the long mountain, as if all the light
    and glory were for the valley only.
Day and night, in sunlight and starlight, and in the light
    of the moon,
Beautiful, beautiful is the valley of brooks.
Travelers have said that in the whole earth there is none
    more beautiful.
Why have I stayed away so long?
I think I will come again and again before I die —
And perhaps after I have died; for in the white graveyard
    on the hill
Rest, in the long sleep, some whom one day I should like
    to join.
I wonder shall I seem to them as strange as now to me
The image of my own self as I was in the days of child-
    hood:
An image that haunts me hourly while here I wander
    and dream,
And makes me strange to myself in a curious double
    existence.

The old friends seem to know me — but I am never de-
    ceived;
The one that I am is not the one that I was — yet truly
No one but I ever knew the youth who departed,
And the youth who departed still lives in the elder re-
    turning,
In whose bosom revive the days that forever are gone —
The old love and the old sweet longings;
The old love for the old place, that deepens as age comes
    closer,
And the heart keeps sighing and singing:
There's no place like the old place!

GLEN GILDER

How curves the little river through Glen Gilder, O Glen
    Gilder;
Now it runs and now it rushes, now it sings and now it
    hushes
O'er the rocks and by the brushes in Glen Gilder.

All music is the river in Glen Gilder, O Glen Gilder;
It sounds like wild birds singing, and it chimes like bells
    a-ringing —
Birds, too, their songs are flinging in Glen Gilder.

O mighty are the willows of Glen Gilder, of Glen Gilder;
Cool the air and cool the waters 'neath the giant spread-
    ing shadows,
And beyond wide sweep the meadows from Glen Gilder.

O, there's life and fun and frolic in Glen Gilder, in Glen
    Gilder;
And near the men are haying, and here the cows are stray-
    ing,
And the lambs and colts are playing in Glen Gilder.

Spring and autumn bring a change to fair Glen Gilder,
      O Glen Gilder;
Above the banks and under come the freshet's rage and
      thunder,
And men look with awe and wonder on Glen Gilder.

O, white the world of winter in Glen Gilder, in Glen
      Gilder;
'Neath ice the waves are creeping, or down in dark
      pools sleeping,
Or with sound of sleigh-bells leaping in Glen Gilder.

O, beautiful the morning in Glen Gilder, in Glen Gilder;
But, O, most dear and tender when blooms the sunset
      splendor,
At dying day's surrender in Glen Gilder.

And now the lingering sunlight leaves Glen Gilder, O
      Glen Gilder;
While moony shades are stalking, is it the wavelets talk-
      ing,
Or whispering lovers walking in Glen Gilder?

SONG

MARIA mia! all in white
Your fairy form against the night,
                    Maria!

Maria mia! in the night
Gleams like a ghost your form so slight,
                    Maria!

Maria mia! like a sprite
Burn those eyes in dusky light,
                    Maria!

Maria mia! sweet and wise
Those darkling, deep, Italian eyes,
                    Maria!

Maria mia! starry skies
Hold no such brightness as those eyes,
                    Maria!

Maria mia! turn, O turn
Those eyes away that beam and burn,
                    Maria!

Maria mia! when those eyes
Burn close, O close, I am not wise,
                    Maria!
         I am not wise,
                    Maria!

OBSCURATION

THIS night, when I blew out my candle flame,
The window's dark square suddenly turned white! —
I had not known the half-moon shone so bright,
And that a cool, sweet, silent moonbeam came
Through summer air, faint-touched with autumn frost,
And poured upon my floor a pool of light!
Pure, heavenly visitant — and almost thou wert lost.

"I DREAMED"

I DREAMED a tender and mysterious dream
Of one who, threading paths of earthly fate,
In a rich twilight walked, with heart aglow,
And all his soul vibrant with unheard tones,
"Drawn, drawn by the soft splendor of a face."

IMPROMPTUS

"FROM LOVE TO LOVE"

(FOR A WEDDING)

From love to love she passes on this day;
Yet all the love she leaves with her doth stay;
Deep, deep, the new love, in her heart of hearts,
And the old love follows her when she departs:
So is she richer than she was before,
For of true love she hath a mightier store.

"I ASKED YOU TO READ MY POEM"

I asked you to read my poem, so shameless was I,
    I not used such boon and service to ask;
This my excuse — when you hear, you will not deny
    The prayer of the poet, who saw the soul through the
       mask.

The singer sails in a sea beyond sight or ken,
    And he flings his plummet of song by night and by
       day;
With his poems he sounds the depths of the souls of
    men —
    In your soul my song I flung to fathom the way.

NAZIMOVA

From every motion, every lovely line,
Breathe art and passion; music from those lips;
The tragic Orient from those lustrous eyes.

A WARRIOR OF TROY

Let other gray-beards mourn the flight of years,
Finding no gains of eld to match its fears;

I have no feud with fate, nor age, nor time,
Who knew great Helen in her golden prime.

THE OBELISK (1881)

BENEATH a stone wrenched from Egyptian sands
Six rivers run through six imperial lands;
Nile, Bosphorus, Tiber, Seine, and Thames, till now
The Hudson wears the jewel on her brow.
Land that we love! O be thou, by this sign,
Tho' last, the noblest of the mighty line.

CROWNED ABSURDITIES

I ASKED me: what in all the world so odd
And laughable to men, and unto God —
The hight of comedy in earthly things?
That lot of little men pretending to be kings!

TO "LITTLE LADY MARGARET" — WITH A BOOK OF POEMS

THEY who love the poets
Will never lack a friend —
Up the road, and down the road,
And to the very end.

SACRILEGE

WED, thou, with sweet and silent Death,
Rather than join the prurient throng
Would soil, with foul, empoisoned breath,
The sanctity of song.

TO THE HERO OF A SCIENTIFIC ROMANCE

IF you wish, go be a pig,
In and out of season;
But do not bore us with a big
Philosophic reason.

THE WATCHMAN ON THE TOWER

(JANUARY, 1907)

Watchman! What seest thou in the New Dawn?

Far off, across the seas, I behold men pursuing men and helpless women with dreadful massacre; borne on the eastern wind I hear the horrible cries of the murdered and bereft.

And what seest thou nearer, O Watchman of the Tower?

Nearer I see dark and cowering forms of crime and frightened innocence, alike given pitilessly to the green tree and the red flame.

And what else nearer dost thou see, O Seer of Evil Things?

I see smoldering fires and drift of black smoke where all manner of shames have been burned in the market-places, befouling the pure air of heaven.

And now, again, thou seest — ?

I see scared creatures, in shape of men, fleeing from the light, and hiding in clefts of rocks, and in far places of the earth.

Look well, O Watchman, look near and wide, and tell us, who wait, what other things thou dost behold!

I see the shining faces of little children from whose backs heavy burdens have been lifted; I see rich men eagerly scattering their wealth among those who need — lifting up the stricken and restoring the power of self-help to the sturdy, and striving to make less hard the lot of them who work; I see those who labor winning an ampler share in the profits of their toil — in wage, and comfort, and safety, and time for rest; I behold Science conquering the secrets and guiding the forces of nature, and creating new and wondrous devices for human happiness — working miracles in culture of the soil, and in the cure of sickness; I behold Art going up and down the land, making homes and cities more beautiful; I behold Service honored above possessions; I see men as brothers, — in times of calm and in days of monstrous calamity, — stretching hands to one another over lands and seas, and across the ancient barriers of race, and religion, and condition; I see the hearts of men go out, in new love and care and understanding, to the beasts of the field and to the birds of the air; I hear the voices of poets and prophets troubling the hearts and lifting up the souls of all mankind; and in all these I see the mind of the Son of Man, and the power of the Will Eternal.

O Seer of Good and Evil, what else, what else?

Near by I behold the Angel of a People, and in his hand he bears a standard whereon is writ, in letters of light, the one word *Truth;* higher he bears the standard than ever before, and the people, in gathering numbers, follow the Word.

And what of the evil things that late thou sawest?

Still I see them, and many more, but fainter are they growing, as by some element of light consumed. Yet doth one strange and greatly evil thing loom with menace against the dawn — the shadow of false and self-seeking men who seize the banner of righteousness and with unclean hands uplift it, to the deceiving of many; and yet even here, I know, it is the love of Right and not of Wrong which doth mislead; and as the light increases, surely the pure in heart shall know their own and shun the deceiver of souls.

And what of the good that late thou sawest?

O still I see the good, and with clearer eyes; and, lo, it

doth appear that, in the light of the New Dawn, greater
and always greater grows the good, and nearer and always nearer. For now, with the rising sun, a company of
angels in new flight lift their wings and come upon the
day, and one is the bright Angel of Freedom, and one the
strong Angel of Justice, and one is the undaunted Angel
of Peace, and one the Angel of Hope Everlasting. With
a great and wonderful burst of light they come, and with
loud music of instruments and many voices.

*O Watcher of the Dawn! thou seest what is, but canst thou
see what yet shall be?*

O ye who doubt! In the visible present lives the invisible future, and the hour that is brings the hour that shall
be. If the Light grows, it shall not cease to grow; and the
good that is brings the good that is to come. As with
separate souls, so with peoples — the New Year, tho' it
holds inheritance of shame and loss, holds, also, inheritance of striving, and accomplishment, and divine aspi-
ration. Lo, the Light is climbing, not only of a New Year,
but of a New Era for the awakening world.

UNDER THE STARS

A REQUIEM FOR AUGUSTUS SAINT-GAUDENS

I

O KINDRED stars, wherethrough his soul in flight
Past to the immortals! 'neath your ageless light
I stand perplext, remembering that keen spirit
Quenched in mid-strength; the world, that shall inherit
His legacy of genius, all deprived
Of wealth untold, the still ungathered fruit
Of that great art! What honey all unhived;
What unborn grandeurs; noble music mute!

II

O silent stars! even as I harken here,
Heart-heavy, a murmurous and mysterious voice,
Blent with sweet wiry tones, on the inward ear
Strikes, and I hear the summons: "O rejoice,
Rejoice and mourn not!" Then that wondrous star
Now drawn near earth, — named for the god of war, —
The fiery planet cries across the night:
"Victory, Victory, he hath won the fight!"

III

O star of fire! he was thy very child!
Mixt with his blood thy fierce, ensanguined ray!
'Gainst the proud forces of the sordid day
He battled valiantly, all unbeguiled
By what might tempt or foil a lesser soul.
Not wealth, nor ease, nor praise unworthily won
Could touch his spirit; — "There the swift course to run!"
"There, there, O see! the bright, immortal goal!"

IV

Thou star of blood and battle! rich and sweet
Thy liquid gleam, where, in the twilight sky,
Thou shinest greatly! So did his art repeat
Thy strength, thy loveliness; thy ministry, —
In a dark, harmful world, — of Beauty's guerdon; —
Beauty that broods, enlightens, and makes endure
The heart of man beneath its heavy burden,
Lifting above the strife a deathless lure.

V

O starry skies! O palpitant winds whose throbbings
From out the vast of heaven pulse and flow!
In light and sound eterne our human sobbings

Are lost. — How dear to him who lieth low
The garment wonderful wild nature throws
About its inner life: green glades withdrawn;
Anger of ocean; radiance of the rose;
The pomp superb of sunset and of dawn.

VI

White, trembling fires of the unknown universe! .
Ye speak of some august, inscrutable Power
Creative, from whose hand, to bless or curse,
Ye were sent forth — thrillingly, in an hour
Of force stupendous, swift, immeasurable;
To-night those unconsuming fires tell
Of one who, in the splendor of his passion,
Alas! tho' mortal, could the immortal fashion.

VII·

O stars that sing as in creation's prime!
He whom, with love and tears, we celebrate,
He, like the Power that made ye, could create —
Bringing to birth new beauty for all time:
Once, lo! these shapes were not, now do they live,
And shall forever in the hearts of men;
And from their life new life shall spring again,
To souls unborn new light and joy to give.

VIII

Ye stars, all music to the spirit's ear!
Before the imperial music-masters knelt
This master of an art sublime, austere;
The very soul of music in him dwelt,
So in his lines the haunting strains of lyres,
From gracious forms deep tones symphonic spring;
Once more we hear the sound of heavenly wires,
Again the stars of morn together sing.

IX

Red star of war! thy sons did he enshrine
In glorious art — fighters on sea and land;
In bronze they give again the brave command;
In bronze they march resistless, in divine
Ecstasy of devotion, not in wrath;
The fire and fury of battle he made real,
But like God's prophets moved they on their path
Led and uplifted by the great Ideal.

X

O fateful stars! that lit the climbing way
Of that dear, martyred son of fate and fame, —
The supreme soul of an immortal day, —
Linked with his name is our great sculptor's name;
For now in art eternal breathes again
The gaunt, sweet presence of our chief of men —
That soul of tenderness; that spirit stern,
Whose fires divine forever flame and burn.

XI

Stars of white midnight! tho' unseen by day,
Imagined! He the unseen could subtly see
And image forth in most divine array:
Blest Charity, and Love, and Loyalty,
And Victory, and Grief; and, with a touch
Made tender by heroic years of pain, —
Telling in art what words might not contain, —
The calm, sweet face of Him who suffered much.

XII

Mysterious sky! where orbs constellate reign!
Toward which the heart of man through endless ages

IN HELENA'S GARDEN

IN HELENA'S GARDEN

PART I

IN HELENA'S GARDEN

THE SUNSET WINDOW

THROUGH the garden sunset-window
    Shines the sky of rose;
Deep the melting red, and deeper,
    Lovelier it grows.

Musically falls the fountain;
    Twilight voices chime;
Visibly upon the cloud-lands
    Tread the feet of Time.

Evening winds from down the valley
    Stir the waters cool;
Break the dark, empurpled shadows
    In the marble pool.

Rich against the high-walled grayness
    The crimson lily glows,
And near, O near, one well-loved presence
    Dream-like comes and goes.

"THE GRAY WALLS OF THE GARDEN"

THE gray walls of the garden
    Hold many and many a bloom;
A flame of red against the gray
    Is lightning in the gloom.

The gray walls of the garden
　Hold grassy walks between
Bright beds of yellow blossoms,
　Golden against the green.

And in the roof of the arbor
　. Leaves woven through and through, —
Great grape leaves, making shadows, —
　Shine green against the blue.

And, O, in the August weather
　What wonders new are seen!
Long beds of azure blossoms
　Cool blue against the green.

The gray walls of the garden
　Hold paths of pure delight,
And, in the emerald, blooms of pearl
　Are white against the night.

THE MARBLE POOL

THE marble pool, like the great sea, hath moods —
Fierce angers, slumbers, deep beatitudes.

In sudden gusts the pool, in lengthened waves, —
As in a mimic tempest, — tosses and raves.

In the still, drowsy, dreaming midday hours
It sleeps and dreams among the dreaming flowers.

'Neath troubled skies the surface of its sleep
Is fretted; how the big drops rush and leap!

Now 't is a mirror where the sky of night
Sees its mysterious face of starry light;

Or where the tragic sunset is reborn,
Or the sweet, virginal mystery of morn.

One little pool holds ocean, brink to brink;
One little heart can hold the world, I think.

THE TABLE ROUND

I

WHAT think you of the Table Round
Which the garden's rustic arbor
In pride doth harbor?
And what its weight, how many a pound?
Or shall you reckon that in tons?
For this is of earth's mighty ones:
A mill-stone 't is, that turns no more,
But, on a pier sunk deep in ground,
Like a ship that's come to shore,
Content among its flowery neighbors
It rests forever from its labors.

II

Now no more 'mid grind and hammer
Are the toiling moments past,
But amid a milder clamor
Stays it fast.
For the Garden Lady here,
When the summer sky is clear,
With her bevy of bright daughters
(Each worth a sonnet)
To the tune of plashing waters
Serves the tea upon it.

III

And when Maria, and when Molly,
Frances, Alice, Grace, Cecilia,
Clara, Bess, and Pretty Polly,

Lolah and the dark Amelia,
Come with various other ladies,
Certain boys, and grown-ups graver —
Then, be sure, not one afraid is
To let his wit give forth its flavor,
With the fragrant odor blent
Of the Souchong, and the scent
Of the roses and sweet-peas
And other blossoms sweet as these.
Then, indeed, doth joy abound
About the granite table round,
And the stream of laughter flowing
Almost sets the old stone going.

THE SUN-DIAL

On the sun-dial in the garden
  The great sun keeps the time;
A faint, small moving shadow,
  And we know the worlds are in rhyme:

And if once that shadow should falter
  By the space of a child's eye-lash —
The seas would devour the mountains,
  And the stars together crash.

"SOMETHING MISSING FROM THE GARDEN"

Something missing from the garden?
  But all's bright there;
Color in the daytime,
  Perfume in the night there.

Something wanting in the garden?
  Yet the blossoms

Bring the hum-birds to the sweetness
    In their bosoms.

And by day the sunlight golden
        On the granite
Glistens, and by night the silver starlight
        From some near planet.

Something missing from the garden?
        But the mountain
Ceaseless pours a secret streamlet
        Filmy from the fountain;

And that streamlet winds blow, wave-like,
        Down the flowers,
And, in the mist, faint, flickering rainbows
        Flash through mimic showers.

Something wanting in the garden
        When all's bright there?
Color in the daytime,
        Perfume in the night there?

Then what missing from the garden
        Spoils its pleasance? —
Just a breath of something human;
        Just one presence.

THREE FLOWERS OF THE GARDEN

THREE blossoms in a happy garden grow —
Have care, for this one, lo, is white as any snow:
Its name is Peace.

Three flowers — and one, in hue, a delicate gold;
A harsh breath, then its golden leaves shall droop and fold
Its name is Joy.

Three flowers — and one is crimson, rich and strong;
This will, if well entreated, all others outlive long:
Its name is Love.

EARLY AUTUMN

The garden still is green
    And green the trees around —
But the winds are roaring overhead
    And branches strew the ground.

And to-day on the garden pool
    Floated an autumn leaf:
How rush the seasons, rush the years,
    And, O, how life is brief!

THE LAST FLOWER OF THE GARDEN

One by one the flowers of the garden
    To autumn yielded as waned the sun;
So prisoners, called by the cruel Terror,
    To death went, one by one.

Roses, and many a delicate blossom,
    Down fell their heads, in the breezes keen,
One by one; and the frost of autumn
    Was the blade of their guillotine.

And at last an hour when the emerald pathways
    Grew from green to a wintry white;
And a new, strange beauty came into the garden
    In the full moon's flooding light.

For a radiance struck on the columned fountain
    As it shot to the stars in a trembling stream,
And a rainbow, springing above the garden,
    Was the dream of a dream in a dream.

And we who loved well that place of flowers
  Looked with awe on the wondrous birth,
And knew that the last flower of the garden
  Was something not of earth.

PART II

THE LION OF TYRINGHAM

MIDWAY the valley, fronting the flusht morn,
The huge beast stretches prone, as by the Nile
The enormous Sphinx; so nature mimics nature,
And man's own art — tho' never such vast shape
By man was fashioned. Thus through ages long
Hath he the tempest and the rain endured;
And the all-rending frost, and the great sun,
And the remorseless winters of the world.

What shall that immemorial rest disturb?
His monstrous head down prest betwixt huge paws,
How well he sleeps! Not deeper slumber holds
The dead in the white city far below.
And shall he waken? — Shall the dead awake?

THE VOICE OF THE HIGHT

I

OF a dream I would sing and a river I saw in a dream —
Of souls that the river divided, so wide was the stream,
So wide and so deep that neither the other beheld.
And they gazed on the ocean near, by terror com-
    pelled —
On the infinite ocean whither their barks had been hurled
In a tempest that drove from the ultimate, unseen world.

By that ocean they stood in awe, and remembrance, and
      wonder;
Troubled their hearts with the ceaseless surge and the
      thunder —
Till in fear they turned, and they gazed on the inland
      hight,
And the mountains that called by day and beckoned by
      night,
And, each to the other unknown, by that call was shaken:
O, lost is the soul that the voice of the hight shall not
      waken,
Nor heavenward climb by the paths high hearts have
      taken.

II

Inland the new souls urged, by river and marsh,
Treading with stedfast feet the roadways harsh.
Inland and up through fields of flower or thorn,
Through forests rude, and through desert ways forlorn —
Upward and on by meadows blossoming bright
Or where, under pestilent breath, the earth was blight;
Onward and up — and still by the river's brink
Where, nigh unto death, they lived by the living drink.

III

And now, behold, they nearer and nearer drew
Till each pilgrim soul the other beheld and knew,
And climbing thus ever higher, they came more nigh,
Above the enfolding mists, 'neath the bending sky —
Till at last at the river's source, near the mountain's
      crest,
At the selfsame spring they drank, and the waters of rest;
For they followed the paths high hearts have climbed to
      the sun,
And the souls that the river divided became as one.

A SONG OF FRIENDSHIP

WE have come nearer, friend!
The thought of each, to each
Shines clearer, dearer, friend!

All doubts have fled away;
Strange deeds and baffling speech
Now are clear as day.

Naught between us, naught
To hurt or separate;
No battles to be fought.

Friends now, in more than name;
Forever friends, our fate —
Tho' never again the same.

We have come nearer, friend!
Would it were not so late,
But all the dearer, friend!

What sorcery, new and strange,
What word, what mystic token,
Has worked the wondrous change?

No word of secret powers,
Nothing sung or spoken,
Only the near, dear hours

Under the starry sky;
Trust and peace unbroken;
Silence, and a sigh.

A ROSE OF DREAM

I DREAMED a rose; it bloomed
　Beyond compare;
Of all wild blossoms by the wayside
　Most rich, most sweet, most rare.

So lovely was the rose
　I could but love it,
As, drinking deep its fragrant soul,
　I bent above it.

O tenderly its leaves
　Outbreathed their beauty;
Humbly to worship at that shrine
　Was my dear duty.

Once, when in the twilight hour,
　Its spirit drew me —
O wonderful! I was aware
　That wild rose knew me.

Knew me, my inmost heart —
　And, O above
All joy imagined! lo! my rose
　Gave love for love.

SONG

O, WHITHER has she fled from out the dawning·and the
　　day?
Empty is the dark of her, and twilight silver gray,
For the world that she makes happy now is far and far
　　away.

Strange, because a girl is gone the stars are not so
 bright,
The sunset sky not fair as once, nor morning after
 night,
While from the day has past away a dear and lovely
 light.

Come back, come back, my darling girl, and set the stars
 aglow;
And make the daylight dear again, and make the blossoms blow;
Come back, come back, my golden girl, never again to go.

"WHEN THE GIRLS COME TO THE OLD HOUSE"

I

When the girls come
To the old house, to the old, old home;
When the girls race through it,
How will they endue it
With light and warmth and fun,
Beyond the touch of the sun.

II

When the girls run through it,
How the old house will awaken!
Never fear! It will not rue it
When it feels its old bones shaken,
From ancient sill to centuried rafter,
With sweet girl laughter.

III

When the girls race through it,
How each old ghost in its own old nook,

That it never forsook,
How it will run
When the girls pursue it
With frolic and fun!

IV

Old house! old home! Come, light
The fires again on the dear hearths of old.
All must be bright;
Not a room shall be cold;
And on the great hearth, — where, in the old days,
Beside the fierce blaze
There was room, and to spare, for each grown-up and
        child, —
High let the fire be piled!

V

Old house! Old home! You need no wine
To cheer you now, for the joyous ripple
Of girlish laughter is quite enough tipple!
O, what liquor
Like the innocent shine,
The sparkle and flicker,
In the eyes of youth!
And, of a truth,
'T is youth, old house! 't is youth that fills you;
Youth that calls to you; youth that thrills you.

VI

Old house! Old home! O, do not dare
To be sad, tho' aware
Of the golden, and the raven, and the pretty, pretty curls,
Of the little dead girls —
Treasures put away in the old chest in the garret.
Be glad, old house! the new girls have come to share it:
The great, deep hearth, with room and to spare;

The dark garret, and the wide hall, and the quaint, old
    stair —
And to bring back to earth
The old, sweet mirth.

THE SONG OF A SONG

I

"WHEN in the morning you wake,"
Said the Song;
"You shall remember me
All the day long,
As the bird remembers the tree,
As the swan remembers the lake.
And when the stars go, one by one,
Like bright souls banished,
Your heart shall echo the Song of the sad Stars vanished.

II

  "When comes the day, with rush and run,
Over the roofs the shadow from the rising sun that falls, —
Over the roofs and down the walls,
Along the roofs and over the brink, —
This shall make you think
Of the Song that sang the Shadow, and sang the Sun.

III

  "And the narrow street,
This have I sung so sweet
That you cannot, even if you would,
Lose the Song; and your feet
Its music shall repeat,
As a bird sings in a wood —
Cheerily, cheerily sings,
Remembering lovely things.

IV

"And the vine on the house where you live,"
Said the Song,
"The vine that I sang in blossom, or wintry bare —
You shall sing to yourself the air
Of the Song of the Vine; it shall follow you every-
        where;
Of the vine like a silent, purple cataract pouring down,
Here in the midst of the noise and the dust of the
        town.
Are you gay? Do you grieve? —
The Song will find you;
Whether you stay or go the Vine will remind you
Of the Song of the Vine, the Song of the House of the
        Vine —
The Song of Home, and Children, and Love Divine.

V

"And the Song of the Stars, and the Shadow, and the
        Rising Sun,
And the Song of the Street,
Whose music is in your feet,
And the Song of the Vine, and the House of the Vine —
One poet has sung them all,
And they are but one,"
Said the Song.

THE NET

CAUGHT in the golden net of the poet's song,
And held there close and long,
How many a marvelous thing!
A humming-bird's invisible wing;
A rose that sent its luring fragrance through night air,
Taken all unaware;

The star of dawn that knew not human eyes
Dared its inviolate secrecies;
A tear shed by an archangel who looked down
On an unpitying town;
A maiden's dream wherefrom she woke
And into secret, silent tremors broke;
And (O, ye wandering, wan and wayward feet,
Beware that music piercing sweet —
That all too ravishing art!)
Caught in the golden net of the poet's song,
(Pray Heaven there come no wrong!)
One little, fluttering heart.

SONG

O PURER far than ever I!
    Be nobler than to choose me:
Flee from me, Sweet; I fain would die
    If thou shouldst not refuse me.

And when I'm dead, and thou, too, Sweet,
    Because I did refuse thee;
Perhaps our new-born souls may meet
    And know, and I not lose thee.

SONG

I AWOKE in the morning not knowing
What it was that had set my heart glowing;
Something had come to me
That was the sum to me
Of all human happiness — crown of life's bliss.
Tho' drowsyhead sleep its image might blot,
I knew it was there, tho' its shape I forgot.
My mind was blue sky with nothing but joy in it;

Not even a dream of the night had employ in it;
No cloud dimmed the blue;
Then I said: "Shall I miss
My nameless, new bliss?"
When sudden it came
Like lightning, like flame;
And, ah, it was this —
It was you!

"WHEN THE WAR FLEET PUTS TO SEA"

WHEN the war fleet puts to sea,
　And the great guns thunder,
Our hearts leap up in glee
　And awe and wonder —
When the war fleet puts to sea.

Let it be peace, not war,
　The strong ships carry;
Two coasts that stretch afar
　Now meet and marry —
Let it be peace, not war.

And let no ill befall!
　Be kind, ye fates!
Stern skies preserve them all
　In the stormy straits —
O, let no ill befall.

And if dread war shall loom
　In far-off days,
Let the shotted cannon boom
　In prayer and praise —
If dreadful war shall loom.

Behind the bellowing guns
　　That do their part,
Let stand the nation's sons
　　All pure in heart —
Behind the bellowing guns.

Then not in pride or hate
　　Let one shot speed;
Be righteous souls elate
　　To do the deed —
O, not in pride or hate.

And thou, Eternal Power!
　　Bring swift the day
When Right shall rule the hour,
　　And Peace alone have sway —
O, high Eternal Power!

ART

(MISS GERALDINE FARRAR IN " MADAMA BUTTERFLY ")

A LITTLE, loosened leaf of painted paper
　　Slow quivering down
From a stage Nagasaki cherry-tree
　　That screens a painted town.

And flitting back and forth in silken robes
　　A figure slight,
With orient gestures, and fixt orient smile,
　　And voice of pure delight.

And every note she sang and word she spoke
　　Was for her writ;
Not nature here, but art and artifice,
　　And cunning human wit.

Yet when that paper petal trembled down,
    Spring thrilled the air;
And when she sang, I knew love's hight and depth
    And passion and despair.

IN PRAISE OF PORTRAITURE [1]

MYRIADS of souls from out the unknown vast
Flash forth and swift return. Tho' something stays, —
Remembered words and deeds, — the look they wore
Were lost forever save for the art we praise —
The art that holds the fleeting spirit fast:
Afield, in household ways, at rest, a-dance;
The sweet, companionable presence; the austere
Demeanor, hiding a rich heart; the glance,
Intense and penetrant, that says a soul is here.

A soul is here, even as in life it lived,
It wantoned, it impassioned, joyed and grieved;
So might an angel through life's doorway peer,
Half drawing back as if in mortal fear;
So might a lost soul linger, leaving here
Remembrance of the horror of its doom:
A living soul, defiant of the tomb.

Great were the masters of the art we praise,
In other lands, in past and splendid days.
What souls the chief Venetian in his art
Makes to the eye apparent, and the heart!
What warriors, princes, women all of grace:
Beauty of body, loveliness of face!
Master of color, he, well-nigh supreme,
Who nobly drew that which before was dream!
    Glorious is Spain in the proud souls that breathe

[1] Address, presenting Cecilia Beaux to the Provost of The University of Pennsylvania for the degree of LL. D., February 22, 1908.

In that most delicate and subtle touch, —
The art miraculous, the not too much, —
Of him whose brows the generations wreathe
With laurel on laurel, as the world grows old,
And all its annals one Velasquez hold.

And by the northern seas his art sublime
That trembles with the tragedies of time —
His art who knew all mysteries of light,
Not less the heart of man; for in his sight
No secret could endure, and on his page
The soul's dark pathos lives from age to age.

They live indeed, whom art has made to live —
How real from the canvas forth they look
And judgment seem on our own selves to give
As we judge them.
     Miraculous art, that took
Through all the centuries the tongue of praise,
And worthy all honors, not for the old days
Alone, and painters gone before — no less
For those who dare discipleship confess
And in the footsteps of the mighty tread.
With modern skill the ancient mode they keep;
On the old altar burns the authentic fire;
Priests of the ancient faith, that never sleep;
They, with new masters of the sacred lyre,
And all the sons of genius, still aspire
Purely and greatly; rendering our late time,
Not less than that long gone, imperial, sublime!

Lady, shrink not that you, to-day, we name
In the same breath with the age-conquering fame
Of them most glorious in a mighty line.
Not for the living is it to assign
Rank to the living, in the long roll of art.
But blame us not if here we crown the intent

Not less than the sincere accomplishment.
We only know the art we see and love
Is beautiful, intense, most subtile, rare,
And tho' with something from our New World air
Athrill, yet is it masterful, above
All else, with the old mastery — not old
But fresh forever as the dawn's new gold.

And in your art, that follows down the line
Of the world's noblest, — the most high, divine
Kinship of them who painted the deep soul, —
Glows a clear, individual attribute;
Something whereof the praiser would be mute
Save that he needs must tell the very whole
And in his office utterly faithful be:
Something that means swift vision of the truth;
The flame of life; the flush of endless youth;
A trait compounded all of Poesy;
A tone most exquisite, illuminate
With the keen sense of Beauty which even art
Can lift above itself; a throbbing heart;
An element that sets the noonday beam
Vibrant with tints; that makes the little, great;
And while the artist would another render
Reveals his own bright spirit in radiant splendor.

IN TIMES OF PEACE

'T WAS said: "When roll of drum and battle's roar
Shall cease upon the earth, O, then no more

"The deed, the race, of heroes in the land."
But scarce that word was breathed when one small hand

Lifted victorious o'er a giant wrong
That had its victims crushed through ages long;

Some woman set her pale and quivering face,
Firm as a rock, against a man's disgrace;

A little child suffered in silence lest
His savage pain should wound a mother's breast;

Some quiet scholar flung his gauntlet down
And risked, in Truth's great name, the synod's frown;

A civic hero, in the calm realm of laws,
Did that which suddenly drew a world's applause;

And one to the pest his lithe young body gave
That he a thousand thousand lives might save.

IMPROMPTUS

EDWARD EVERETT HALE

PATRIOT, and sage, and lover of his kind —
The love he gives a thousandfold returns:
His is the wealth of love a great heart earns
By giving all that heart and soul and mind.

BARDS OF BRITAIN (1908)

THE poets silent and the poets fled?
Not till these two that pluck the lyre are dead!
He of the patriot heart and Milton's line,
With soaring song and melody divine;
And he who makes the old days breathe again,
Yet sings the hour that is, and hearts of living men.

CALVÉ

SWEETNESS and strength, high tragedy and mirth;
And but one Calvé on the singing earth!

IN A CONCERT ROOM

Two streams of music beat upon my heart —
  That which now is; that which was silent long:
Sacred this temple of a deathless art,
  Whose very walls thrill with remembered song.

THE LONESOME WILD

  LOVELIER, lovelier this place
  Since here she brought her maiden grace;
  Dearer far this lonesome wild
  Since here she wandered, here she smiled.

NEW FRIENDS AND OLD

  How wonderful and sweet
New friends, as if forever known, to greet!
The warm, new, kindred touch; the dear surprise
To find an answer in new dawning eyes.
  But when old friends draw nearer —
  O dearer, dearer!

SHADOW AND SUN

I LOOKED from the window with hungry eyes
On the day long longed for, that must be bright:
(That day of days, of the long, long night!)
When, O dear Shadow! by thy divining
I knew that the morn was bright:
I knew by the shadow the sun was shining.

A NAVAL SURGEON OF THE WAR FOR THE UNION

HERE was as loyal soul as ever drew
  The breath of battle, and the air of home:
  He duty followed, lonely and far to roam;
To country, kindred, God, forever true.

A MOTHER'S PICTURE

SWEET dignity and tenderness and grace,
  Devotion, and the power to draw the heart:
  This her inheritance, her dower, her art;
All these are radiant in that mother face.

ON A YOUNG HERO

TOO soon? But heroes always die too soon!
  This, this it is that makes them dear and great.
Grant us, O kindly Heaven, the supreme boon
  To give our lives too soon — not die too late!

A HERO'S BRIDE

WHAT tragic loss! but, O, what gain sublime,
  What golden memory, life-enduring pride.
What shall it matter, brief or long the time?
  Love of a noble soul — a hero's bride.

TO ONE WHO PRAISED "THE GAY LIFE"

GAY! — as the hot crater's crust all lightning-lit —
But one tread more, and horror of the pit!
Gay! Yes, for a moment, and then weeping sorrow,
With wild remorse to meet the dawning morrow.

LYRIC LIVES

THERE are more poets than the rhyming race;
Souls beautiful of thought, and full of grace;
The spirit of poetry in them breathes and thrives;
They write not poems, but lead lyric lives.

SONG

A LITTLE longer still in summer suns,
On wintry hights, and where the wild brook runs,
    To rest or wander;

A little longer left for human joy;
To win and lose, — man's masterful employ, —
   To dream and ponder.

A little longer! But, O, sweeter this
Than any lesser grace or lowlier bliss
   In earth's wide blindness:
A little longer left for lifting hearts,
Healing hurt souls, for earth's most heavenly arts —
   For love and kindness.

THE SINGING RIVER

I

I read the poet's verses by the stream
Where late with him I walked; the twilight gleam
Faded, the page darkened, and from the sky
The day, withdrawing gradual, came to die
Slowly, into a memory and a sigh.

II

There as I read, the poet's lyric dream
Mixt with the silvery clamor of the stream,
And, tho' the night fell, and I read no more,
Still on and on the mingled measures pour:
"Beauty is one," they murmur o'er and o'er.

THE SOLACE OF THE SKIES

WHEN fell the first great sorrow of my life, —
   He dying from whom my mortal frame was drawn, —
   Into the night I fled, long ere the dawn,
Succor to bring for her, the stricken wife.

Then first I knew the solace of the skies,
  And that mysterious mingling of the soul
  With the still beauty of the infinite whole;
  My heart was melted, and grew strangely wise.
I was a child then, having little lore
  Taken from books, or the wide world of men,
  But something suddenly through my soul did pour
Beyond all thought, all dream, all hope; since then
  Nor Death, nor Life, has been the same to me:
  Can grief the spirit kill, once touched by deity?

THE WINDING PATH

The winding path
Come let us follow
Along the lane
And down by the hollow;
For I would fain
The way it passes, —
Through the long grasses,
The meadows, the woods, —
Seek and learn it:
What the moods,
What true uses
Lead and turn it,
What abuses
Break it, cloak it,
Twist it, choke it.
  Now 't is a span;
But onward still,
Over the hill
It wider grows,
It firmer flows.
The subtle path

Its own thought hath;
It is more wise
Than you or I;
As if with eyes
That peer and try,
It feels its way
Across the day.
    What little feet
Hard have packed it!
What great hoofs
Gouged and wracked it!
Rude water-courses
Cut across it,
Rocks emboss it;
A lichened cliff
Its route enforces.
Yet on it goes,
And upward flows
Through the dark pines
In wayward lines;
Past the birches
Skyward it lurches:
One more flight —
And on the hight
At last we stand,
And catch the vision
Of sky and land.

"WHAT MAKES THE GARDEN GROW"

WHAT makes the garden grow
In beauty and delight —
A place to linger in by day or night,
But chiefly when the long and level light

Makes shadows that still glow
With burning blossoms — the heart's home
Wherefrom our charmèd feet reluctant roam.
Not pride, nor envy, nor crude wealth
Can bring the drooping roses health,
Nor lift the sanguine poppies, row on row,
Nor from their bed of green
Make every iris spread it like a queen;
While all along the wall
The jeweled colors call.
O, not from these can come the art
That touches the deep heart,
That makes the small blades shove
Through the soft earth into a pictured balm above;
Not sordid thoughts and low
Can make the garden grow
In beauty and delight,
A place to linger in by day or night —
Not these, not these, but love.

"IF, ONE GREAT DAY"

IF, one great day, the God I see
Aflame in blade and bush and tree,
In the white dawn and passing sun —
Shall I not joy in that clear sight
And tell in song my strange delight,
Tho' come a day when mist and cloud
Shall the celestial presence shroud?
O, shall I not be bold,
And cry, "Behold!"
Tho' swift the vision darkens and is done?

MUSIC BENEATH THE STARS

Music beneath the Stars! remembering him
  Who music loved, and who on such a night
  Had, through white paths celestial, winged his flight,
  Hearing the chanting of the cherubim —
Which even our ears seem now to apprehend,
  Rising and falling in waves of splendid sound
  That bear our grieving spirits from the ground
  And with eternal things lift them and blend.
Now Bach's great Aria charms the starlit dark;
  Now soars the Largo, high angelical,
  Soothing all mortal sorrow on that breath;
And now, O sweet and sovereign strain! now hark
  Of mighty Beethoven the rise and fall.
  Such music 'neath the stars abolished death.

THE BIRDS OF WESTLAND

PRINCETON, JUNE, 1908

O birds of Westland, singing on
  As blithely as of yore!
Do ye not know how deep he sleeps
  Behind yon closèd door?

Do ye not know that he who hailed
  Your music, dawn by dawn,
Hath, since he harkened yesterday,
  From hearing been withdrawn?

O happy birds! I think ye know
  He loved your joyful song,
And therefore in the growing light
  Ye carol loud and long.

O birds! ye know he would not wish
  To hush that singing sweet,
Tho' since he heard your music last
  That great heart ceased to beat.

THE VEIL OF STARS

O VEIL of stars! O dread magnificence!
  Not unto man, O, not to man is given
  The power to grasp with human sight and sense
  Him, clothed upon by all the stars of heaven
And thou, O infinite littleness! not more
  Doth infinite distance and immensity
  That Presence veil, whom fain we would adore,
  If mortals might the immortal dimly see.
Atoms and stars alike the Eternal hide,
  Nor know we if in light or darkness dwells
  The Ever Living! No voice from out the wide
Intense of starlight the great secret tells;
  No word or sign in earth or skies above,
  Save one — the godhead in the eyes of love.

INDEX OF FIRST LINES

INDEX OF TITLES

The Riverside Press
CAMBRIDGE . MASSACHUSETTS
U . S . A